AF848789

THE UNIQUE FAMILY LAW IN THE STATE OF ISRAEL

Touro University Press Books

Series Editor

MICHAEL A. SHMIDMAN, PhD (Touro College, New York)
SIMCHA FISHBANE, PhD (Touro College, New York)

THE UNIQUE FAMILY LAW IN THE STATE OF ISRAEL

YITSHAK
COHEN

NEW YORK
2021

Library of Congress Cataloging-in-Publication Data

Names: Cohen, Yitshak, 1971- author.
Title: The unique family law in the state of Israel / Yitshak Cohen.
Description: Brookline, MA: Academic Studies Press, 2021.
Identifiers: LCCN 2020048081 (print) | LCCN 2020048082 (ebook) | ISBN 9781644695401 (hardback) | ISBN 9781644695418 (adobe pdf) | ISBN 9781644695425 (epub)
Subjects: LCSH: Domestic relations--Israel. | Domestic relations (Jewish law) | Domestic relations--United States.
Classification: LCC KMK540 .C64 2021 (print) | LCC KMK540 (ebook) | DDC 346.569401/5--dc23
LC record available at https://lccn.loc.gov/2020048081
LC ebook record available at https://lccn.loc.gov/2020048082

Copyright © Itshak Cohen, 2021
Please do not copy or photocopy without the written permission of the author

Published by Touro University Press and Academic Studies Press
Typeset, printed and distributed by Academic Studies Press

ISBN 9781644695401 (hardback)
ISBN 9781644695418 (adobe pdf)
ISBN 9781644695425 (epub)

Touro University Press
Michael A. Shmidman and Simcha Fishbane, Editors
320 West 31st Street, Fourth Floor,
New York, NY 10001, USA
tcpress@touro.edu

Book design by PHi Business Solutions Limited
Cover design by Ivan Grave.

Academic Studies Press
1577 Beacon Street
Brookline, MA 02446, USA

press@academicstudiespress.com
www.academicstudiespress.com

To my dearly beloved in-laws, Nehemiah and Rachel Stern

”כִּי בִי יִרְבּוּ יָמֶיךָ וְיוֹסִיפוּ לְךָ שְׁנוֹת חַיִּים.“ (משלי ט, יא)

Contents

Acknowledgments

I wish to take this opportunity to thank several of my teachers and mentors. First, I must express my profound gratitude to Professor Berachyahu Lifshitz, who supervised my doctoral dissertation and advised me on the articles that followed it.

I am grateful to my mentors at the Institute for Advanced Torah Studies, Bar-Ilan University, and to my rabbi, Rabbi Aaron Katz. For many years I was privileged to study with Rabbi Katz and learn from his leadership skills. I must also gratefully acknowledge my rabbis and teachers at Yeshivat Shaalvim who first introduced me to high-level Torah study and taught me to love the Torah.

For approximately fifteen years, I have been a faculty member at Ono Academic College, an institute that has become a warm and supportive home for me. I thank Mr. Ranan Hartman, founder and chairman of Ono Academic College, for his personal guidance; Professor Dudi Schwartz, to whom I owe most of my academic development; and Dr. Rivi Cohen, the vice president, whose administrative talents have enabled me to dedicate a significant amount of my time to research.

I am grateful to Rabbi Dr. Michael A. Shmidman, dean and professor of medieval Jewish history and editor in chief of Touro University Press, for his very significant assistance and wise advice during our work together on both this book and my previous publication *The Unique Judicial Vision of Rabbi Meir Simcha of Dvinsk: Selected Discourses in Meshekh Hokhmah and Or Sameah* (2016).

I wish to sincerely thank Alisa Shilor, the translator of this book, for her professional, dedicated, diligent work, and especially for her patience and warm welcome throughout the years of working together. I also thank Mr. Stuart Allen for his professional and dedicated editing work.

The gratitude that I owe my parents and parents-in-law is immeasurable. With genuine love, I wish to bless my parents, Mordecai and Esther, for their boundless dedication and self-sacrifice that instilled in me a love of learning and awe of Heaven. Likewise, I wish to offer my heartfelt blessings to my in-laws, Nehemiah and Rachel Stern, and I wish to thank them for their assistance and for remaining by our side throughout the years. May the Lord grant my parents and in-laws many years of health and happiness.

Last, but not least, I must thank my own family: to my wife Shuli, my earthly partner, for her great faith in me, her never-ending encouragement, and her tireless devotion to the education of our children—Efrat, Tamar, Naama, Gilad, Ariel, and Hila; and to my children, who gave up their time with me so that I could devote it to the publication of this book.

Words cannot express my gratitude to the Creator of the World for all the goodness that He has bestowed upon me. I humbly ask that He continue to enable me to study His Torah and to lead our family on the path of righteousness, and that He bestow upon myself and my family His grace and blessings. May the Torah remain in my mouth and in the mouths of my offspring in perpetuity. "May the words of my mouth and the meditation of my heart be acceptable in Thy sight" (Psalms 19:15).

Introduction

This book is as relevant to the general public as it is to family law practitioners, since divorce has not only negative consequences for the spouse and his or her family unit but also ripple effects on society as a whole.

Divorce matters affect everyone and determine the quality of life of an individual, a family, and a nation. In the State of Israel, the unique family law derives from ancient Jewish law, different *halakhic* traditions, and an extensive legal tradition spanning many centuries and geographic locations. It will be emphasized on the background of a comparison with the corresponding law in the United States and other countries around the world. This analysis is intended to illuminate some issues in legal systems worldwide.

First, it is important to indicate that Israeli family law is substantially different from other legal systems. The Israeli system is primarily controlled by the religious law of the parties. Thus religious courts were also established and granted enforcement powers equivalent to those of the civil courts. This is a complex situation because the religious law applied in these courts is not always consistent with gender equality and civil rights practiced in civil court. In contrast, the various state legal systems in the United States and the legal systems in other Western countries separate between religion and state. They provide for family law matters exclusively through secular law. Although rabbinical courts have also been established in different countries, they lack enforcement and execution powers. Their authority is contingent upon the consent of both spouses. Nevertheless, there are many similarities between the systems that can also contribute to one another. The real issues are not simply religion as opposed to secularism, but those defining personhood and rights.

In its legislation promoted by the deputy minister of religion, the Israeli Knesset granted the religious courts exclusive jurisdiction over matters of marriage and divorce for the members of the religion associated with each such court. However, the religious courts and civil courts have concurrent jurisdiction in other matters of personal status that accompany divorce, such as child support, custody, and the division of property. This creates significant tension between the legal systems as applied in religious and civil courts. This book seeks to clarify that tension and offers the solutions suggested in each of its chapters. Spouses who are unaffiliated with any religion or are members of different religions will not be under the exclusive jurisdiction of a religious court. All of their matters will be brought before the civil court. With respect to spouses of different religions, the civil court will request from the head of each relevant religious court an opinion as to annulment of the marriage and whether religious law requires a divorce.

The book also examines comparative legal systems. It seeks to provide the Israeli legal system as well as legal systems worldwide with additional tools for resolving a family dispute. The comprehensive analysis in this book may serve as a guide for those interested in family law both in Israel and in other countries. In divorce disputes this may include civil court judges and rabbinical court judges, lawyers, mediators, arbitrators, and the couples themselves. This book deals with general matters applicable worldwide and not only in Israel. Included among them are issues subject to modification, the right of a minor to independent status, extramarital relationships and joint property. This book may also facilitate the divorce process and thus reduce the suffering of a couple and their children. The following is a brief description of its chapters.

The first chapter discusses the issues subject to modification in family law. The state legal systems in the United States have accepted that issues of child support, custody, and alimony may be modified, even after final judgment or agreement between parties. The standard for when modification is appropri-ate is the occurrence of a "substantial change in circumstances." This unclear standard contributes to prolonged litigation, causes family disputes to remain open, and violates the fundamental principles of finality and *res judicata*. The discrepancy between the decisions of the rabbinical court and those of the civil court in the State of Israel also contributes to the standard's lack of clarity. It urges spouses to repeatedly sue in one of the courts in an attempt to alter a previous ruling given in the other court. Yet when two courts make different determinations, it is difficult to identify the correct standard, the appropriate amount of child support to be determined in each case, and whether the change in circumstances is substantial enough to justify new litigation. This therefore leads to an overabundance of reopened cases. Although the issue of property distribution is very much interrelated with matters subject to modification, it cannot be relitigated along with them. The first chapter challenges both aspects of the current practice.

The first chapter presents two opposing arguments as a basis for a new model that attempts to achieve a good, fair, and efficient balance of competing interests. One argument suggests broadening the application of issues subject to modification and applying it to the distribution of property as well. The second argument, on the other hand, suggests eliminating relitigation and applying, instead, the principle used for the legal system in general: *res judicata*. This principle of the finality of judgment means that it is not possible to relitigate a matter that has already been determined by the court. These two contrasting arguments brought about the present suggestion of a third model.

A new model suggests both following an intermediate path and adopting the system of periodic payments from tort law, with its accompanying fixed legislative rules providing clear guidelines for relitigation and modification. The model proposes defining the present substantial change in circumstances standard through clear guidelines for modification, such as a time period before allowing relitigation and a fixed percent above or below the support payment determined in the original decree. The chapter further suggests enhancing this model with an innovative approach called "effective support." This approach ensures the consideration of property matters that are involved in issues subject to modification, while also preventing their relitigation. In other words, property matters will not be relitigated between spouses, and the judicial decision in their matter will be final. Relitigation for a modification will take place only regarding the amount of the spousal support payment, as customary in all legal systems worldwide.

Any modification of support will relate to all the effective support and not only to the amount of an actual monetary payment. The new model is fairer from the perspective of tax considerations, avoids the need for indemnification stipulations, and prevents the court from selling family property. Such a proceeding usually takes place when the individual that pays support does not have available cash. The spouses will not, for example, have to sell their house against their will, but will be able to transfer portions of their property to one another instead of the payment of support in cash. This is consistent with the principle of "clean break," and assists both the couple and the legal system in delineating a clear and stable roadmap with respect to disputes following divorce.

The second chapter examines a minor's right to independent status in matters of family law, the importance and benefits of that right, the interests it competes with, and possible new approaches for the future. The right of a minor to independent status was intended to resolve a concern that parents, while undergoing divorce proceedings and focused on their own interests, might compromise the interests of their children. This concern has developed into a legal presumption that parents compromise the interest of minors in divorce proceedings. However, this presumption contradicts the assumption, fundamental to every legal system, that parents are natural guardians who safeguard the interests of their children in every decision involving the welfare, education, and health of the child. The best interest of the child does not assume joint custody unless shown otherwise, but depends upon the particular circumstances in each case. The best interest is a judge's finding and might ignore religious or cultural preferences of the parents where safety or health issues are involved—plus psychological assessments and educational attitudes. It is also important to remember that while the principle of the best interests of the child is the determining factor in all legal systems worldwide, both under religious law and under secular law, each court interprets it differently. It is certainly possible that a religious court might determine a place of religious education is better for the child, in contrast to the determination of a civil court. In addition, the development of a minor's right to independent status has several negative impacts on divorce proceedings, including among them contractual uncertainty, lack of finality of judgment, waste of judicial resources, and prolonged divorce proceedings between parents.

The second chapter offers the following three models for protecting the interests of the minor: (i) requiring the court to comprehensively determine the best interests of the child, using expert opinion in rabbinical courts as well, and then granting a presumption of validity to the court's determination. That determination should also serve as binding precedent for a subsequent court in accordance with the principle of finality of judgment, unless there would be a change in circumstances; (ii) legislating clear considerations and guidelines for defining the best interests of the child and thereby reducing future relitigation. Without guidelines, each court sees the best interests of the child differently, although the same factual reality is presented before all of them; and (iii) appointing independent representation for the minor. The chapter discusses the age at which such representation is suitable and appropriate. These models may serve to create a more appropriate formula for balancing the competing interests in family law proceedings.

The third chapter examines whether extramarital relationships should be taken into consideration in determining the distribution of family property. Under the state legal systems within the United States, opinions differ as to whether this fault should be a factor in distribution of family property. The controversy is influenced by and arises from an earlier disagreement that followed the "no-fault" revolution of the 1970s, which focused on the role of fault in divorce proceedings. The discussion of fault with regard to property distribution took place without in-depth consideration of the underlying basis and rationales for the principles of joint property and, even more importantly, without relating to their modern, theoretical and current bases. The third chapter fills this void, clarifies the modern bases for the principles of joint property, and through them sheds new light on the role of fault. An example is the question of whether a person, who had an extramarital relationship which brought about the end of the marriage, should receive a smaller portion in the distribution of family property. This analysis produces a new model for examining the relevance of fault in property distribution. Although the model does not answer all the questions, it certainly offers a more accurate and fairer formula for dealing with the issue of extramarital relations and the sanction for them.

In order to clearly and precisely focus on the theoretical rationales for joint family property and the establishment of a new model, this chapter also examines the Israeli legal system. It is important to mention that in Israel the religious law applies to matters of marriage and divorce, but not to the distribution of property. With regard to matters of property distribution, regular civil law applies in accordance with the civil principles that are also customary throughout the world. Therefore, the Israeli case law in this matter can both benefit from and provide a new balance to that which is customary in the world. At the end of the 1970s, one court decision determined, without explanation, that extramarital relationships are not a relevant consideration in property distribution. The third chapter analyzes the theoretical bases of property distribution principles under both Israeli law and Jewish religious law, including the ways in which these legal systems each relate to extramarital relationships.

The fourth chapter discusses the arrangement for balancing marital resources. This arrangement was established to replace the presumption of sharing that had applied in Israel until 1973. The presumption of sharing allowed claims for unregistered rights in family assets, failed to maintain certainty of property ownership and value, and did not protect the interests of third parties. Under the presumption of sharing, the spouse whose property is not registered in his or her name may claim ownership of half of the registered property, although there is no evidence of his or her right in the Land Registry. As a result of this claim, a third party that purchases the property in reliance upon the Land Registry loses half of the property for the benefit of the spouse whose ownership was not registered at all.

However, the arrangement for the balancing of resources addresses all of these concerns. The difficulty is that a failure in the structure of the

Property Relations Law prevented implementation of the legislature's intent. The Supreme Court tried to remedy this flaw based on a flexible application of general property law. The chapter argues that the flexible interpretation of the general property law is relevant only before Amendment 4 to the Property Relations Law was enacted. After the amendment, which allowed for property distribution prior to divorce, this construction was no longer justified.

The fourth chapter analyzes and is inspired by legal systems worldwide. It proposes a new model, suggesting the return to the basic requirements of the Property Relations Law as designed by the legislature. This model will provide for protection of property, clarity among creditors, increase in the family's property value, and relief to engaged or married individuals who are concerned about their separate assets.

The fifth chapter discusses the recognition of foreign civil marriages. The State of Israel has no separation of religion and state in matters of divorce and marriage. Religion is the only determining factor in these matters. Thus, marriages prohibited by religious law do not formally take place in all four major religions in Israel: Christianity, Islam, the Druze religion, and Judaism. Two examples of such marriages are a marriage between spouses of different religions which is prohibited by Jewish law, or a marriage between same-sex spouses which is prohibited by all religions. However, an individual who enters a marriage prohibited by religious law can be married in countries outside of Israel. Upon presentation of an official public record from those countries, that individual is entitled to be registered in the Population Registry as married. If the spouses have no religion, there are no religious restrictions but only civil restrictions for their marriage. Included among them are bigamy and the prohibition of the marriage of minors.

The discussion under Israeli law should have ended here with regard to civil marriage performed in a foreign country, especially marriage prohibited by Jewish law such as marriage between spouses only one of whom is Jewish. Prohibited marriage has no place in a state in which religious law prevails in matters of status.

However, the Israeli courts, unlike the legislature, have more of a civil orientation than a religious one. They look for ways to bridge the gap between religious law and the rules of private international law that seek to recognize or respect civil legal actions carried out in a foreign country. In some cases, the courts have recognized the status of civil marriages even when such marriages are prohibited by state law. In order to avoid the serious conflict between religious law and the domestic rules of private international law, the court has explained that this is not a matter of personal status, but rather an administrative question which purely concerns the Population Registry.

The decisions made in these matters are greatly disputed and reflect the constant prevailing tensions regarding Israel not only as a Jewish state (characterized by religious law) but also as a democratic state (characterized, among other factors, by recognition of the rules of private international law). Although the Basic Laws stipulate that Israel is both, in practice these values conflict and often collide. This tension is clearly reflected in and may be analyzed through the issue of civil marriages performed in a foreign country and prohibited by religious law in Israel. This issue also illustrates the uniqueness of the book that tells the Israeli story which combines civil secular law with religious law. While some matters are determined by religious law and others by civil law, the Supreme Court frequently tries to balance between them.

The sixth chapter deals with the issue of document disclosure in family courts. In 1995 the Family Court Law established family courts in Israel. The law determined that various family matters, previously under the separate jurisdictions of different courts, would all be brought before one judicial authority. For example, before the family court was established, the issue of alimony was determined by the district court, while the dissolution of couple's apartment was brought before the magistrates' court. In contrast, child custody was in the jurisdiction of the juvenile court. The establishment of the family court concentrated all these issues under its authority.

Together with the establishment of the family courts, the need arose to determine their applicable procedures. The rules of procedure that apply to general proceedings were not fitting for sensitive family disputes. Therefore, a unique section of family court procedures was incorporated into the general rules of procedure in order to address the special needs of the family dispute. The seventh chapter analyzes the tension between the general rules of procedure and those of the family court, especially with regard to mandatory disclosure.

The restrictive family court procedural rule that prohibits courts from ordering disclosure of documents between the couple prevents the courts from ascertaining the truth for efficient and just conflict resolution. It is also inconsistent with the family court's purpose of achieving speedy and effective dispute resolution with the consent of the parties. When one party is unable to see the documents of the other, each one strongly maintains his or her position, is unwilling to compromise, and refuses to personally come to terms with a judicial decision given on the basis of an incomplete picture. The chapter argues that the family courts should be granted even broader authority for issuing document disclosure orders than is customary in the general courts. Such authority could also prevent suspicions and concerns between married spouses with respect to the preservation of documents. They will be assured that the legal system will protect them should the need arise. This suggestion is also inspired by other legal systems around the world.

The first chapter is based on an article that was published in 2014 in the *Drake Law Review* (volume 62, p. 313). The second chapter is based on an article that was published in 2015 in the *Northwestern Journal of Law and Social Policy* (volume 9, issue 2). The third chapter is based on an article that was published in 2015 in the *Missouri Law Review*. The fourth chapter is based on an article that was published in 2017 in the *International Journal of the Jurisprudence of the Family*. The fifth chapter is based on an article that was published in 2017 in the *Yearbook of Private International Law*. The sixth chapter is based on an article that was published in 2014 in the *Houston Journal of International Law*.

CHAPTER 1

Issues Subject to Modification in Family Law

I. INTRODUCTION

In legal systems throughout the world, family law includes an exceptional practice: modification of certain matters that have already been adjudicated. This practice allows litigants to revisit legal proceedings that would otherwise have been settled, provided that the standard of a "substantial change in circumstances" is met. This practice deviates from the principles of *res judicata* and the finality of judgments that are customary in all the other areas, such as tort law and contract law. Most significantly, the vague standard for relitigation worsens an already problematic and ongoing connection between the spouses, in violation of the principle of a "clean break."[1] Modification has also resulted in the development of indemnification stipulations within divorce agreements.[2] Guarantors were usually sought to ensure adherence with the agreements. These indemnification requirements delay the completion of the divorce settlement and are detrimental to the economic efficiency that the legal system seeks to promote.[3]

The scholarly literature has not focused upon the practice of modification and relitigation because it is relevant only in post-divorce proceedings with regard to a change in circumstances. The purpose of this chapter is to review the appropriateness, justification, and scope of the modification practice. It also examines the corresponding relationship of that practice with other issues that are not subject to modification, particularly the distribution of marital

1 *See* Mary Ann Glendon, The New Family and the New Property 60 (1981); June Carbone, *Feminism, Gender and the Consequences of Divorce*, *in* Divorce: Where Next? 181, 189 (Michael Freeman ed., 1996).

2 *See, e.g.*, Lay v. Lay, 912 S.W.2d 466, 472 (Mo. 1995) (discussing spouses' separation agreement, which provided that "the party found to be in default in any enforcement proceedings would be responsible for reasonable attorney fees").

3 *See* Zollie Steakley & Weldon U. Howell, Jr., *Ruminations on Res Judicata*, 28 Sw. L.J. 355, 359 (1974).

property.[4] After analyzing this practice[5] and highlighting its weaknesses as reflected in two opposing arguments,[6] the book offers a new model that may better address the conflicting interests.[7] This model may bring about greater certainty, clarity, and predictability; lessen the amount of litigation in family disputes; delineate a clear plan of action for resolving future conflicts; and more fairly consider the involvement of property distribution in matters subject to modification. The model can be applied worldwide. In this way, it may even decrease the level of tension subsequent to divorce proceedings that eventually becomes engrained in the lives of the spouses, their children, and even in the entire community.

II. ISSUES SUBJECT TO MODIFICATION IN FAMILY LAW

In family law, certain issues are excluded from the principles of *res judicata* and the finality of judgments.[8] In those instances, a litigant may reinitiate a proceeding in a matter that has already been decided, provided that the litigant shows a substantial change in circumstances.[9] This is a critical condition. The change

---

4 Determining what property constitutes "marital property" is beyond the scope of this chapter. *See generally* 24 AM. JUR. 2D *Divorce and Separation* §§ 477–478 (2008) (discussing marital property, which is subject to equitable distribution in divorce proceedings).

5 *See* discussion *infra* Parts II–III in this chapter.

6 *See* discussion *infra* part IV.A–B in this chapter.

7 *See* discussion *infra* part IV.C. in this chapter.

8 The doctrine of *res judicata* states "that a cause of action once finally determined, without appeal, between the parties, on the merits, by any competent tribunal, cannot afterwards be litigated by new proceedings either before the same or any other tribunal." Foster v. The Richard Busteed, 100 Mass. 409, 412 (1868); *accord* Cnty. of Wayne v. City of Detroit, 590 N.W.2d 619, 620–21 (Mich. Ct. App. 1998) ("Under the doctrine of res judicata, 'a final judgment rendered by a court of competent jurisdiction on the merits is conclusive as to the rights of the parties and their privies, and, as to them, constitutes an absolute bar to a subsequent action involving the same claim, demand or cause of action.'" (quoting BLACK'S LAW DICTIONARY 1305 (6th ed. 1990)); *see also* Steakley & Howell, *supra* note 3, at 355–57.

9 Professor Joan G. Wexler, in the context of child custody modifications, states:
"Each of the approaches to modification applications ... represents an attempt to balance competing policy interests. Trying to balance the policies behind the res judicata doctrine on the one hand, and the policies in favor of making the best-advised contemporary determination of the child's welfare on the other, the traditional changed circumstances doctrine holds that not just any changed circumstances, but only substantial ones, should warrant changing custody." Joan G. Wexler, *Rethinking the Modification of Child Custody Decrees*, 94 YALE L.J. 757, 779 (1985); *see also* Sally Burnett Sharp, *Modification of Agreement-Based Custody Decrees: Unitary or Dual Standard?*, 68 VA. L. REV. 1263, 1264 n.9 (1982) ("The change of circumstances standard is based on principles of res judicata").

of circumstances standard is intended to prevent unnecessary litigation for the couple and their children.[10] The important question is whether this standard accomplishes its objective. The clearest instances of the practice of modification are in matters of child custody and visitation.[11] Several fundamental reasons form the rationale for preserving the rights to future modification only with respect to these issues, as opposed to other areas of litigation. First, present policies of adjudication usually require the determination of past acts and facts, and not a prediction of future events.[12] In most litigation, the result depends upon the court's determination that some event did or did not take place at an earlier time.[13] However, custody litigation attempts to predict the future rather than to understand the past.[14] Second, custody disputes require "person-oriented" and not "act-oriented" determinations.[15] In custody disputes a court must evaluate the attitudes, dispositions, capacities, and shortcomings of each parent in order to apply the best-interest standard.[16] Third, evaluating the best interests of the child requires a prediction based in part on the future behavior of the parties.[17] However, most disputes resolved by adjudication do not require appraisals of future relationships.[18] In short, adjudication in custody disputes should look forward toward the continuation of the family in the future, instead of looking back at its past. It is certainly difficult to predict different scenarios, such as a new marriage of one spouse. Therefore, it is always possible to appeal to the court on grounds of change of circumstances.

Certain legal systems have addressed these issues in legislation, in addition to judicial decisions, and have permitted the courts to modify previously issued orders.[19] For example, the law in Alaska states:

---

10 *See* Richard Montes et al., *The Changed-Circumstance Rule and the Best Interest of the Child*, L.A. LAW., Dec. 2001, at 12, 12 ("[O]ne of the purposes of the [changed-circumstance] rule is to recognize the finality of judgments and protect the parties and the child from harmful and needless relitigation of the issues of custody and visitation").

11 *See* Sharp, *supra* note 9, at 1264 ("[I]t is elemental that courts have continuing jurisdiction over matters affecting children, and therefore they may always modify the custodial provisions of a decree." (footnote omitted)).

12 Robert H. Mnookin, *Child-Custody Adjudication: Judicial Functions in the Face of Indeterminacy*, LAW & CONTEMP. PROBS., Summer 1975, at 226, 250.

13 *Id.* at 250–51.

14 *Id.* at 251.

15 *Id.* at 250.

16 *Id.* at 251 (emphasis omitted).

17 *Id.* at 252.

18 *Id.* at 253.

19 Wexler, *supra* note 9, at 760.

> An award of custody of a child or visitation with the child may be modified if the court determines that a change in circumstances requires the modification of the award and the modification is in the best interests of the child.[20]

The authority of the court to modify orders also applies to child support awards, based upon the same rationale.[21] This practice is also customary with respect to alimony. Indeed, every state within the United States permits its courts to modify alimony awards when a party can demonstrate a change in circumstances.[22]

---

20 ALASKA STAT. § 25.20.110(a) (2012); *accord* Lee v. Cox, 790 P.2d 1359, 1361 (Alaska 1990); Garding v. Garding, 767 P.2d 183, 184–85 (Alaska 1989). Other countries beyond the United States use standards similar to the changed circumstances and best interests rules when considering custody orders. *See, e.g.*, Divorce Act, R.S.C. 1985, c. 3, s. 17(5) (Can.) (providing that before making a variation to a custody order, "the court shall satisfy itself that there has been a change in the condition, means, needs or other circumstances of the child ... [and] the court shall take into consideration only the best interests of the child"); *Sampson v Hartnett (No. 10)* (2007) 215 Fam LR 155, 164 (Austl.) (explaining the need to consider the child's best interests, as well as whether an order is "reasonably practicable," when making parenting orders). Although many courts must consider the child's best interests foremost in parental custody orders, when third-party visitation rights are concerned (including grandparents or adult siblings) such consideration must often be balanced with the parents' own parental rights. *See generally* Melissa Curry, *Who Gets to Visit? A History of Third-Party Visitation Rights in Family Court*, 16 J. CONTEMP. LEGAL ISSUES 289 (2007) (discussing the interaction of parental decisionmaking rights, third-party visitation, and the best interests of the child).

21 *See, e.g.*, WIS. STAT. ANN. § 767.59(1f) (West 2009) (providing that a modification of a child support order may be made only if there has been a substantial change in circumstances affecting the parties). The change in circumstances standard is also used in other countries when courts consider modifications of child support orders. For example, in Malaysia,

> [i]t is common ground that [the Law Reform (Marriage and Divorce) Act of 1976] give[s] to the court a general power to vary or rescind any subsisting periodical payments for the wife and/or the children of the marriage where it is satisfied that ... there has been any material change in the circumstances.

Gisela Gertrud Abe v. Tan Wee Kiat, [1986] 2 M.L.J. 297, 298 (Malay.) (citations omitted).

22 Newsome v. Newsome, 984 So. 2d 463, 465–66 (Ala. Civ. App. 2007) ("At trial, the party seeking to modify a trial court's judgment regarding alimony must make a showing that, since the trial court's previous judgment, there has been a 'material change in the circumstances of the parties.'" (quoting Posey v. Posey, 634 So. 2d 571, 572 (Ala. Civ. App. 1994)); ALASKA STAT. § 25.24.170(b) (2012); ARIZ. REV. STAT. ANN. § 25–327 (2007); ARK. CODE ANN. § 9-12-312(a)(7) (Supp. 2013); CAL. FAM. CODE § 3591 (West 2004); COLO. REV. STAT. § 14-10-122(1)(a) (2013); CONN. GEN. STAT. ANN. § 46b-86(a) (West 2009); DEL. CODE ANN. tit. 13 § 1519(a)(4) (2009); D.C. CODE § 16-914.01 (LexisNexis 2008); FLA. STAT. ANN. § 61.14(1)(a) (West 2012); GA. CODE ANN. § 19-6-19 to -20 (West 2010); HAW. REV. STAT. § 580-47 (2006); IDAHO CODE ANN. § 32-709 (2006); 750 ILL. COMP. STAT.

Interestingly, these courts are typically authorized to modify not only previously issued decrees but also written agreements between the spouses, regardless of whether they are incorporated into decrees. For example, Florida law states:

> When the parties enter into an agreement for payments for, or instead of, support, maintenance, or alimony, whether in connection with a proceeding for dissolution or separate maintenance or with any voluntary property settlement, or when a party is required by court order to make

---

ANN. 5/510(a-5) (West Supp. 2013); IND. CODE ANN. § 31-15-7-3 (LexisNexis 2007); IOWA CODE § 598.21C (2013); KAN. STAT. ANN. § 23-2903 (Supp. 2012); KY. REV. STAT. ANN. § 403.250 (LexisNexis 2010); LA. REV. STAT. ANN. § 9:311(A)(1) (Supp. 2014); ME. REV. STAT. ANN. tit. 19-A, § 951-A(4) (Supp. 2013) (providing for modification "when it appears that justice requires"); MD. CODE ANN., FAM. LAW § 11-107(b) (LexisNexis 2013); MASS. GEN. LAWS ANN. ch. 208, § 37 (West 2007); MICH. COMP. LAWS ANN. § 552.28 (West 2005); MINN. STAT. ANN. § 518A.39 (West Supp. 2014); MISS. CODE ANN. § 93-5-23 (West Supp. 2013); MO. ANN. STAT. § 452.370(1) (West 2003); MONT. CODE ANN. § 40-4-208(2)(b) (2013); NEB. REV. STAT. ANN. § 42-365 (LexisNexis 2011); NEV. REV. STAT. § 125.150(10)(b) (2013); N.H. REV. STAT. ANN. § 458.33 (LexisNexis 2007); N.J. STAT. ANN. § 2A:34-23(c) (West 2010); N.M. STAT. ANN. § 40-4-7(B)(2)(a) (2006); N.Y. DOM. REL. LAW § 236(B)(9)(b)(1) (McKinney 2010); N.C. GEN. STAT. § 50-16.9 (2013); N.D. CENT. CODE § 14-05-24.1 (2009 & Supp. 2013); OHIO REV. CODE ANN. § 3105.18(E) (LexisNexis Supp. 2013); OKLA. STAT. ANN. tit. 43, § 134(C) (West 2001 & Supp. 2014); OR. REV. STAT. ANN. § 107.135 (West Supp. 2013); 23 PA. CONS. STAT. ANN. § 3701(e) (West 2010); R.I. GEN. LAWS § 15-5-16 (2013); S.C. CODE ANN. § 20-3-170 (Supp. 2012); S.D. CODIFIED LAWS § 25-4-41 (2004); TENN. CODE ANN. § 36-5-101(a)(1) (2010 & Supp. 2013); TEX. FAM. CODE ANN. § 8.057(c) (West 2006); UTAH CODE ANN. § 30-3-5(8)(i)(i) (LexisNexis 2013); VT. STAT. ANN. tit. 15, § 758 (2010); VA. CODE ANN. § 20-109(A) (2008); WASH. REV. CODE ANN. § 26.09.170 (West Supp. 2014); W. VA. CODE ANN. § 48-8-103(b) (LexisNexis Supp. 2013); WIS. STAT. ANN. § 767.59(1k) (West 2009); WYO. STAT. ANN. § 20-2-116 (2013); Schmir v. Schmir (*In re* Marriage of Schmir), 35 Cal. Rptr. 3d 716, 719 (Ct. App. 2005) (noting that a change in circumstances warranting modification has occurred when there has been "a material change since the entry of the previous order"); DeGrazia v. DeGrazia, 741 A.2d 1057, 1058–59 (D.C. 1999); *In re* Marriage of Ehinger, 121 P.3d 467, 471 (Kan. Ct. App. 2005) ("Maintenance may be reduced upon a showing of a material change in circumstances ..."); Kelley v. Kelley, 835 N.E.2d 315, 320 (Mass. App. Ct. 2005) ("Although the power ... to modify an alimony judgment under G.L. c. 208, § 37, is 'broad and general,' it has nevertheless been held 'repeatedly ... that *no modification can be made unless the party seeking modification shows a change of circumstances since the entry of the earlier judgment*.'" (second alteration in original) (quoting Binder v. Binder, 390 N.E.2d 260, 263 (Mass. App. Ct. 1979)) (internal quotation marks omitted)); Lemmen v. Lemmen, 749 N.W.2d 255, 257 (Mich. 2008) ("There would be no need to adjust the amount of spousal support unless there had been a change in the circumstances of either party."); Lee v. Lee, 699 N.W.2d 842, 846 (N.D. 2005) ("Spousal support will be modified upon a showing of a material change in circumstances." (citing Wheeler v. Wheeler, 419 N.W.2d 923, 925 (N.D. 1988));

> any payments, and the circumstances or the financial ability of either party changes ..., either party may apply ... for an order decreasing or increasing the amount of support, maintenance, or alimony, and the court has jurisdiction to make orders as equity requires, with due regard to the changed circumstances.[23]

Moore v. Moore, 763 N.W.2d 536, 539–40 (S.D. 2009); Maher v. Maher, 90 P.3d 739, 743 (Wyo. 2004) ("[T]his court has clarified that a party seeking modification of alimony must establish that there has been a material and substantial change of circumstances which outweighs the interest of society in applying the doctrine of *res judicata*").

Despite the prevalence of alimony modification across the United States, its continued presence in family law jurisprudence has been questioned by academics. For example, Professor Robert Kirkman Collins has argued

> [o]f the three financial issues raised by divorce—asset division, child support, and spousal maintenance—the question of alimony is typically the least predictable and the most contentious. With assets, judges even in equitable distribution jurisdictions tend to apply a presumption of equal division in most marriages of significant duration. ... On the issue of child support, while there remains room for bargaining by higher-income parents, most couples settle within the shadow, if not by strict application, of statutory child support guidelines. Only with regard to alimony is there no fixed frame of reference for discussions. Spousal support negotiations are particularly difficult because of the absence of any objective standard for judging fairness or predicting outcomes. Statutes simply list factors for trial courts to consider without providing any guidance as to how the judge should weigh or apply them.

Robert Kirkman Collins, *The Theory of Marital Residuals: Applying an Income Adjustment Calculus to the Enigma of Alimony*, 24 HARV. WOMEN'S L.J. 23, 23 (2001).

23 FLA. STAT. ANN. § 61.14(1)(a) (West 2012); *accord* Armstrong v. Armstrong, 544 P.2d 941, 943 (Cal. 1976) ("When a child support agreement is incorporated in a child support order, the obligation created is deemed court-imposed rather than contractual, and the order is subsequently modifiable despite the agreement's language to the contrary." (citing CAL. CIV. CODE § 4811 (1976)). However, some states apply a different standard for modification between decrees and agreements. The Supreme Court of Kansas, for instance, has held that when a custody decree is entered in a default proceeding, and the facts are not substantially developed and presented to the court, the trial court may later, in its discretion, admit and consider evidence as to facts existing at the time of the earlier order, and upon the full presentation of the facts the court may enter any order which could have been made at the initial hearing whether a "change in circumstances" has since occurred or not. Hill v. Hill, 620 P.2d 1114, 1119 (Kan. 1980). Thus, a consensual award is always subject to judicial review under a pure best interests standard, but if initial custody was awarded after litigation, the traditional modification test applies. *See id.*; Wexler, *supra* note 9, at 767–68. Kansas is one of several jurisdictions that rejected the changed circumstances rule for nonlitigated decrees. *See* Stewart v. Stewart, 383 P.2d 617, 619–20 (Idaho 1963); *Hill*, 620 P.2d at 1119; Friederwitzer v. Friederwitzer, 432 N.E.2d 765, 768 (N.Y. 1982); Kolb v. Kolb, 324 N.W.2d 279, 283 (S.D. 1982); Elmer v. Elmer, 776 P.2d 599, 603 (Utah 1989); McDaniel v. McDaniel, 539 P.2d 699,

In North Carolina, agreements between spouses must preserve the rights to future modification on three issues:

> It is the policy of this state to allow, by agreement of all parties, the arbitration of all issues arising from a marital separation or divorce, except for the divorce itself, while preserving a right of modification based on substantial change of circumstances related to alimony, child custody, and child support.[24]

Furthermore, a stipulation agreed upon by the parties is unenforceable on grounds of public policy.[25] Thus, a trial court will always be able to modify a child support agreement regardless of a stipulation between the parties.[26]

III. BARGAINING AND INDEMNIFICATION IN DIVORCE AGREEMENTS

In 1984, the United States Congress noted its concern about possible harm to the rights of children if custodial parents are not awarded adequate child support.[27] The determination of low amounts of support places a heavy burden on assistance organizations in the United States.[28] Thus, Congress conditioned its aid to states and assistance organizations on the determination of clear child support guidelines.[29] In 1988, Congress further demanded that these guidelines be given the validity of a presumption in a legal proceeding, so that whoever wishes to change them must provide written justification.[30] In light of these

---

701 (Wash. Ct. App. 1975); Wendland v. Wendland, 138 N.W.2d 185, 191–92 (Wis. 1965). *But see* Kraft v. Kraft (*In re* Marriage of Kraft), 868 N.E.2d 1181, 1188–89 (Ind. Ct. App. 2007) (holding that regardless of whether child support was based on a court hearing or a mediated agreement, the change in circumstances standard should be interpreted in the same way).

24 N.C. GEN. STAT. § 50-41.

25 *See, e.g., id.* at §§ 50-42.1(c), -56.

26 *See, e.g.,* Fernandez v. Fernandez, 222 P.3d 1031, 1034–35 (Nev. 2010).

27 *See* Child Support Enforcement Amendments of 1984, Pub. L. No. 98-378, § 23, 98 Stat. 1305, 1329–30.

28 *See generally* Gale M. Phelps & Jerald L. Miller, *The New Indiana Child Support Guidelines*, 22 IND. L. REV. 203, 204–5 (1988) (discussing the need for statewide child support guidelines as seen by Congress prior to 1984).

29 Child Support Enforcement Amendments of 1984 § 18 (codified as amended at 42 U.S.C. § 667).

30 Family Support Act of 1988, Pub. L. No. 100-485, § 103, 102 Stat. 2343, 2346 (codified at 42 U.S.C. § 667).

requirements, guidelines have been defined in each of the states.[31] The amount of basic child support is calculated as a certain percentage of parental income, which differs significantly among the states.[32] Thus, in all 50 states, clear standards and guidelines have been determined and legislated for calculating child support and enforcing payment.

In some states, child support might differ from the guidelines as a result of other elements in the parties' financial settlement. For example, the obligor may consent to compromises in the distribution of property or agree that the custodial parent remain in the marital home, in exchange for a lower amount of child support than that determined by the guidelines.[33] The spouses could maintain this approach by setting contractual limitations upon the right to modify child support.[34] Some courts have questioned such efforts to restrict the court's authority to modify child support due to a party's change in circumstances.[35] These courts seem to take into consideration that such agreements might have undesirable impacts upon the well-being of children.[36] Certain

31 *See, e.g.*, CONN. GEN. STAT. ANN. §§ 46b-215a to -215b (West 2009), GA. CODE ANN. § 19-6-15(c)(1) (West 2010 & Supp. 2012), LA. REV. STAT. ANN. § 9:315.1-.19 (2012), MD. CODE ANN., FAM. LAW §§ 12-202, -204 (LexisNexis 2013), MISS. CODE ANN. § 43-19-101 (West Supp. 2013), NEB. REV. STAT. ANN. § 42-364.16 (LexisNexis 2011), N.C. GEN. STAT. § 50-13.4(c1) (2013), N.D. CENT. CODE § 14-09-09.7(4) (2009), OR. REV. STAT. ANN. §§ 25.275, .280 (West 2013), WYO. STAT. ANN. § 20-2-304 (2013).

32 *Compare* WYO. STAT. ANN. § 20-2-304, *with* LA. REV. STAT. ANN. § 9:315.19.

33 *See, e.g.*, Kelley v. Kelley, 449 S.E.2d 55, 55–56 (Va. 1994).

34 *See, e.g.*, *id.*

35 *See, e.g.*, Guille v. Guille, 492 A.2d 175, 179 (Conn. 1985) ("Although [the agreement] may have been effective to define permanently the support obligations of the divorcing parties as between themselves, [it cannot] be held binding as to their minor children, who were unrepresented during both the negotiation of the stipulation and the dissolution proceedings."); Lieberman v. Lieberman, 568 A.2d 1157, 1163 (Md. Ct. Spec. App. 1990) ("A parent cannot agree to preclude a child's right to support by the other parent, or the right to have that support modified in appropriate circumstances."); Brenneman v. Brenneman, No. WD-90-33, 1991 WL 49998, at *5 (Ohio Ct. App. Apr. 5, 1991) ("[T]he obligor parent cannot, by means of his own contract, totally relieve himself/herself of the obligation to support a minor child and the custodial parent cannot barter away the child's right to that support."); *In re* Marriage of Wood, 806 P.2d 722, 723 (Or. Ct. App. 1991) ("Parents cannot, by their agreement, avoid the continuing obligation to contribute to the support of their children."); *see also* Elliot L. Epstein, *The Enforceability of Extra-Statutory and Repudiated Divorce Settlement Agreements*, 8 ME. B.J. 144, 145 (1993) (discussing policy concerns surrounding such extra-statutory settlement agreements).

36 One Maryland court noted that such agreements jeopardize the child's best interest in not becoming a ward of the state: "The [s]tate has a vested interest in requiring a responsible parent to support his or her child. Otherwise, the [s]tate could be responsible in whole or in part for the support of a minor child, even though a parent is financially able to meet those

opinions even determine that parents may not restrict a court's ability to modify child support.[37]

Because family law includes issues subject to future modification, and courts tend not to enforce a stipulation limiting such modification, one spouse (or that spouse's legal counsel) may be concerned that the other will request a modification of the agreement's terms, and in that way disrupt the balance of interests achieved by the settlement. Waiver of the right to modification will not be helpful. The courts view the possibility of modification as an integral part of the agreement, even if the parties were either silent or agreed not to relitigate in the future. Therefore in some jurisdictions, including the Israeli legal system, it is common practice for the spouse who is concerned about future claims to attempt to seek protection within the divorce agreement itself, through an indemnification stipulation.[38] It establishes that if one of the spouses initiates a future modification proceeding, then that party also promises to indemnify the other spouse, whether by financial payment or by return of a portion of the property received under the terms of the divorce agreement.[39]

The goal of the stipulation for indemnification is preventative. It aims to block in advance future claims for modification of the terms of the agreement.[40] When the stipulation does not succeed in doing so, and a claim is brought after the divorce to adjust one of the matters subject to modification, the defendant

---

obligations. We hold that a parent may not, even potentially, shift the burden of support to the [s]tate."

Lieberman, 568 A.2d at 1163–64.

37 *See, e.g.*, Mora v. Mora, 861 S.W.2d 226, 228 (Mo. Ct. App. 1993) ("Only a court of law has the power to alter future child support payments."); Comeaux v. Comeaux, 767 S.W.2d 500, 503 (Tex. App. 1989) ("We reject the sterile concept that, if the child support payments [provided in an agreement] are approved in the divorce decree, the same cannot be ... attacked collaterally once the judgment is final. ... [S]uch conceptualistic, unrealistic thinking is simply out of place in the modern-day world of numerous, tragic divorces involving minor children."); Grimes v. Grimes, 621 A.2d 211, 214 (Vt. 1992).

38 *See, e.g.*, DN 4/82 Kot v. Kot 38(3) PD 197 [1984] (Isr.).

39 The following is an example of an indemnification stipulation in an agreement incident to divorce: "In the event [wife] should ever petition any [c]ourt of competent jurisdiction for support and maintenance of [the children], and should a Court grant any such child support award, the said [wife] hereby covenants and agrees to pay directly to [husband], any amount of support that he is directed to pay to any party. In other words, [wife] is agreeing to hold harmless [Husband] from the payment of any amount of child support, regardless of the circumstances under which he is paying same." *Kelley*, 449 S.E.2d at 55–56 (alterations in original).

40 Sometimes the indemnification mechanism is ensured by a guarantee. *See, e.g.*, DN 4/82 Kot v. Kot 38(3) PD 197 [1984] (Isr.).

spouse has no other choice but to require implementation of the indemnification as well.

For example, it is not unusual for the noncustodial spouse to have difficulty providing monthly child support or alimony payments. Therefore, in some divorce agreements the couple consents to a less-than-customary amount of child support or alimony,[41] and agrees that this amount will not be increased in any way whatsoever.[42] In exchange, the noncustodial spouse transfers his or her portion of the family home to the custodial spouse.[43] In order to ensure the custodial spouse's obligation not to increase the amount of child support or alimony, the indemnification stipulation is formulated so that if the custodial spouse breaches this obligation and files suit for modification of the child support or alimony, the obligor will be indemnified.[44]

When the custodial spouse brings a claim to increase child support, the court will generally grant the request if it is in accordance with the child's best interests and the substantial change in circumstances standard. The noncustodial spouse then asks the court to implement the indemnification stipulation, which protects that spouse's interests, and attempts to regain half of the home. However, the court avoids ruling on the property matter (half of the home) in the second proceeding because under most legal systems, the distribution of property is not subject to future modification. An order issued with respect to property division is a final order, even if the circumstances with regard to other matters subsequently change.[45] In contrast to the aforementioned issues,

---

41 This happens even in light of the guidelines. *See, e.g.*, Kraft v. Kraft (*In re* Marriage of Kraft), 868 N.E.2d 1181, 1183 (Ind. Ct. App. 2007) ("This agreement is a compromise between the parties of several competing positions expressed during mediation and may not be consistent with the Indiana Child Support Guidelines").

42 *See, e.g.*, *Kelley*, 449 S.E.2d at 55.

43 *See, e.g.*, *id.*; HCJ 8638/03 Amir v. Supreme Rabbinical Court (Apr. 6, 2006), Nevo Legal Database (by subscription) (Isr.).

44 *See, e.g.*, *Kelley*, 449 S.E.2d at 55–56. Ultimately, the Supreme Court of Virginia did not look favorably upon including this type of provision in an agreement incident to divorce: "Clearly, the parties contracted away the [h]usband's legal duty to support his children and, in effect, placed upon the [w]ife the sole duty of support. Additionally, the [w]ife's ability to contribute to the support of the children was adversely affected. Thus, the children's rights to receive support from both parents were substantially abridged, and the court's power to decree support was diminished. We hold, therefore, that the challenged provision of the [a]greement is null and void because it is violative of clearly established law." *Id.* at 56.

45 *See, e.g.*, Mo. Ann. Stat. § 452.330(5) (West 2003) ("The court's order as it affects distribution of marital property shall be a final order not subject to modification ..."); Rosato v. Rosato, 822 A.2d 974, 979 (Conn. App. Ct. 2003) ("[T]he assignment of property may only be made at the time of the marital dissolution and it is not thereafter subject to

property distribution is presently considered "act-oriented" so that the courts usually require the determination of past acts and facts, and not a prediction of future events.[46]

IV. ISSUES SUBJECT TO MODIFICATION—A NEW MODEL

This chapter reexamines the appropriate use of the change in circumstances standard and the practice of modification and relitigation in general, as well as its interrelationship with the distribution of marital property as described in the previous section. I will present two arguments in support of a new model that represents another balance among modification issues and other issues in a divorce dispute.

A. Argument I: Broadening Issues Subject to Modification

1. *A Theoretical View*

It seems that the legal rationale at the basis of issues subject to modification is also applicable to the distribution of property. The customary reasons for categorizing a matter as subject to modification also hold true with respect to the distribution of marital property. For example, the classification of child support as an issue subject to modification is explained as follows:

> By its nature, this matter is different in its purpose from other obligations for payment of money. Generally, when a monetary claim is brought before a court the judge's work is completed with the issuing of a decision. However, with respect to child support, the payment obligation may change even subsequent to the judgment. If the father's income decreases, he is allowed to request that the court decrease the amount of support that

---

modification. ..."); Ricciuti v. Ricciuti, No. FA0004353345, 2003 WL 21716434, at *1 (Conn. Super. Ct. July 7, 2003) ("Pensions are treated as property in financial orders in a dissolution, and are therefore nonmodifiable." (citations omitted)); Ratliff v. Ratliff, No. 97APF10-1294, 1998 WL 514039, (Ohio Ct. App. Aug. 18, 1998) ("The division of marital assets pursuant to [Revised Code §] 3105.17.1 does not provide for modification due to change of circumstance ..."); *see also* Norma Harwood, A Woman's Legal Guide to Separation and Divorce in All 50 States 34 (1985) ("There is one other steadfast rule recognized by all courts in all states: No part of a court-ordered property division can later be changed by the court unless the court expressly reserves the power in the original decree").

46 *See supra* notes 12–18 and accompanying text (discussing the rationale for allowing modification of custody orders).

> he is obligated to pay. If the child's needs increase, the custodial mother may demand an increase in the child support that was allocated to her. Every change in circumstances that is a factor in determining the amount of the obligation justifies returning to the court which will reexamine its decision.[47]

This paragraph apparently explains why the possibility of relitigating child support must be preserved.[48] However, the deeper one looks into it, the more it seems that there is no true distinction between a determination of child support and a decision regarding the distribution of marital property. In the equitable distribution of marital property, courts consider the mutual contributions of the spouses, their professional status at the time of separation, and the abilities they acquired during the marriage. The court fashions the division of property accordingly.[49]

It is therefore fitting to modify the division of property in the event of a change in circumstances in order to rebalance the strengths of the spouses. It seems fair to continue to grant an additional advantage to the weaker spouse whose weakness results from having waived professional development during the marriage. If the income of one spouse decreases, that spouse should be permitted to request that the court readjust the property distribution. If the needs of one spouse increase, that spouse should be entitled to demand an increase in the distributed property. After all, the property distribution was formed in

---

47 HCJ 59/53 Housman v. Director of Jerusalem Center for Execution of Judgments 7 PD 1142, 1147 [1953] (Isr.).

48 *See id.*

49 For example, the Uniform Marriage and Divorce Act provides that, in distributing marital property, [t]he court shall consider the duration of the marriage, and prior marriage of either party, antenuptial agreement of the parties, the age, health, station, occupation, amount and sources of income, vocational skills, employability, estate, liabilities, and needs of each of the parties, ... and the opportunity of each for future acquisition of capital assets and income.

UNIF. MARRIAGE & DIVORCE ACT § 307 Alt. A, 9A U.L.A. 288 (1998). Courts across the United States use similar factors to determine whether the distribution of marital property, if not equal, is equitable. *See, e.g.*, Giammarco v. Giammarco, 959 A.2d 531, 534 (R.I. 2008). In one such case, the Supreme Court of North Dakota explained why the trial court awarded the husband nearly $4,500 more property than the wife: "This marriage was of relatively short duration, and ... [the husband] brought considerably more property into the marriage. ... At the time of the hearing [the wife] was earning more than [the husband]. Furthermore, [the husband] is 43 years old while [the wife] is only 27 years old, so [the wife] has both greater income and presumably more years to accumulate an estate. Therefore, the [trial] court could have concluded [the husband] has a greater need to be awarded additional property now." Schmidkunz v. Schmidkunz, 529 N.W.2d 857, 860 (N.D. 1995).

accordance with particular circumstances. When those circumstances change, the original distribution of property may no longer be equitable because it does not take into account the later occurrences. Therefore, it becomes appropriate to adjust the distribution of property.[50]

The argument has been made that child support and custody, unlike property distribution, are classified as matters subject to modification because they deal with the best interests of the child. In contrast, property distribution focuses only on the relationship between the parents. This approach may be refuted by two counterarguments. First, the protection of the child may be ensured through the principle of the right of a minor to independent status.[51] Second, judicial decisions classify alimony as a matter subject to modification.[52] The customary rationale for this is that the matter involves an ongoing relationship, as well as decisions that determine future rights and obligations.[53] Therefore, changes in the needs of the obligee or in the earning capacity of the obligor serve as justifications to relitigate and modify an earlier judgment to meet the changed circumstances. Thus, what is in the best interests of the child is not the exclusive factor for designating which matters are subject to modification.

In fact, marital property distribution as alimony is also a decision that determines future rights and obligations. Property distribution defines which

---

50 The well-known determination that distribution of property is not modifiable appears to be incorrect, at least in Alaska and in connection with a pension. *See* ALASKA R. CIV. P. 60(b)(6); Lowe v. Lowe, 817 P.2d 453, 458–59 (Alaska 1991) (noting that a party is entitled to modify the distribution of property in a final divorce decree under "extraordinary circumstances" based on four factors: "(1) the fundamental, underlying assumption of the dissolution agreement ha[s] been destroyed; (2) the parties' property division was poorly thought out; (3) the property division was reached without the benefit of counsel; and (4) the [asset in controversy] was the parties' principal asset"); Gearhart v. Gearhart, No. 17725, 1999 WL 1043894, at *3 (Ohio Ct. App. Nov. 19, 1999) (noting that modification of the distribution of a pension "can be granted when confusion arises over the interpretation of a particular clause of the [order]" or when the original order "did not contemplate unforeseen contingencies and leads to absurd and unintended results").

51 *See* Simcox v. Simcox, 546 N.E.2d 609, 611 (Ill. 1989) ("[C]hildren are *not* privies of their parents [in dissolution proceedings], because the interests of children are not properly represented in such proceedings."); Guillermo v. Guillermo, 252 N.Y.S.2d 171, 181 (Fam. Ct. 1964) ("No parent should be able to bind a child by buying matrimonial freedom at the price of selling a child's material or other security, even if a court approves such agreement. ... No child support decree should be sacrosanct if 'incidental' to, and inequitably incidental to, the problems of adults").

52 *See supra* notes 22–23 and accompanying text.

53 *See supra* notes 12–18 and accompanying text (discussing similar rationale for allowing modifications of custody orders).

property will remain in the hands of each of the spouses and sometimes where they will live, so that it is not only a determination regarding the past but also relates to the future. Property distribution can become unjust in light of future changes. Changes in an obligee's needs or in an obligor's earning capacity should serve as grounds for redetermining property distribution. If one of the spouses ceases to earn an income and the original property distribution took earning capacity into consideration, it is necessary to modify a judgment even though it is included in the property distribution. More than the practicality of this argument, it clarifies the rationale and justification for the relitigation.

Furthermore, a number of recent foreign family court decisions have dealt with the distribution of career assets and earning capacity, which are clearly matters of property.[54] They ruled that in these matters it is appropriate to determine renewable, periodic payments that are modifiable when there is a change in circumstances.[55] Property distribution is a decision that anticipates the future and, as such, it should take into consideration a change in a spouse's circumstances. Just as a support payment is subject to modification, property distribution or at least a portion of the parameters that make up the claim for property distribution should also be subject to change.[56]

The ideological closeness between the concepts of property distribution and alimony is reflected in Professor Ira Ellman's proposal that the concept of alimony should be replaced with a new mechanism of compensation for loss of career, which is clearly a matter of property.[57] Furthermore, Professor Rosen-Zvi clearly explains:

> In litigation regarding the rights of spouses, at the time of their separation the determination of support payments must take into consideration the distribution of property, and the reverse is also true. To a certain extent, after the divorce the determination of alimony may also serve as a

54 *See, e.g.*, FA 1033/03 (TA) A. v. L. (Apr. 19, 2004), Nevo Legal Database (by subscription) (Isr.); FamilC (TA) 37181/97 T. v. T, PM 5761, 577, 623 (2001) (Isr.).

55 *See* FA (TA) 1033/03 A. v. L. (Apr. 19, 2004), Nevo Legal Database (by subscription) (Isr.); FamilC (TA) 37181/97 T. v. T, PM 5761, 577, 623 (2001) (Isr.).

56 For example, a change of circumstances should not relate merely to future earning capacity but also to a change in mortgage payments. *See* Passamano v. Passamano, 612 A.2d 141, 143 (Conn. App. Ct. 1992) ("The order to pay the mortgage and real estate taxes on the house was not a property award because it did not alter the parties' respective ownership interests. … Because this order resulted from the defendant's *continuing duty to support his family*, it is … modifiable." (emphasis added)), *rev'd*, 634 A.2d 891 (Conn. 1993).

57 *See* Ira Mark Ellman, *The Theory of Alimony*, 77 Calif. L. Rev. 1, 49–51 (1989).

> means to correct or complete the property distribution in an individual case. English Law and Australian Law went even farther and established the granting of support after divorce in one-time payments. In that way, they brought the two issues very close together. Moreover, under these legal systems, that include judicial discretion regarding the distribution of property during divorce, there is no longer any separation, either in the proceedings or in the judgment, between these two factors. The considerations that the court must weigh in these two issues are identical or very closely related. In that way, granting alimony through a one-time payment can serve the purpose of adjusting property within the family. The system of discretion has a double advantage: It prevents artificial division at the time of the decision making in two complementary areas, and it allows for the settlement at one time of all the economic questions between the spouses. Satisfaction of all the needs requires weighing all the different resources available to the family.[58]

The courts therefore recognize the distribution of property as a matter in which circumstances are subject to change, and thus provide for the option of periodic and modifiable payments.[59] Therefore, the basis for associating the "characteristic of finality" with property distribution is not that firm.[60] When viewed as a practical determination, it raises other troubling concerns as well.

2. *A Practical View*

A divorce settlement usually weighs all the relevant issues and interests. It is an economic package, with a reciprocal relationship among its elements. The customary practice in some countries is the equal distribution between spouses of property obtained in their joint efforts. Even in such a system with clear rules for distribution, the courts still have broad discretion to deviate from the equal division of all the property. In other countries, the customary practice is the fair and just distribution of such property between the spouses. In those countries with equitable distribution, no clear rules exist for property distribution. It remains in the broad discretion of the court. Certainly not only in the latter countries but also in the former, as shown below, property distribution is

---

58 Ariel Rosen-Zvi, The Law of Matrimonial Property 24 (1982).

59 *See, e.g.*, FA (Jer) 4623/04 Anonymous v. Anonymous, para. 24 (Aug. 26, 2007), Nevo Legal Database (by subscription) (Isr.).

60 *Id.*

determined according to its relationship with the other matters under discussion. Those matters, in turn, are considered with respect to their relationships with property distribution. Thus, for example, the division of property is sometimes interrelated with child custody. The custodial spouses may receive a larger portion of the property than they would have received had they not taken on this responsibility.[61] Sometimes the level of child support is decreased from the presumptive guideline amount in exchange for transferring a larger portion of the property to the custodial parent.[62] The determination of the amount of spousal support also takes the property distribution into account.[63] Moreover, it is not always easy to distinguish whether a payment from one spouse to the other is made in connection with the distribution of property, or is perhaps related to alimony.[64] In one case, the voluntary agreement to contribute to the expenses of

---

61 *See* Carbone, *supra* note 1, at 194–95. *But see* Elizabeth S. Scott, *Pluralism, Parental Preference, and Child Custody*, 80 CALIF. L. REV. 615, 626 (1992) (suggesting that the gender-neutral best interests rule leads women, who typically "care more about having custody than do men," to "trad[e] away claims for support and property" to ensure custody).

62 Courts often have little power to modify such agreements absent changed circumstances. For example, Texas law provides: "If the parties agree to an order under which the amount of child support differs from the amount that would be awarded in accordance with the child support guidelines, the court may modify the order only if the circumstances of the child or a person affected by the order have materially and substantially changed since the date of the order's rendition." TEX. FAM. CODE ANN. § 156.401(a-1) (West Supp. 2013).

63 In Ohio, for instance, when considering whether spousal support is appropriate and reasonable, and in determining the nature, amount, and terms of payment, and duration of spousal support, "the court shall consider ... [t]he income of the parties, from all sources, including, but not limited to, income derived from property divided, disbursed, or distributed under section 3105.171 of the Revised Code [governing the equitable division of marital property]." OHIO REV. CODE ANN. § 3105.18(C)(1)(a) (LexisNexis Supp. 2013).

64 Some states use cumbersome tests to distinguish these payments. For example, the Supreme Court of North Dakota has noted several [f]actors which may indicate that the payments are distributions of property include: payments that do not terminate after the obligee dies; payments that continue even after obligee remarries; excluding the payments in controversy, a large disparity in the property divided which is otherwise unexplained; [and] payments that do not terminate on the obligor's death. In addition, ... security for payment may tend to indicate property distribution since deferred-property payments are dischargeable in bankruptcy, unlike spousal-support payments. In contrast, factors which may indicate the amount paid is spousal support include: payments that are monthly; [and] payments that terminate upon the obligee's death or remarriage.

Redlin v. Redlin, 436 N.W.2d 5, 8 (N.D. 1989) (citations omitted). Furthermore, states are split as to whether certain types of payments under a divorce order constitute alimony or a division of property. *Compare In re* Marriage of Johnson, 781 N.W.2d 553, 557 (Iowa 2010) (holding that court-ordered support payments for wife's health insurance policy were modifiable alimony), *with* McCoy v. McCoy, 687 S.E.2d 82, 85 (Va. Ct. App. 2010) (holding that

the child, post-divorce, was not characterized either as spousal maintenance or as child support,[65] even though it was.[66] Sometimes, property distribution also takes into consideration the amount of support paid to the wife, until the time that the property is divided,[67] as well as a variety of other factors.[68]

It is therefore unreasonable to divide up divorce agreements or decrees and view only certain issues as subject to future modification, while treating others as impossible to change. Any change in one of the elements of the agreement should require a change in the other elements, since they are all interrelated. The property settlement and spousal support can impact the child support obligation. Any system for modifying child support should view a divorce settlement as a financial package.

Indeed, in some legal systems courts have determined that when there is a change of circumstances, it is appropriate to modify a property settlement if it is interconnected with a maintenance order.[69] Furthermore, in Indiana, when issues subject to modification are combined with other matters, property distribution must be modified due to the change in circumstances.[70] Other courts have

---

payment of health insurance premiums under divorce decree was not alimony and therefore did not end upon wife's remarriage).

65 Snow v. England (*In re* Marriage of Snow), 862 N.E.2d 664, 667–68 (Ind. 2007).

66 *See id.* at 665–66.

67 *See, e.g.*, CA 6557/95 Avneri v. Avneri 51(3) PD 541, 545 [1997] (Isr.) (discussing support in relation to the husband's monthly pension, and stating "[t]he result will be, that the respondent is entitled to the greater of the two: the amount of support that was ordered or the relative portion that she is entitled to in the monthly pension of the appellant"); FamilC (TA) 67910/00 Anonymous v. Anonymous (Apr. 10, 2007), Nevo Legal Database (by subscription) (Isr.).

68 *See* Robert H. Mnookin & Lewis Kornhauser, *Bargaining in the Shadow of the Law: The Case of Divorce*, 88 YALE L.J. 950, 960–63 (1979) (discussing the effect of additional "money elements" on bargaining between spouses, including alimony and child support, and lump-sum payments versus periodic payments).

69 *See, e.g.*, Lau Hui Sing v. Wong Chuo Yong, [2008] 5 M.L.J. 846, 853 (Malay.) ("There are one or two exceptions to [the] 'clean break' concept. For example, [a] consent order for a property settlement is a final order. However, if the said consent order is inextricably interwoven with [a] maintenance order, the court has discretion to amend [it]." (citation omitted)).

70 *See* Dewbrew v. Dewbrew, 849 N.E.2d 636, 646 (Ind. Ct. App. 2006). Although the Indiana Court of Appeals determined that the property division in this case was ambiguous and had to be remanded to the trial court, the court noted that notwithstanding that conclusion, it would nevertheless have remanded this case to the trial court for recalculation of the entire division of marital property based on [the court's] partial modification of the property settlement agreement in terms of child support and spousal maintenance. It is well established that a partial modification of a property settlement agreement will likely upset the division of

also provided that if the parties consent to modify their agreement in the event of a change in circumstances, the court should enforce this condition, even with respect to property distribution.[71] Moreover, if a court order reserves its right to change the division of property in the future, it has the authority to do so.[72]

It also seems that as a matter of legal policy, property distribution should be categorized among those issues subject to modification, and its adjustment permitted due to a change of circumstances.[73] Furthermore, the possibility of change may serve as an internal defense mechanism. It is not impossible to avoid the need for various indemnification provisions, as well as the need for finding guarantors to ensure such indemnifications.[74] The party wishing to modify a matter subject to change in circumstances, such as child support, will carefully consider doing so, knowing that the modification may also influence the interrelated division of property. It seems this internal defense mechanism is preferable to the practice of indemnification stipulations and will be more beneficial in helping to avoid repeated proceedings.

According to this first argument, the recognition of issues subject to modification should be broadened and applied to property distribution. This argument suggests a better and certainly fairer balance among the existing interests within family law. Under the present system, some issues in divorce are designated as subject to modification in the event of a substantial change of

---

property equation in the divorce decree. The adjustment of one asset or liability may require the adjustment of another to avoid an inequitable result or may require the reconsideration of the entire division of property.

Id. (citation omitted) (citing Dusenberry v. Dusenberry, 625 N.E.2d 458, 461 (Ind. Ct. App. 1993)).

71 *See, e.g.*, Hale v. Hale, No. 2936-M, 2000 WL 109101, (Ohio Ct. App. Jan. 26, 2000) ("Although the trial court cannot modify a division of property, the parties themselves may modify the property division. ... Such an order [enforcing a postdecree modification by the parties] does not violate the principle that the court does not have jurisdiction to modify a property division." (citation omitted) (citing Myers v. Myers, No. 16696, 1994 WL 687202, at 2 (Ohio Ct. App. Dec. 7, 1994)).

72 Harwood, *supra* note 45.

73 In some states, courts have noted that modification can apply to property issues. *See, e.g.*, Osborne v. Osborne, 428 N.E.2d 810, 816 (Mass. 1981) (noting that antenuptial agreements settling alimony and property rights of the parties post divorce are only enforceable if (1) the agreement is fair and reasonable at the time of enforcement, (2) the agreement is subject to judicial modification the same as if it had been entered into after the marriage subject to divorce, and (3) the agreement does not contravene public policy by unreasonably encouraging divorce).

74 *See supra* notes 38–44 and accompanying text (discussing the use of indemnification clauses as a possible defense in divorce agreements against subsequent modification).

circumstances, while others are designated as final and unchanging. This situation does not properly balance competing interests.

The following section presents a contrasting argument that is also likely, in its own way, to better maintain a balance among the interests in family law. It may even contribute to resolving other aspects of a marital controversy as well. This argument will be guided by the aspiration of a couple to shorten, as much as possible, the path to the full and effective elimination of their relationship and the establishment of a clean break.

B. Argument II: Eliminating Modification in Divorce Settlements

The categorization of certain issues in family law as subject to modification in the event of a substantial change in circumstances was developed many years ago.[75] This created an exception that is taken for granted. This practice requires renewed review in light of developments in family law and in the entire legal system. If one steps back a little from family law, modification may be viewed more broadly through the general values of civil procedure, such as effectiveness, certainty, finality, and predictability.[76] Questions then arise as to why the courts accept issues subject to modification as a concept that cannot be reversed. Normative harmony needs to be established among all the branches of the law, and this practice in family law should be discontinued.

Moreover, upon also considering the emergence of the clean break theory and the "no-fault divorce" philosophy, it seems that the time has come to eliminate the practice of designating issues as subject to modification.[77] Today,

75 *See, e.g.*, Crater v. Crater, 67 P. 1049, 1050 (Cal. 1902) ("It is well established that in divorce proceedings the court has the power to vary and modify its decree as to the custody of the minor children from time to time as circumstances change"). While this is the standard for most modifications, see *supra* part II, the Uniform Marriage and Divorce Act adopted a stricter standard for child support modification: modification is permitted only when the circumstances of the parties have changed so much that the order has become unconscionable. *See* UNIF. MARRIAGE & DIVORCE ACT § 316(a), 9A U.L.A. 102 (1998).

76 *See* Stephen Goldstein, *The Influences of Constitutional Principles on Civil Procedure in Israel*, 17 ISR. L. REV. 467, 481 (1982); Lawrence B. Solum, *Procedural Justice*, 78 S. CAL. L. REV. 181, 188 (2004) ("[F]rom the ex ante point of view, procedure has another role—to guide action after the formal legal proceedings have ended and the judgment has become final. This is the real work of procedure—to guide primary conduct after the judgment is rendered." (footnote omitted)).

77 *See* Herma Hill Kay, *An Appraisal of California's No-Fault Divorce Law*, 75 CALIF. L. REV. 291, 313–14 (1987) (arguing that, because no-fault divorce seeks a clean break between spouses, continuing financial relationships should be minimized); Milton C. Regan, Jr., *Spouses*

judicial decisions in divorce disputes are not final rulings but may be reopened from time to time,[78] hindering the spouses from setting out in new directions.

It is difficult to say that the substantial change in circumstances requirement serves any practical role as a filter, blocking any petitions for modification. First, although it is possible that the burden of the change in circumstances standard will result in the denial of the claim,[79] without any fixed rules the requirement does not prevent, in advance, the claim's submission to the court. In that way, litigation expenses also increase. Second, the decision with respect to a change in circumstances is subject to broad judicial discretion.[80] In addition, judicial systems, including family courts, are already burdened with very heavy caseloads.[81] The current vague standard of substantial change in circumstances potentially increases that caseload. The benefit of categorizing issues as subject to modification to suit changing circumstances may not even be preferable to

---

and Strangers: Divorce Obligations and Property Rhetoric, 82 Geo. L.J. 2303, 2314 (1994) (analogizing a business partnership dissolution to the clean break idea of divorce); Cynthia Starnes, *Divorce and the Displaced Homemaker: A Discourse on Playing with Dolls, Partnership Buyouts and Dissociation Under No-Fault*, 60 U. Chi. L. Rev. 67, 108 (1993) (noting that a core concept of the partnership model of marriage is a clean emotional and financial break as an ideal divorce outcome).

78 *See supra* part II.

79 *See, e.g.*, Kelley v. Kelley, 835 N.E.2d 315, 320–21 (Mass. App. Ct. 2005); Moore v. Moore, 763 N.W.2d 536, 544–45 (S.D. 2009); Maher v. Maher, 90 P.3d 739, 744–45 (Wyo. 2004).

80 For example, a family court in New York exercised this broad discretion when it ruled, even though there was justification in its words, that the "freedom" obtained through the divorce is in itself a change in circumstances: "As soon as the parent's marital freedom is adjudicated, the parent's 'circumstances' thereby ipso facto are changed by the new freedom itself. Having been safely separated, divorced or the marriage annulled, the parent for the first time is in a radically 'changed' position—to litigate freely, to strive vigorously for an equitable order of support without fear of refusal by the other parent to cooperate in the separation, divorce or annulment by consenting to appear, or by declining to controvert the proof. Here in the Family Court, the judge is for the first time given both sides of the circumstances as contended for by the respective parents, and he can find the facts as they are rather than as a separation agreement and mute parents made them appear to another court." Guillermo v. Guillermo, 252 N.Y.S.2d 171, 181 (Fam. Ct. 1964).

81 Judges consistently express concerns that family law disputes will overload court calendars. As one appellate judge noted, "An announcer for a soap opera would bill this proceeding as yet another episode in the continuing saga of the Rand family. ... Unfortunately, this is not a soap opera. Real people are involved; and, for the fourth time in less than seven years an appellate court of this State is called upon to resolve the post-marital financial disputes between these warring parties. Would only that [their daughter] have had the benefit of the fortune invested in this seemingly interminable litigation." Rand v. Rand, 392 A.2d 1149, 1150 (Md. Ct. Spec. App. 1978).

the costs resulting from that classification. The following subpart questions the practice of modification from three perspectives.[82]

1. The Perspective of Contractual Obligations: Breach of Agreements

A distinct interest of every legal system is that the parties involved in a dispute will settle their differences by agreement. If that is true regarding any conflict, it is even more so in a family law dispute that affects sensitive third parties who are the children of the couple.[83] Therefore, the legal system is expected to ensure that the agreements between parties to a conflict will be preserved and not be altered or subject to cancellation, except under extraordinary circumstances.[84] Otherwise, the parties will not be motivated to resolve their dispute by agreement and will need to resort to the complex process of the judicial system.[85]

This interest accompanies and guides judicial decisions, including those in matters of family law. A divorce agreement usually covers many issues of controversy, and it needs to be examined in its entirety. One must believe it will be stable and reliable in order to develop agreed upon arrangements between parties who are unable to resolve their dispute. Otherwise, there will be little value to the divorce agreement. It will only be an interim stage before returning to the court.[86]

In light of this interest in establishing stability and credibility in divorce settlements, it is unclear why the courts and the legislatures continue to support the practice of modification. There is certainly an important benefit in the possibility of modification since the needs of the child change. However, it also has a complicated price when it becomes unclear that the benefit is greater than the cost. Perhaps it is also in the best interests of the child that the conflict between the parents come to an end and not be repeatedly litigated.

---

82 Aside from the disadvantages and costs that will be detailed below, we should not forget that the possibility of modifying payments downward may sometimes also harm the recipient of the support—for example, when an event occurs that lowers the income of the obligor.

83 *See* Andrew J. Cherlin et al., *Longitudinal Studies of Effects of Divorce on Children in Great Britain and the United States*, 252 Sci. 1386, 1386 (1991). For a thorough discussion on the effect of changing family structures on children, see generally Sara McLanahan & Gary Sandefur, Growing Up With A Single Parent: What Hurts, What Helps (1994).

84 *See, e.g.*, CA 5490/92 (Jer) Pegas v. Pegas (Dec. 29, 1994), Nevo Legal Database (by subscription) (Isr.).

85 *See, e.g.*, *Rand*, *supra* note 81, 392 A.2d at 1150 (noting the couple's divorce decree was in front of the appellate court for the fourth time in seven years).

86 CA 4515/92 (Jer) Stein v. Stein (June 13, 1994), Nevo Legal Database (by subscription) (Isr.).

The adverse consequences of this practice must be considered seriously. It complicates the litigation procedures; allows one party not to honor an agreement with the other party; enables one side to be in breach of an agreement without it being considered a breach; transforms family law agreements into conditional agreements; or may bring about an unjust result, abuse, uncertainty, lack of confidence, and even more undesirable consequences.

This practice incentivizes spouses not to reach agreements. Without an effort to settle their differences, the dispute remains open and the parties are left with an unresolved conflict. This uncertain condition of "separation without separation" or of not achieving a clean break imposes difficulties upon the couple and upon their children who may remain subject to legal proceedings for a number of years.[87] This situation also goes against the best interests of the child. For the child's benefit, it is preferable that the parents resolve their dispute willingly and by agreement.[88] Without a stable agreement, the dispute will be determined through a demanding and oftentimes consuming judicial process.[89]

If spouses nevertheless decide to enter into an agreement, they will do all they are able to avoid the risks that may arise from it. Individuals who are apprehensive about a future claim due to the vague change in circumstances standard will insist on defense mechanisms such as indemnification stipulations.[90] It is customary in some jurisdictions to ensure such provisions by the signatures of third-party guarantors.[91] This requirement makes completing the agreement all the more complicated. It is not easy to find a third-party guarantor for an indemnification, effective upon any claim related to a change in circumstances. Courts have also looked unfavorably upon certain indemnification stipulations.[92] In a number of rulings, it intervened in the contractual freedom of the parties, cancelled the provisions, and left a party to the contract exposed to

87 *See, e.g.*, *Rand*, *supra* note 81, 392 A.2d at 1150.

88 As Justice Elon of the Supreme Court of Israel noted, "Giving effect to and honoring these agreements, essentially, are in the best interests of the minor. It is good and desirable also from the perspective of his welfare and education, that the arrangement of financial matters between his parents, who are separated from one another, each going his own way and to his new home, will be completed willingly and by agreement, without quarrels and conflicts, that become embedded first and foremost in the sensitive minds of young children." CA 255/81 Kent v. Kent 36(1) PD 236, 243 [1981] (Isr.).

89 *See, e.g.*, *Rand*, *supra* note 81, 392 A.2d at 1150.

90 *See supra* notes 38–44 and accompanying text.

91 *See, e.g.*, CA 4262/96 Wayeh v. Wayeh 51(5) PD 231 [1997] (Isr.).

92 *See, e.g.*, Kelley v. Kelley, 449 S.E.2d 55, 56 (Va. 1994) (holding the indemnification provision was null and void because it both abridged the rights of the child and diminished the court's power against established law); CA 4262/96 Wayeh v. Wayeh 51(5) PD 231 [1997]

damages arising from the change in circumstances practice without the ability to properly protect that party's own interests.[93]

2. The Perspective of Public Policy: The Ongoing Destructive Relationship

The general approach of the courts, reflected in the concept of *res judicata*, holds that the litigant needs to be given protection from repeatedly dealing with the same matter after it has already been decided.[94] The litigants should be able to go their own way, make plans with certainty, and follow a clear process without concern they may be called to court an additional time by an adversary.[95] Thus, for example, in *Hasal v. Hasal* the wife requested annual calculations of the profits from a business registered in her husband's name.[96] She argued that due to their joint efforts in establishing the "tree" during the marriage, there was no reason she should not benefit from her share of the "fruits" after the divorce.[97] These were among the considerations of the court that denied her request:

> Another reason to discontinue giving spouses their portions of the "fruits" of formerly joint property is to avoid forcing couples who have separated to prolong their relationship. A monetary arrangement that connects the spouses to one another after their separation is not desirable, and it unnecessarily lengthens the difficult process of separation.... In this area, experience also teaches that it is preferable for the separated spouses to quickly, completely, and finally divide their property, without leaving traces of open issues for them to go back and dig through.[98]

(Isr.) (holding that both the indemnification stipulation and the guarantee were void for public policy reasons).

93 *See, e.g., Kelley*, 449 S.E.2d at 56; CA 4262/96 Wayeh v. Wayeh 51(5) PD 231 [1997] (Isr.).

94 *See* Steakley & Howell, *supra* note 3, at 355.

95 As Justice Abella of the Supreme Court of Canada argued, "While some issues, like custody and access, have an inherent fluidity that tracks a child's evolutionary needs, and while support may vary if a material change in circumstance occurs, property matters can usually be ascertained with sufficient clarity to permit the parties to exit from a marriage with an economic map delineating clearly marked boundaries. No matter the issue, subject always to the transcendent duty of fairness, the goal is to create enough certainty that each spouse can make personal and financial decisions about the future based on legitimate and enforceable expectations." Stein v. Stein, [2008] 2 S.C.R. 263, para. 35 (Can.) (Abella, J., dissenting).

96 CA 5640/94 Hasal v. Hasal 50(4) PD 250, 258 [1997] (Isr.).

97 *Id.*

98 *Id.*

Thus, even though it is reasonable to assume the immediate annual calculation will be fairer, the Supreme Court prefers the values of certainty and planning for the future (expressed in the finality of judgments principle) over the value of fairer distribution of property (expressed in the principle of substantive change in circumstances).[99] This clear attempt to "avoid preserving any economic connection between the parties" contradicts the designation of issues subject to modification that, instead, creates a permanent and interdependent connection between them.[100]

Moreover, maintaining an economic connection between the spouses may be harmful to the public interest of their rehabilitation after separation. Although Professor Nina Zaltzman wrote the following with respect to tort law, it is appropriate to the present matter as well:

> [This approach] opens before each of the litigants the means with which to bother the other with capricious claims regarding "substantial change in circumstances." In that way, not only is the principle of finality of judgments significantly harmed, but public policy may be harmed with respect to the rehabilitation of the injured. It is easy to imagine that the latter will not have the motivation to be rehabilitated as long as he can bring a claim against the person who harmed him, on the one hand, or as long as he expects to be constantly followed by his adversary, who is seeking to find any grounds to claim a decrease in compensation, on the other hand.[101]

In the present context, it is easy to imagine that noncustodial spouses who owe child support and alimony will not be motivated to rehabilitate themselves and increase their income since that may expose them to a claim for increased

---

99 *Id.*

100 If the court found it correct to separate property between the spouses, why did it not do the same with respect to support? *See id.* This question becomes stronger in light of the ideological closeness between payment of support and distribution of property. *See supra* notes 66–73 and accompanying text. This does not necessarily mean that the support will be paid in a one-time payment. There may be problems that cause cash flow difficulties for the individual obligated to make payment. However, it is certainly possible to determine monthly payments, which are not subject to modification, or a single amount divided into several installments. These considerations brought about the development in English law of the clean break doctrine. *See* Dunford v. Dunford, [1980] 1 W.L.R. 5, 9 (C.A.) (U.K.). According to this approach, an effort should be made to achieve complete separation after divorce, and to prefer a single payment over ongoing support payments following divorce. *See, e.g., id.*

101 Nina Zaltzman, Res Judicata in Civil Proceedings 295 (1991).

support due to a change in circumstances.[102] Indeed, courts have expressed concern that modification of child support could encourage underemployment.[103] In the same way, the custodial spouse may not be motivated to rehabilitate himself and increase household income after the divorce because it may expose that spouse to a claim for decreasing child support or alimony.

Classifying these matters as issues subject to modification is therefore harmful to the public interest in the rehabilitation of the family with its two new households.[104] It encourages the parties not to rehabilitate themselves and perhaps even to worsen their situations.[105] It is unfortunate enough that when judicial proceedings are first initiated and then become ongoing, spouses may attempt to hide their income and their property in order to influence the amount of support awarded. Legal systems should not encourage extending this unhealthy period and transforming it into a routine way of life.

3. *The Perspective of Normative Harmony: Monetary Claims*

The rationale at the basis for determining that certain issues are subject to modification is likely to be relevant both with respect to tort matters and to monetary disputes in general. Actually, the same justifications raised above for classifying property distribution as an issue subject to modification[106] are applicable to a significant portion of regular monetary disputes and tort matters. Even in each of those areas, however, the compensation awarded may or may not forecast future needs. If in the future it proves to be inadequate, there may be reason to adjust the compensation. This is especially the case following circumstances affecting, for example, earning capacity or mobility.

---

102 This argument is not intended to conflict with research that shows that the standard of living of the husband significantly increases after divorce. *See, e.g.*, LENORE J. WEITZMAN, THE DIVORCE REVOLUTION: THE UNEXPECTED SOCIAL AND ECONOMIC CONSEQUENCES FOR WOMEN AND CHILDREN IN AMERICA 339 (1985) ("Men experience a 42 percent improvement in their [postdivorce] standard of living, while women experience a 73 percent decline." (emphasis omitted)). First, it is possible that the standard of living of the wife could increase even more if she does not fear prosecution. Second, although the level of support will be determined from available income, legal expenses increase as litigation over a divorce continues, decreasing the income available for support.

103 *See, e.g.*, Roszko v. Roszko, 705 P.2d 951, 954 (Ariz. Ct. App. 1985); *In re* Marriage of Powell, 474 N.W.2d 531, 534 (Iowa 1991).

104 *See* FamilC (CD) 28050/04 A.G. v. A.M (Mar. 20, 2006), Nevo Legal Database (by subscription) (Isr.).

105 *See, e.g.*, *id.*

106 *See supra* part IV.A.

Moreover, the same rationale provided in academic literature and judicial decisions in support of periodic payment in tort may also be used to justify the designation of monetary claims and certain tort claims as issues subject to modification.[107] Therefore, it is unclear why the legal system chose to distinguish between monetary claims and matters of family law, applying the principle of finality to the former while subjecting the latter to modification.

From an opposite point of view, the rationale at the foundation of *res judicata*, applicable to every monetary dispute, holds true for family law as well. The principle of the *functus officio* ("having performed his or her office")[108] is intended to ensure an end to proceedings and disputes between parties in order to achieve certainty and legal security, and to avoid calling upon litigants after the completion of legal procedures.[109] It is also intended to ensure that the judicial system does not need to repeatedly deal with previously determined matters while many other cases are awaiting initial litigation.[110]

Family law is not immune to the disadvantages of multiple proceedings. It also needs to ensure the stability and certainty of the binding power of a judicial act, even after a substantive change in circumstances. It is certainly possible to understand that exceptional institutions in family law developed out of the unique qualities of family disputes,[111] but those unique characteristics have nothing to do with not applying *res judicata*. It therefore seems fitting to review the justifications for disrupting normative harmony and applying different rules to matters of such similar and close natures.

Even the attempt to avoid creating exceptional doctrines within the legal system by securing the possibility of relitigation through existing principles raises other challenges.[112] Professor Zaltzman explains:

> Without a specific provision in the contract itself, making it subject to change, from the nature of a contract, the court reads into it an implied

---

107 A. Barak et al., Dine Ha-neziḳin [The Law of Civil Wrongs: The General Part] 339, 341 (G. Tedeschi ed., 1976).

108 Black's Law Dictionary 743 (9th ed. 2009).

109 *See* Mandl v. Bailey, 858 A.2d 508, 520 (Md. Ct. Spec. App. 2004) (discussing principle in context of family law arbitration).

110 *See id.*

111 *See supra* notes 12–18 and accompanying text.

112 *See* Zaltzman, *supra* note 101, at 209.

> provision that a change in circumstances allows for a return to judicial proceedings.... What is the nature of this provision that the court reads into the agreement and thus "imposes" on the parties a situation of uncertainty in the future ... a possibility that is doubtful whether the parties were really prepared to consider when they drew up the contract, since they themselves specifically avoided relating to it.... [What is the nature of the implied provision] when the sides explicitly expressed their opinion that they want to put an end to the legal proceedings? Doesn't that indicate that the parties specifically rejected the possibility of including an implied provision that conflicts in content, with what they specifically agreed upon?[113]

Therefore, by relying upon existing doctrines it is difficult to find theoretical justification for the possibility of relitigation in the future. In addition, the same implied provision "forced" upon the parties can be read into every tort decree, and just as it is incorrect in tort law, it is also incorrect in family law.

4. The Limitations of Modifying Judicial Decisions

Different legal systems have dealt with the question of what constitutes a change in circumstances that justifies modifying a previously issued order.[114] Indeed, the lower courts have broad discretion in this matter,[115] and their decisions will not be easily overturned on appeal.[116] This broad discretion brought about different interpretations of the change in circumstances standard,[117] resulting

113 *Id.* at 290.

114 *See* Ada Orakwusi, *Child Custody, Visitation and Termination of Parental Rights*, 8 GEO. J. GENDER & L. 619, 632–33 & nn.70–83 (2007) (offering examples of how various states have applied the change in circumstances standard).

115 *See id.* at 632.

116 *See, e.g.*, Pridgeon v. Superior Court, 655 P.2d 1, 3 (Ariz. 1982) ("The trial court has broad discretion to determine whether a change of circumstances has occurred. ... [Its] decision will not be reversed absent a clear abuse of discretion." (citation omitted)); Kirk v. Kirk, 770 N.E.2d 304, 307 (Ind. 2002) ("We set aside judgments [of modifications] only when they are clearly erroneous, and will not substitute our own judgment if any evidence or legitimate inferences support the trial court's judgment." (citing *In re* Marriage of Richardson, 622 N.E.2d 178, 179 (Ind. 1993)).

117 *See* Scott Bassett, *Changing Circumstances, Changing Agreements: Standards for Modification Are Uniform, but How the Courts Apply Them Varies*, 8 FAM. ADVOC., no. 2, 1986, at 29, 29–30 (providing examples).

in a lack of normative uniformity.[118] In certain states within the United States, court rulings have even determined that the change of circumstances standard is not a "strict" standard, and prior decisions can be modified, even without regard to this principle.[119] There is no need to emphasize the importance of clarity of court rulings in matters dealing with couples and their children during the crisis of separation. Certainty and stability are essential to the parties involved. The use of the vague standard of substantive change of circumstances, without clear guidance, only intensifies the difficulty.

Therefore, several legal systems that were not satisfied with this current standard for modification found different ways to limit it. One approach is to make it difficult to reinitiate a proceeding due to a change in circumstances, even if the change is substantive.[120] Moreover, in Ohio a court is not authorized to modify the amount of alimony or its duration if the agreement between the spouses did not specifically authorize the court to do so. In the case of a judicial decree, if the alimony or duration was not explicitly authorized by the court order, no modifications can be made.[121]

---

118 As Judge Richard Montes, Harold Cohn, and Shelly Albaum have noted: "The changed-circumstance rule is a judicially created doctrine rooted in the concept of res judicata. The intent of the rule is to supplement the statutorily mandated 'best interest of the child' standard by recognizing the child's right to stability and continuity in his or her living arrangements. In the application of the rule, however, what is or is not a change of circumstances has been inconsistently defined, ill-defined, and most often not defined at all." Montes, *supra* note 10.

119 *See, e.g.*, Goto v. Goto, 338 P.2d 450, 453 (Cal. 1959). Professor Wexler has noted that states have attached this standard from both sides: "Despite its apparent rationality, the changed circumstances standard has been rejected by some courts and legislatures on the ground that the interests of the children far outweigh the policies behind the res judicata doctrine, and that therefore a pure best interests standard is preferable. Criticism of the traditional standard has also come from the opposite pole, with the assertion that there is no inconsistency between res judicata policies and an individual child's best interests; children are more likely to fare best when left with their current custodian." Wexler, *supra* note 9.

120 As the Supreme Court of Canada has described, ". . . the preliminary threshold test ensures that child support orders will not be reassessed by courts anytime a change, however minimal, occurs in the circumstances of the parties or their children. This approach recognizes the value in some degree of certainty and stability between the parties. Parties must be encouraged to settle their difficulties without coming before the courts on each and every occasion." Willick v. Willick, [1994] 3 S.C.R. 670, para. 101 (Can.).

121 Ohio Rev. Code Ann. § 3105.18(E) (LexisNexis Supp. 2013). This is different from the Israeli legal system, which does not require specific consent in order for a court to be authorized to modify a previous order; it is sufficient that the parties or the order were

Other systems determine that certain circumstances discussed and foreseen during the original agreement process or in the first court decision will not serve as a basis for initiating procedures due to a change in circumstances.[122]

Courts in Texas have also taken the approach of making relitigation more difficult when initiated on the basis of a change in salary or in the economic status of one of the spouses.[123] At the same time, Texas courts have held that an alimony agreement that was incorporated into the final divorce decree and became a part of the final judgment is binding on the parties and interpreted under general contract law.[124] For example is the provision, "[A]bsent consent of the parties, the provisions of the agreement will not be modified or set aside except for fraud, accident, or mutual mistake of fact."[125]

C. An Intermediate Path—Comprehensive Legislative Rules for Modification

The preceding sections presented two opposing arguments. The first argument favors broadening the practice of designating issues subject to modification and including within it the distribution of marital property.[126] In contrast, the second argument prefers eliminating the practice of modification and relitigation, and applying the principle of *res judicata* to all issues in family law.[127] The advantages of the first argument (flexibility, adjustment of payments, etc.) are the disadvantages of the second. The disadvantages of the first (multiple proceedings,

---

silent. *See* CA 363/81 Fayga v. Fayga 36(3) PD 187 [1982] (Isr.). If, in their agreement, the sides explicitly restrict the possibility of change it will be of no effect because agreements in these matters are seen as inherently including the possibility of modification. *See id.*

122 *See, e.g.*, Wheeler v. Wheeler, 548 N.W.2d 27, 31 (N.D. 1996); Holley v. Holley, 864 S.W.2d 703, 706–07 (Tex. App. 1993); Michel v. Michel, (1988) 67 O.R. 2d 60, para. 10 (Can. Ont. Sup. Ct.); Gaudet v. Gaudet, (1988) 70 Nfld. & P.E.I.R. 107, para. 9, 11 (Can. P.E.I. Sup. Ct.). *But see* Manners v. Manners, 706 P.2d 671, 675 (Wyo. 1985) ("The fact that a change in circumstances was foreseeable is not fatal to a petition to modify a decree of divorce." (citing Mentock v. Mentock, 638 P.2d 156, 159 (Wyo. 1981)).

123 *See, e.g.*, Warren v. Warren, No. 13-05-00429-CV, 2008 WL 668213, at *2 (Tex. App. Mar. 13, 2008); Payne v. Dial, 831 S.W.2d 457, 459 (Tex. App. 1992).

124 *See, e.g.*, Schwartz v. Schwartz, 247 S.W.3d 804, 806 (Tex. App. 2008).

125 *Id.* (citing Boyd v. Boyd, 545 S.W.2d 520, 523 (Tex. Civ. App. 1976)). Some states specifically allow the parties to agree to have their alimony terms not subject to review. *See, e.g.*, MINN. STAT. § 518.552(5) (2006).

126 *See supra* part IV.A.

127 *See supra* part IV.B.

lack of certainty, discouragement of rehabilitation, etc.) are the advantages of the second.

These conflicting considerations may be resolved through an intermediate model that incorporates advantages found in the first two arguments. In fact, the rationale for the two arguments forms the basis for the new model. In proposing a new model, it is essential to consider that while nonmodifiable child support and alimony orders would preserve the obligor's incentives and the finality of judgment,[128] they could also be undesirable in several other respects.

First, it is unjust that an obligor will continue making the same level of payments if the obligor becomes unemployed or ill. Second, child support might be decreased when the obligor has to support additional children. Third, a system that will not increase the obligation for a child who develops special needs, places the entire burden of all such costs on the custodial parent. Fourth, it may be fitting to change the amount of spousal support when the obligee, for example, remarries or becomes unemployed.

Therefore, a system for modifying child support and alimony seems both fair and even unavoidable. The intended purposes of child support and alimony are to address the needs of the children and the spouse, to balance the standards of living in the two households, and to protect children from negative financial impacts of divorce.[129] Some possibility for modification must be made available in order to achieve each of these purposes. The next section presents a proposal for balancing between the need for certainty and stability in a spousal agreement and the need for addressing unforeseeable changes.

1. Defining the Changed Circumstances Standard through Fixed Rules

The principles of the new model should be based on setting fixed legislative rules for modification that are not subject to judicial discretion. Such rules would include, among other considerations, time requirements restricting the modification of an order due to a change in circumstances. For example, under Wisconsin law, unless a party can show physical or emotional harm to the child's best interests, a custody order can only be relitigated after a period

128 *See supra* part IV.B.2–3.

129 *See* June Carbone, *Income Sharing: Redefining the Family in Terms of Community*, 31 Hous. L. Rev. 359, 362 (1994); Milton C. Regan, Jr., Commentary, *The Boundaries of Care: Constructing Community after Divorce*, 31 Hous. L. Rev. 425, 442, 448 (1994).

of two years.[130] Montana, on the other hand, restricts certain modifications for a two-year period.[131] Texas limits modification for a period of three years.[132] In Indiana, modification is restricted for only one year.[133] Minnesota law specifies time periods that may vary, depending upon certain circumstances.[134]

Other legal systems have legislated not only a time period before allowing relitigation but also a restriction on the extent of the modification. For example, Texas law sets forth that the court may modify an order when the monthly amount of the child support award under the order differs by either 20 percent or $100 from the amount that would be awarded in accordance with the child support guidelines.[135] Indiana law provides a similar formula,[136] as do additional states.[137]

However, an in-depth look at those legal systems shows that the vague substantial change in circumstances standard is retained in their legislation.[138] This standard is still a very important factor, and may in itself result in a modification of a previous order.[139] Alongside this standard, and always as an alternative,

---

130 Wis. Stat. Ann. § 767.451(1)(a) (West 2009). After the two-year period, these orders may be modified upon a substantial change in circumstances if in the best interests of the child. *Id.* § 767.451(1)(b).

131 *See* Mont. Code Ann. § 40-4-208(2)(a) (2013) (providing that modifications to a divorce decree, other than modifications relating to maintenance or support, may only be made within two years of the decree).

132 *See* Tex. Fam. Code Ann. § 156.401(a) (West Supp. 2013) (providing that if circumstances have not materially and substantially changed, a child support order can only be modified after three years and if the award differs from the guidelines by 20 percent or $100).

133 Ind. Code Ann. § 31-16-8-1(b) (LexisNexis 2007) (providing that, absent substantial, continuing, and unreasonable changed circumstances, maintenance and child support may only be modified if the child support amount differs from the guidelines by 20 percent and it has been at least 12 months since the order or last modification).

134 *See* TN. Stat. Ann. § 518.18(a)–(b) (West 2006) (stating a general rule of one year from an initial custody order before filing any petition for modification, and two years between one petition for modification and a subsequent one); *see also* Unif. Marriage & Divorce Act § 409(a), 9A U.L.A. 439 (1998) (providing a general rule of no modification until two years after custody order).

135 Tex. Fam. Code Ann. § 156.401(a).

136 Ind. Code. Ann. § 31-16-8-1(b).

137 *See, e.g.*, Colo. Rev. Stat. § 14-10-122(b) (2013) (specifying 10 percent); Conn. Gen. Stat. Ann. § 46b-86(a) (West 2009) (specifying 15 percent); Ky. Rev. Stat. Ann. § 403.213(2) (LexisNexis 2010) (specifying 15 percent).

138 *See* Tex. Fam. Code Ann. § 156.401(a)(1); Ind. Code Ann. § 31-16-8-1(b)(1); Ky. Rev. Stat. Ann. § 403.213(1); Colo. Rev. Stat. § 14-10-122(1)(a); Conn. Rev. Stat. § 46b-86(a).

139 *See, e.g.*, Tex. Fam. Code Ann. § 156.401(a)(1).

fixed rules were also established for modifying a previous order.[140] These two options for discretionary or mandatory modification are not cumulative, but alternative.[141] Thus according to the first option, the court still has broad discretion, without clear guidance as to when a previous order may be modified. While broad discretion is beneficial for a legal system, it also presents the risk of legal arbitrariness which leads to different decisions in similar cases.

The vague change in circumstances standard encourages actions for modification in an attempt to implement the court's discretion and avoid the alternative fixed rules.[142] Moreover, if the spouses originally agree upon an amount of child support in the order that differs from the guidelines, there are no fixed rules for modification of the order at all, and only the changed circumstances standard will apply.[143]

The desirable balance between fixed rules and discretion has been repeatedly considered in Anglo-American law.[144] Family law commentators have also examined the issue.[145] Judges traditionally have been granted broad discretion under family law as separately determined by each of the states within the United States.[146] Some family law scholars have proposed restricting this discretion.[147]

---

140 *See, e.g.*, TEX. FAM. CODE ANN. § 156.401(a)(2).

141 *See, e.g.*, IND. CODE ANN. § 31-16-8-1(b).

142 *See* Jeffry C. Sorenson, Note, *Changing the Changed Circumstances Requirement: A New Standard for Modifying Permanent Custody Orders*, 23 J. JUV. L. 90, 97 (2002–2003) (discussing judicial advocacy for the pragmatic application of the discretionary changed circumstances rule). Unlike my proposal, Sorenson concluded that the best interests of the child standard should replace the change in circumstances standard. *See id.* at 99. However, I suggest that the best interests of the child standard is no less problematic with respect to judicial discretion. *See also* Jon Elster, *Solomonic Judgments: Against the Best Interest of the Child*, 54 U. CHI. L. REV. 1, 43–44 (1987) (arguing the best interests of the child standard is problematically indeterminate).

143 TEX. FAM. CODE § 156.401(a-1).

144 *See, e.g.*, Louis Kaplow, *Rules Versus Standards: An Economic Analysis*, 42 DUKE L.J. 557 (1992); Kathleen M. Sullivan, *Foreword: The Justices of Rules and Standards*, 106 HARV. L. REV. 22, 57–58 (1992) (discussing the rule versus standard debate and its effect on constitutional issues and the Supreme Court).

145 *See, e.g.*, Mary Ann Glendon, *Fixed Rules and Discretion in Contemporary Family Law and Succession Law*, 60 TUL. L. REV. 1165 (1986); Carl E. Schneider, *Discretion, Rules, and Law: Child Custody and the UMDA's Best-Interest Standard*, 89 MICH. L. REV. 2215 (1991).

146 *See* Mnookin, *supra* note 12, at 262.

147 *See, e.g.*, *id.* ("More rule-like standards would avoid or mitigate some obvious disadvantages of adjudication by an indeterminate principle."); Elster, *supra* note 142, at 36–43 (suggesting three alternatives to the best interests principle: "(1) a return to the maternal presumption rule; (2) a primary caretaker presumption; and (3) some form of compromise between the parents ... [including] the choice of a custodial parent by the flip of a coin").

Critics note that a system of discretion may have undesirable consequences. First, results are less predictable, thereby discouraging early settlement and increasing litigation costs.[148] Second, discretionary judgments may be somewhat influenced by a judge's personal beliefs and biases, thus resulting in inconsistent results.[149] Different results could, in turn, be detrimental to the public's trust in the judicial system.[150] However, a system allowing significant judicial discretion is more flexible and able to respond to changing social needs without legislative action.[151] Therefore, a discretionary system is able to respond more rapidly to social change and to encourage creativity.

On the other hand, the resulting predictability of rules reduces litigation costs and assists settlement.[152] Rules require decision makers to treat similar cases alike, thus decreasing arbitrariness or bias. However, fixed rules are a somewhat strict regulatory device, intended to be technically implemented. Fixed rules set forth in a statute may only be changed by the lengthy process of legislative amendment. When rules are set forth by the legislature, the legislature determines important policy choices. However, a policy of discretion generally enables judges to make such choices. It is very unusual to find a regulatory system that either includes a "pure" rule or allows for unlimited discretion.

The acceptance of child support guidelines shows a preference for rules more than discretion. Guidelines are presumptive standards presently used in all states in determining an initial child support award.[153] However, there are no true guidelines for the modification of those awards. Modification is usually determined according to the first statutory alternative, the vague change in circumstances standard which is dependent upon broad judicial discretion.[154] It is more appropriate to define the change in circumstances standard

---

148 Mnookin, *supra* note 12, at 262.

149 *Id.* at 263.

150 *See id.* ("Because of the scope of discretion under [an indeterminate] standard, there is a substantial risk that decisions will be made on the basis of values not widely shared in our society . . ").

151 *See* Kaplow, *supra* note 144, at 616–17.

152 Jane C. Murphy, *Eroding the Myth of Discretionary Justice in Family Law: The Child Support Experiment*, 70 N.C. L. Rev. 209, 223 (1991).

153 *See supra* notes 27–32, and accompanying text; *see also Child Support Guideline Models by State*, Nat'l Conf. St. Legislatures (Apr. 2013), http://www.ncsl.org/research/human-services/guideline-models-by-state.aspx (providing links to each state's child support guidelines).

154 *See supra* notes 138–43, and accompanying text.

by fixed rules that would provide guidance in the implementation of judicial discretion.

To establish greater certainty, an objective standard for what constitutes a substantial change in circumstances should be determined by clear, presumptive rules. For example, a policy could presume a substantial change in circumstances if a child support award calculated under the then current rules would vary by more than a defined percentage from the initial award.[155] Indeed, even the several states that have legislated what constitutes a change in circumstances have only considered some of the relevant aspects. They have requested limits to judicial discretion in order to preserve uniformity and clarity of judgments. For example, in Alaska, a change in circumstances is presumed if it reflects an amount 15 percent above or below the support payment determined in the original decree.[156]

Another example is in Florida, where a parent's residence is considered to have been changed only when the new residence is fifty miles away from the place of residence determined in a previous decree.[157] In Wisconsin, statutory law determines when certain matters may be considered a change in circumstances, restricting judicial discretion.[158] While in Canada the family law acts vary from province to province, Canada has a Federal Charter of Rights and

---

155 *See, e.g.*, Colo. Rev. Stat. § 14-10-122(b) (2013) (providing that a less-than-10-percent change is not a substantial and continuing change in circumstances); Conn. Gen. Stat. Ann. § 46b-86(a) (West 2009) (providing that a less-than-15-percent deviation is not a substantial change); Ky. Rev. Stat. Ann. § 403.213(2) (LexisNexis 2010) (same). Although more states define when a modification can occur based upon a percentage change from the guidelines, they do not go so far as to define a "change in circumstances" as such. *See, e.g.*, Ind. Code Ann. § 31-16-8-1(b) (LexisNexis 2007); Tex. Fam. Code Ann. § 156.401(a) (West Supp. 2013).

156 Alaska R. Civ. P. 90.3(h)(1).

157 Fla. Stat. Ann § 61.13001(1)(e) (West Supp. 2013). For further discussion on state approaches to and restriction of the relocation of the custodial parent, see Charles P. Kindregan, Jr., *Family Interests in Competition: Relocation and Visitation*, 36 Suffolk U. L. Rev. 31, 37–38 (2002); Merle H. Weiner, *Inertia and Inequality: Reconceptualizing Disputes Over Parental Relocation*, 40 U.C. Davis L. Rev. 1747, 1755 (2007); Ruth Zafran, *Children's Rights as Relational Rights: The Case of Relocation*, 18 Am. U. J. Gender Soc. Pol'y & L. 163, 174–76 (2010).

158 The Wisconsin law provides: "[A] court may not modify [legal custody or physical placement] orders before 2 years after the final judgment determining legal custody or physical placement is entered ..., unless a party seeking the modification ... shows by substantial evidence that the modification is necessary because the current custodial conditions are physically or emotionally harmful to the best interest of the child[.]"Wis. Stat. Ann. § 767.451(1) (West 2009).

Freedoms. Federal Canadian law also establishes rules for defining changes in circumstances that allow for the modification of a previous child support order.[159] These legal systems redefined the change in circumstances standard through guidelines and did not merely add them as alternatives to modification.

In order to ease the strict requirements of a standard defined by rules, payments could be linked to the cost of living index. This linkage could be adjusted automatically, without requiring additional legal proceedings. Otherwise, inflation might cause the actual value of the payments to erode over time.[160] This erosion would obviously have substantial negative effects on the standard of living for the custodial parent and the child.[161] However, linkage could preserve the value of the payments and its psychological impact might also result in decreased relitigation.

The determination of guidelines for modification requires the consideration of an additional issue. Will the guidelines for modification of child support focus on the child's needs or perhaps on the parents' incomes? The initial determination should take into consideration both these factors. However, with respect to modification, the focus must be only on the changing needs of the child, not on the changing incomes of the parents. Focusing on the parents' incomes could result in underemployment, hidden employment, concealment of income, or lack of motivation to rehabilitate oneself and increase one's salary. It could also create an ongoing and interdependent connection between the spouses, resulting in a significant amount of tension.

The standard for modifying child support should be "needs-based." This standard determines child support according to evidence of the child's expenses

---

159 For example, the Canadian Divorce Act of 1985 states: "Before the court makes a variation order in respect of a child support order, the court shall satisfy itself that a change of circumstances as provided for in the applicable guidelines has occurred since the making of the child support order or the last variation order made in respect of that order." Divorce Act, R.S.C. 1985, c. 3, s. 17(4) (Can.). Canada's Federal Child Support Guidelines then provide that a change in circumstances occurs in three specific (yet also broad) instances:
(a) in the case where the amount of child support includes a determination made in accordance with the applicable table, any change in circumstances that would result in a different child support order;
(b) in the case where the amount of child support does not include a determination made in accordance with a table, any change in the condition, means, needs or other circumstances of either spouse or of any child who is entitled to support; and
(c) in the case of an order made before May 1, 1997, the coming into force of section 15.1 of the [Divorce Act] ... Federal Child Support Guidelines, SOR/97-175 s. 14 (Can.).

160 Phelps & Miller, *supra* note 28, at 210.

161 *See id.*

rather than the incomes of the parents. Modification should focus exclusively upon the needs of the child. If the needs significantly change in a specified percentage above the calculation that was made when the order was issued, then there is reason for seeking modification. This model is closer to the best interests of the child principle since it concentrates on the child's needs, and not on the parents' incomes. The percentage-of-income model implies that a child has a right to a certain portion of the obligor's income, while the needs-based standard is focused, instead, on meeting the child's own needs. This approach is also appropriate, with the necessary changes, for spousal support modifications. Although automatic adjustment mechanisms such as a percentage of the obligor's income will decrease the need for post decree modification, they will not eliminate it altogether.[162]

Moreover, modification of support payments in accordance with the obligor's income could also result in calculations of the parents' earning potentials.[163] Such calculations would dramatically broaden the court's discretion,[164] with all of the related concerns discussed above.[165] For example, a California court may exercise its discretion to attribute income to either party.[166] Therefore, child support may be determined by the parents' earning capacity instead of by their actual earnings.[167]

Furthermore, a change in circumstances could include anything impacting the finances of either party, for example a shift in the stock market and thus in the finances of a shareholder. However, if the support amount is dependent upon the parents' incomes, every change in the value of the stock market could result in a claim for modification due to a change in circumstances. It may also be detrimental to the well-being of the child if a change in the value of the market results in a claim to reduce the amount of child support.

---

162 It is of interest to note that courts have approved orders that set a maximum amount that the obligation can increase, regardless of how much the obligor's income increases. *See, e.g*, Edwards v. Edwards, 665 P.2d 883, 884–86 (Wash. 1983) ("[T]he trial judge must set a maximum dollar amount, *relating to the children's need*, above which the support award cannot rise." (emphasis added).

163 *See* Phelps & Miller, *supra* note 28, at 218–19.

164 *See id.*

165 *See supra* notes 146–51, and accompanying text.

166 "The court may, in its discretion, consider the earning capacity of a parent in lieu of the parent's income, consistent with the best interests of the children." CAL. FAM. CODE § 4058(b) (West 2013).

167 *Id.; see, e.g.*, Othman v. Hinman (*In re* Marriage of Hinman), 64 Cal. Rptr. 2d 383, 389 (Ct. App. 1997); *accord* Schlakman v. Schlakman, 886 N.Y.S.2d 758, 759 (App. Div. 2009).

A fluctuation in the value of the stock market should not necessarily result in a modification of the support payment. Investors in securities know that their investments are measured over time. It is unreasonable to allow every change in value to bring along with it a claim to increase or decrease the level of support payments. The obligor that invests in stocks would not want the court to restrict the ability to invest in the stock market and order the obligor to put aside a portion of that money for child or spousal support. In the same way, the obligor must absorb and manage losses, rather than allow those dependent upon support payments to suffer from the market fluctuations.

The adoption of fixed rules for defining the change in circumstances standard as the sole standard for modification would be helpful both to legal systems and to litigants. It would establish a more precise system for the modification of judgments and could also prevent unnecessary post-divorce litigation. An exclusive, objective standard for the modification of child support would be beneficial. Both the parties and the judge would more accurately recognize when modification is appropriate.

2. The Effective Support Approach

The following approach is intended to complete the foregoing model and help ensure a fair result when a court decides a modification request. The underlying principle should be that the distribution of property is a final decision that generally cannot be relitigated. The discussion of the second argument, above, describes the justifications for this view.[168] However, in cases when property distribution is closely interrelated with issues customarily subject to modification, then the modification of those issues may also result in an adjustment to the property matter as well.[169] An example of such a case would be when part of the property is transferred as a support payment and the actual distribution of property does not conform to customary practice. It is both possible and preferable to avoid relitigation of property matters by implementing an approach referred to in the present model as "effective support."

When preparing the agreement, the couple should define the amount of effective child or spousal support. The couple must formulate the child support

168 *See supra* part IV.B.

169 *See supra* notes 49–50, and accompanying text.

or alimony and indicate that it is a certain effective amount. This amount is made up of two portions. The first portion is paid and transferred monthly to the custodial parent for the benefit of the minor or the spouse. The second portion is paid at the time of the agreement by the transfer of property to the custodial parent or to the spouse.

When the court considers a modification, it will not compare the new modified amount, then being sought, with the amount of support actually paid. Rather, it will compare it with the entire amount of effective support, including both the portion actually paid and the additional portion transferred as property. If the court finds that the amount of support should be increased, the calculation will take into consideration the entire amount of effective support, not only the amount actually paid. Only such an approach prevents relitigation of the distribution of property in a just way. It also preserves the balance of interests that the spouses achieved at the time of formulating their agreement.[170]

This approach may be illustrated further with the help of an example. If the parties agree that the level of child support for their two children is $2,000 per month, they must specifically indicate that in their agreement. This is the amount of effective support. Next the parties must designate how payment will be made. For example, they could indicate that $1,000 will be a monetary monthly payment, and $1,000 will be paid by the transfer of property to the custodial parent. A subsequent claim for modification will have to relate to the amount of effective support, which is $2,000, and not to the support that was actually paid in the amount of $1,000.

If the modification meets the legislative guidelines and the court determines that there is reason to increase the amount of support to $2,500, it will require payment only of the difference between $2,000 and the new amount to be paid in light of the change that occurred. Thus, the obligor will increase the payment amount by only $500. The court will not order the payment of the difference between $1,000 and the new amount, $2,500. Through this process, the court does not relitigate the division of property. Instead, it recognizes the earlier agreement between the parties and considers the involvement of property with issues subject to modification.

This approach allows the parties greater freedom in negotiating a divorce agreement without concern that the courts may ignore the arrangements they

---

170 *See supra* notes 59–68, and accompanying text.

agree upon.[171] Sometimes the spouse obligated to pay support does not have the direct means to make payments, but can exchange that with the distribution of property. The effective support approach allows the spouse to do so and makes it easier for the parties to reach an agreement. This approach may also prevent the various types of indemnification provisions that arise, among other reasons, out of concern that the court might disregard the transfer of property as part of the support payment.[172]

This approach is also preferable from the perspective of preserving the value of the family's property. If the court does not take into consideration the transfer of property between the parties in exchange for the support obligation, the parties will be forced to sell all or part of their property for cash. Generally, the sale of property during divorce proceedings is not beneficial to the family. The value received for the property is usually lower than its value in a sale between a willing buyer and a willing seller.[173] The effective support model prevents the sale of the couple's property and retains the property within the family. This better preserves the value of the property rather than selling it during divorce.

This approach is also more appropriate from a tax perspective. The contractual determination of effective support, and not the amount of support actually paid, entitles the payor to take tax deductions for payments in the amount of effective support.[174] If the payor gave up his or her portion of the home in exchange for the entire amount of support, that must be calculated for

---

171 *See supra* part IV.B.1.

172 *See supra* notes 38–40, and accompanying text.

173 For a discussion on the difficulties individuals face when attempting to sell their home during a divorce, see generally Kathleen Lynn, *The Great Divide: Divorce and Home Sale*, Chi. Trib. (Feb. 17, 2012), http://articles.chicagotribune.com/2012-02-17/news/sc-cons-0216-divorce-homesale-20120217_1_real-state-agents-home-values-coldwell-banker-agent.

174 *See* 26 U.S.C. §§ 71, 215 (1982). Professor Mary Ann Glendon has succinctly summarized how these sections addressing the federal tax effects of alimony work together: "Under federal income tax law, "alimony" is deductible by the payor-spouse and taxable to the recipient. Child support is neither deductible by the payor nor taxable to the payee. When the payor-spouse earns significantly more than the recipient, the tax consequences for both are usually minimized (and more income made available for both) by designating the payments as alimony. ... The domestic relations tax provisions of the Deficit Reduction Act of 1984 have now established a federal standard for determining what types of payments will qualify as alimony and what will be considered child support. Within broad limits, however, the parties are still given substantial freedom to allocate the tax consequences of periodic payments." Glendon, *supra* note 145, at 1174 n.24 (citations omitted).

tax purposes as an expense related to support and be deducted from the payor's income accordingly.[175] This certainly leads to a more just result than ignoring the true nature of the transaction between the parties.

Another option for dealing with the interrelationship between property matters and support issues is to contractually allow modification of the property distribution. This is an option that has been put into practice. In Indiana, for example, property distributions as well as payments constituting property distributions are modifiable if permitted by a contractual provision between the parties.[176] As long as the current legal situation is not changed in accordance with the proposed approach, attorneys should consider this option in formulating the agreement. When the amount of support is low due to the transfer of property, the parties should specifically state that matters of property distribution may also be modified. The courts should enforce such a condition as part of the agreement between the parties.

An additional option relating to the interrelationship between property matters and support issues is to establish a condition that child support shall not be relitigated. However, the court generally does not enforce such provisions because they may be detrimental to the child.[177] Similarly, an agreement restricting the modification of below-guideline child support should only be accepted by the court upon its confirmation that the agreement was freely made and that the custodial parent received some substantial economic concession from the other parent.[178]

This proposed approach creates a more desirable balance among competing interests, permits the restriction of issues subject to modification, leaves the matter of property as one that is not subject to change, and allows modifications

---

175 However, section 71 of the Internal Revenue Code currently only allows taxpayers to deduct "alimony," which is specifically defined as a cash payment. *See* 26 U.S.C. §§ 71(b)(1). This section would need to be amended in order to include the value of the portion of the home given up by the taxpayer as "alimony" and allow this deduction.

176 IND. CODE ANN. § 31-15-2-17(c) (LexisNexis 2007).

177 *See supra* part II.

178 Similarly, under California law, the court shall not approve a stipulated agreement for child support below the guideline formula amount unless the parties declare all of the following: (1) They are fully informed of their rights concerning child support. (2) The order is being agreed to without coercion or duress. (3) The agreement is in the best interests of the children involved. (4) The needs of the children will be adequately met by the stipulated amount. (5) The right to support has not been assigned to the county ... and no public assistance application is pending. CAL. FAM. CODE § 4065(a)(1)–(5) (West 2013).

to be made in accordance with fixed rules as stated above, without ignoring the transfer of property from one party to the other.

3. The Tort Model

The proposed model can also be based on and inspired by the existing model of periodic payment as is found in Israeli tort law. In matters involving "continuing expenses," the Israeli legislature allows the court to award compensation to the injured party in periodic payments as monthly support payments.[179] In tort law, a past decision may be unjust to either of the parties in the future. Therefore, the legal system has a clear interest in adjusting compensation to changed circumstances. In order to balance these interests, the court did not create an exceptional practice such as in the determination of issues subject to modification based on a discretionary standard.[180] Instead, the balance in tort is achieved by legislating clear criteria for adjusting compensation through periodic payments.[181] In order to avoid an abundance of litigation and to ensure greater certainty, a number of rules must be met before bringing a claim for an increase in payments. For example, Regulation 2 of the Compensation Regulations sets forth as follows:

> Request for increase in payments:
>
> 2. (a) The victim is entitled to request that the court increase payments awarded if the two following conditions are fulfilled:
>   (1) The condition deteriorated, including earning capacity, as a result of the traffic accident. ...
>   (2) Six months have elapsed since the last decision in his matter.[182]

The modification is not subject to the vague changed circumstances standard. Instead, the regulations set fixed and clear rules determining the extent of the deterioration that allows for a claim for modification. Moreover, not every deterioration or substantial change in circumstances can bring about a claim for increased

179 *See* Road Accident Victims Compensation Law, 5735-1975, 780 LSI 234, § 6 (1975) (Isr.); *see also* Road Accident Victims Compensation (Periodic Payment), 1978, KT 3815, 706 (Isr.) [hereinafter Compensation Regulations].

180 *See* D. Mor, Legislation, *Periodical Payments for Road Accident Victims*, 6 Tel Aviv U. L. Rev. 645, 651 (1979).

181 *See id.* at 652.

182 Road Accident Victims Compensation Law, § 6.

payments.[183] The deterioration must be directly connected to a traffic accident.[184] The regulations set a minimum time period before reinitiating a claim.[185]

In addition, not every party is entitled to request modification. A claim for modification may only be brought by the victim, and not by the party liable for the injury.[186] This restriction is designed to protect the interest of the injured to undergo rehabilitation, without concern for constantly being under surveillance by an insurance company.[187]

This model creates an appropriate balance between the interests of the parties in tort law and can be adapted to family law as well. It is not desirable to rely on the substantial change in circumstances standard that is completely dependent upon the broad discretion of the court and leaves the parties with a lack of legal clarity.[188] When there is no defined "cooling off period" prior to relitigation, no restriction as to the extent of the change and its causes, and the claim can be for either an increase or decrease in a support payment, the dispute actually remains open. It is more correct to determine criteria and restrictive provisions in family law, as in the tort model. It is more appropriate to determine, for example, that the possibility of adjusting the amount of support will only be the right of the minor.

This limitation will at least allow the custodial parent to be economically rehabilitated without concern over an exposure to a claim for decreasing support. In tort law, one must focus on the worsening condition of the injured, and not on the improvement of the injured's condition or the economic strength of the insurance company.[189] So, too, in family law, one must focus only on the additional needs of the child, and not on the argument that the child's needs decreased, or on the economic ability of the obligor. The two latter considerations cannot be the basis for a claim for modification.

---

183 Regulation 1(1) of the Compensation Regulations states: "The victim will lose, as a result of the traffic accident, 40 [percent] or more of his future earning ability." Compensation Regulations, 706.

184 If the deterioration derives or results from changes in economic circumstances or from the elimination of an economic field without any connection to the accident, the victim will not be able to request an increase in payments. *Id.* Similarly, section 6 of the Compensation Law states that payments are linked to the Consumer Price Index, and in that way the possibility of further litigation due to inflationary changes is prevented in advance. Road Accident Victims Compensation Law, § 6.

185 Compensation Regulations, 706.

186 Road Accident Victims Compensation Law, § 6.

187 *See* Mor, *supra* note 180, at 652.

188 *See supra* part IV.C.1.

189 *See generally* 86 C.J.S. *Torts* § 1 (2006).

Aside from these advantages, there is no doubt that stricter, legislated rules with respect to a future change will result in greater care while determining the provisions of a divorce agreement. They will bring about a serious attempt to relate at that time to possible future occurrences, and to provide in advance for resolving them.[190] It is also possible that this greater stringency may encourage creative solutions by the couples.[191] Such a model is certainly preferable over the present one, in which an attorney might advise clients that the agreement is just an intermediate stage, and that they do not have to make the effort to think about every eventuality, since the agreement may be modified.

Within this intermediate model, it is also possible to develop various alternatives for the two arguments presented above. Here, too, the different systems existing worldwide in tort law can be a source of inspiration. The President of the Supreme Court of Israel, Aharon Barak, wrote the following in the *Brada* case:

> Most of the Civil Law countries (such as Germany, Italy) take the approach of periodic payments that are modifiable in the future. ... In a number of systems, an intermediate approach is customary, whether by awarding a one-time payment, subject to change with a change in circumstances (such as Norway, Denmark), or whether by awarding a periodic payment, that is subject to change only in exceptional circumstances (such as France, Belgium).[192]

On that basis, one portion of the support payment could be made as a periodic payment. That payment should only be modifiable by linking it to the cost of living index, or by meeting clear legislative rules applicable in exceptional

---

190 *See* Mor, *supra* note 180, at 653 ("It can be assumed that in the Israeli system in which the original defendant does not have the right for reconsideration, the judges will warn that the judgment is final from the perspective of the defendant").

191 As Professor Mor noted: "In France and in Switzerland, for example, there is a huge gap between the written word in the legislation and the customary practice. Despite that in theory the norm there is determining compensation in periodic payments, more than 99 percent of the instances end with a one-time compensation payment, whether through settlements outside of court or by settlements in court. That is the obvious result in light of the position of all the relevant entities that prefer this sort of compensation." *Id.* at 661.

192 CA 357/80 Naim v. Brada 36(3) PD 762 [1982] (Isr.).

circumstances. The other portion of the support obligation should be paid as a one-time fixed payment, not subject to any change.

V. CONCLUSION

A customary ruling in worldwide legal systems is that child support, child custody, and alimony are subject to modification, and may be relitigated upon the occurrence of a substantial change in circumstances. In Israel, the problem is more complex because the civil and the religious courts each have authority to determine the same issues. The gap between their decisions is significant and may encourage the reopening of cases. At the same time, marital property distribution is not subject to modification, and as such, may not be relitigated. An analysis of the rationale for defining issues subject to modification, and an examination of divorce agreements in which issues subject to modification are interrelated with marital property distribution, raise questions as to the fairness of this practice and the desirable standard for modification.

This chapter challenges the present practice allowing for the modification of certain matters in family law according to the vague changed circumstances standard. This standard is subject to broad judicial discretion and generally lacks guidance for its implementation. As a result, a number of problematic issues arise. Included among them are multiple litigations, lack of certainty, lack of fairness, lack of normative uniformity, deterrence from completing the dispute by agreement, and deterrence from rehabilitation. Even more so, other matters that are interrelated with and dependent upon the issues subject to modification are not subject to change at all.

This chapter presents two arguments as a basis for a new model that seeks to balance the conflicting interests in family law issues. One argument suggests broadening the application of the modification practice to all the issues that are part of a divorce dispute, especially marital property distribution. A second argument suggests, to the contrary, completely eliminating this practice. Instead it applies to family law two principles applicable to every branch of law, *res judicata* and the finality of judgments.

A new model provides an intermediate path between these arguments. It incorporates their advantages and suggests that the changed circumstances standard be defined through fixed legislative rules. This model is inspired by the system of periodic payments in tort law, along with its provisions that serve to restrict repeated litigation. Included among these fixed rules are a time restriction before reinitiating a claim, a legislative definition and limitation of the change, and a restriction as to which of the parties may initiate future proceedings. To complete the model, this chapter suggests an innovative approach of effective support when property distribution is deeply interrelated with issues subject to modification.

This approach requires the spouses to explicitly define in their agreement an amount of effective support. They also must designate the portion of that support to be paid monthly, and the portion to be paid through a transfer of property. Accordingly, a claim for modification will relate to the entire amount of effective support, and not only to the amount actually paid. Thus, without relitigating the division of property, the court considers the involvement of property matters in issues subject to modification.

This model, with both its components of guidance for defining the changed circumstances standard, and the effective support approach, is consistent with the principle of achieving a clean break. It is likely to be helpful both to couples and to the legal system in setting a clearer and more stable path with respect to disputes following divorce.

CHAPTER 2

The Right of a Minor to Independent Status

I. INTRODUCTION

In the United States, the number of divorce proceedings is increasing.[1] Accordingly, the number of children involved in such proceedings is growing every year.[2] The decisions made during a couple's divorce proceedings have a crucial effect upon the lives, personal development, tranquility, and security of that couple's children. These decisions will affect the children although they are usually not parties to the proceedings that take place between their parents. The courts have expressed concern over the conflicts of interests between parents and children during divorce proceedings.[3] When parents are involved in a struggle over their interests and personal freedoms, they might neglect or even compromise the interests of their children.

In order to protect a child's interests, the courts established and strengthened the minor's right to independent status by determining that decisions or agreements made in the proceedings between the parents are not binding upon the minor.[4] Children are therefore allowed to subsequently reopen such agreements in a new proceeding initiated on their behalf.[5] In this relitigation proceeding, the best interests of the children appear before the court as separate and

---

1 *See* Randall W. Leite & Kathleen Clark, *Participants' Evaluations of Aspects of the Legal Child Custody Process and Preferences for Court Services*, 45 FAM. CT. REV. 260, 260 (2007) ("Throughout the United States, domestic relations courts experience large, often unmanageable caseloads. In fact, domestic relations cases are the largest and fastest growing segment of state-court civil caseloads") (citations omitted).

2 *See* John David Meyer, *The "Best Interest of the Child" Requires Independent Representation of Children in Divorce Proceedings*, 36 BRANDEIS J. FAM. L. 445, 445 (1998) ("Divorce is a common occurrence that disrupts the lives of over one million children each year, affecting their psychological and physical well-being.") (citations omitted).

3 *See, e.g.*, Jaramillo v. Jaramillo, 823 P.2d 299, 307–08 (N.M. 1991); Ford v. Ford, 371 U.S. 187, 193 (1962).

4 CA 404/70 Evron v. Evron, 25(1) PD 373, 378 [1971] (Isr.).

5 *Id.*

distinct from the matters between their parents.[6] This is the first opportunity for the child to be heard. As a consequence, prior decisions that affect the minor might be changed.

However, excessive use of the minor's right to independent status detracts from the finality of judgments, resulting in certain issues remaining open and unresolved.[7] This uncertainty might also be detrimental to the motivation of the couple to resolve their dispute. The parties may wrongfully use the minor's right to independent status in their own conflict as a couple. It may even burden limited judicial resources with the relitigation of claims, while other parties with new matters wait to come before the court. However, even though the potential for abuse exists, limiting and restricting minors' rights to independent status might be detrimental to the best interests of the children if their interests are compromised in favor of those of their parents.

The first part of this chapter examines the importance of the right to independent status, its necessity for the protection of minors, its place in legal systems today, and possible trends for the future. This right does not exist in a legal vacuum, and it has significant implications for the remaining interests involved in a family law matter. Therefore, the second part of this chapter evaluates the present balance between contractual certainty, the finality of judgments, and the right of a parent not to repeatedly face litigation; as compared with the best interests of the child and his right to independent status. The third and final part of the chapter considers different practical models that have been used to address a minor's right to independent status. This examination may assist in building a formula that more appropriately balances the competing interests in family law matters.

II. IMPORTANCE OF THE MINOR'S RIGHT TO INDEPENDENT STATUS

A. Finality of Judgment

The principle of finality of judgment is fundamental to legal systems. Simply put, finality of judgment means that a matter conclusively decided by a court of competent jurisdiction will not be relitigated between the same parties.[8] The

---

6 *Id.*

7 Leite & Clark, *supra* note 1, at 260–61 ("From a legal point of view, divorce traditionally required a couple to address grounds for the divorce, property distribution, alimony, child custody, and child support. Today, only those issues associated with children remain open issues in most states").

8 *See, e.g.*, Jullie Steakley & Weldo U. Howell, *Ruminations on Res Judicata*, 28 Sw. L.J. 355, 355 (1974) ("The doctrine of *res judicata* ... [states] that a cause of action once finally

principle of finality of judgment includes three cumulative conditions: final resolution by a competent court, identical litigants, and the same claim.[9] The rationales at the basis of this principle include prevention of relitigation, the right of a litigant not to be repeatedly called back to court, the concern over conflicting decisions made by different courts on the same issues, and the efficient use of judicial resources.[10] Therefore, once a court has granted a final judgment, a procedural barrier arises before the parties, preventing any relitigation between them on the same cause of action.[11]

The importance and effectiveness of this principle has resulted in its expansion on several levels. For example, finality of the judgment is not restricted only to the parties who were formally present during the first action, but may also bar the initiation of a proceeding by others who are privy with the parties to the earlier action.[12] The classic example of this sort of privity is the natural guardianship of parents. In matters associated with their children, parents are authorized to represent them both in legal actions and in court proceedings.[13] The legal significance of such representation is, among other considerations, that a decision concerning the minors is binding upon them and prevents them from relitigating the same matter.

---

determined, without appeal, between the parties, on the merits, by a competent tribunal, cannot afterwards be litigated by new proceedings either before the same or any other tribunal").

9 *See, e.g.*, Amstadt v. U.S. Brass Corp., 919 S.W.2d 644, 652 (Tex. 1996) (The elements of *res judicata* are: "(1) a prior final judgment on the merits by a court of competent jurisdiction; (2) identity of parties or those in privity with them; and (3) a second action based on the same claims as were raised or could have been raised in the first action"); Wayne Cnty. v. Detroit, 233 Mich. App. 275, 277 (1998) ("Under the doctrine of res judicata, 'a final judgment rendered by a court of competent jurisdiction on the merits is conclusive as to the rights of the parties and their privies, and, as to them, constitutes an absolute bar to a subsequent action involving the same claim, demand or cause of action.'" (citing Black's Law Dictionary 1305 (6th ed. 1990)).

10 CA 9085/00 Shitrit v. Sharvat Brothers Ltd, 57(5) PD 462, 475 [2003] (Isr.).

11 CA 246/66 Klosner v. Shimony, 22(2) PD 561, 583 [1968] (Isr.).

12 *See, e.g.*, Getty Oil Co. v. Ins. Co. of N. Am., 845 S.W.2d 794, 800–01 (Tex. 1992) (People can be in privity in at least three ways: (1) they can control an action even if they are not parties to it; (2) their interests can be represented by a party to the action; or (3) they can be successors in interest, deriving their claims through a party to the prior action); Mathison v. Public Water Supply Dist. No. 2 of Jackson Cnty., 401 S.W.2d 424, 431 (Mo. 1966) ("to make one 'privy' to an [earlier] action he must have acquired his interest in the subject matter of the action subsequent to the commencement of the suit or rendition of judgment").

13 Capacity and Guardianship Law, 5722—1962, 380 Laws of the State of Israel (LSI) 120, §§ 14–15 (1962) (Isr.).

The rationale behind obligating a minor by a legal proceeding in which he was not even present is sufficiently clear: parents appropriately protect the interest of their children. In representing them, they do the most to ensure that the children's interests are thoroughly considered by the court.[14] Therefore, finality of judgment is intended to prevent the minor's relitigation.

B. Natural Guardianship

The natural presumption that parents safeguard the interests of their children is not as simple as it seems. This presumption is challenged by the concern that parents who are in the midst of divorce proceedings, struggling over their own personal matters including freedom, and sometimes even motivated by the desire for revenge may unknowingly or unintentionally compromise the interests of their minor children. When one spouse focuses on proving his own parenting skills and abilities, or the other spouse's lack thereof, that spouse may fail to properly consider the children's interests.

The picture presented before the court may even be distorted if the atmosphere in the divorce proceedings is controversial and charged. Since the spouses are concerned with personal gain, the interests presented before the court are their own and not necessarily the interests of their children.[15] In addition, divorce proceedings sometimes cause a rift between children and their parents, and consequently, parents may not be sensitive to or aware of the needs of their children.

Moreover, the interests of the parents may sometimes be at odds with their children's interests. For example, while in principle broad visitation arrangements with both parents are in the best interests of the child, it is certainly possible that the noncustodial parent will prefer more restricted visitation that will not burden him in finding new work or in establishing a new family.

Further complications result when the parents have different religions or different attitudes towards religious education and practice. Sometimes parents present arguments with regard to the child's education, while their true aim is to harm the other spouse. For example, for more than a year during a divorce dispute, a mother requested preventing her husband from circumcising their

14 *See Getty*, 845 S.W.2d at 800–801.

15 Donald N. Bersoff, Representation for Children in Custody Decisions: All That Glitters is Not Gault, 15 J. Fam. L. 27, 31 (1977).

child.[16] In another instance, a father who is not religious requested an order from the religious court requiring that his children be given religious education. The father's request was only due to the claim brought by the mother for increased child support payments.[17]

Legal systems worldwide are aware of the gap that exists between the interests of parents and those of their children during divorce proceedings.[18] In the case of *Jaramillo v. Jaramillo*, the court stated:

> When, however, the interests of a third party (or parties—the children) are not only significantly affected by the outcome of the litigation but indeed are paramount in determining that outcome, placing on one party the burden of establishing that his or her interests are the ones that should be vindicated can subordinate the interests of the third party—who may be absent and may not even be represented—in the clash over the other two parties' competing hopes and desires.[19]

Similarly, the alienation that might occur between parents during divorce proceedings could negatively impact their parental judgment with respect to the interests of their children.[20]

C. The Right of the Minor to Independent Status

The concern that parents might compromise the interests of their children is not merely an academic or theoretical issue. A proceeding between parents, especially when uncontested or resolved by agreement, does not bind a subsequent court in matters that only concern the child.[21] Such matters are brought before a court apart from earlier proceedings that involved the parents.[22] A parent is not

16 HCJ 8533/13 Anonymous v. The Supreme Rabbinical Court (June 29, 2014), Nevo Legal Database (by subscription) (Isr.).

17 HCJ 5507/95 Amir v. Supreme Rabbinical Court 50 PD 55 [1995] (Isr.).

18 *See, e.g.*, Short v. Short, 730 F. Supp. 1037, 1039 (D. Colo. 1990); Taff v. Bettcher, 646 A.2d 875, 878 (Conn. App. 1994).

19 Jaramillo v. Jaramillo, 823 P.2d 299, 307–08 (N.M. 1991).

20 Ford v. Ford, 371 U.S. 187, 193 (1962) ("Unfortunately, experience has shown that the question of custody, so vital to a child's happiness and well-being, frequently cannot be left to the discretion of parents. This is particularly true where, as here, the estrangement of husband and wife beclouds parental judgment with emotion and prejudice").

21 CA 42/49 Mashkeh v. Mashkeh, 3(1) PD 88 (1950)(Isr.).

22 *Id.*

permitted to purchase his personal freedom at the cost of his child's peace and safety, even if the court approves such an agreement.

In *Guillermo v. Guillermo*, the family court in Mexico confirmed a divorce agreement, which determined, among other issues, that the father would pay fifteen dollars a week for child support.[23] Eight months thereafter, the mother brought a claim against the father, on behalf of the child, before a different court of parallel jurisdiction.[24] She argued that the amount of support did not meet the needs of the child.[25] The court held that in some cases the mother might be so anxious to end her marriage that she may compromise her children's needs for a matrimonial decree, failing to provide for the children adequately.[26]

The court further stated that there had been no change in either the child's or the father's circumstances since the initial judgment.[27] The court noted that the only change that took place was simply that of the mother's own situation.[28] While she had previously been constrained by her matrimonial dispute, eight months later she was free to litigate.[29] This change for the first time enabled the mother to independently raise the issue of support for her minor child.[30] The court indicated that the ruling of the previous court relied only upon the divorce agreement of the parties. From the evidence brought before the court, there seemed to have been no discussion or interrogation process in the earlier proceeding, or any sort of examination of the needs of the child.[31]

The court concluded that according to the income of the father, he was required to pay child support in an amount fifty percent higher than the amount previously determined.[32] The court stated that when matrimonial litigation is uncontested or results in a settlement between the parties, the incidental provision of child support cannot control a subsequent court in which the best interests of the child are first considered, separate and apart from the earlier proceedings between the parents.[33]

---

23 Guillermo v. Guillermo, 252 N.Y.S.2d 171, 172 (1964).
24 *Id.*
25 *Id.* at 172–73.
26 *Id.* at 173.
27 *Id.*
28 *Id.*
29 *Id.*
30 *Id.**
31 *Id.* at 178.
32 *Id.*
33 *Id.* at 181.

> No parent should be able to bind a child by buying matrimonial freedom at the price of selling a child's material or other security, even if a court approves such agreement. ... No child support decree should be sacrosanct if "incidental" to, and inequitably incidental to, the problems of adults.[34]

A minor has no control over the process or the strategies used. Therefore, the findings should not obligate him. In sum, since children are not privy to their parents in divorce proceedings, they must not be bound by the results of proceedings that take place between their parents.[35]

The most important implication of these concerns is the development of the minor's right to independent status. Accordingly, a voluntary agreement between the parents in matters concerning the child is not binding upon the child, even if approved by the court.[36] Merely including the minors in the proceedings and having the parents declare that they are creating an agreement in the interests of their children does not make any difference.[37] The child is

---

34 *Id.*

35 *See, e.g.*, Simcox v. Simcox, 546 N.E.2d 609, 611 (Ill. 1989) ("We, therefore, hold that children are *not* privies of their parents in dissolution proceedings and, as such, are not bound by findings of paternity in such proceedings unless they are parties to the proceedings.") (emphasis in original).

36 *Id.*

37 In the Israeli legal system, it is insufficient to merely determine that the agreement meets the needs of the child and serves his best interest. Two procedural conditions must be fulfilled for it to be binding upon the minor: (1) a separate claim on behalf of the minor, and (2) a separate proceeding in his matter, that is not connected to the remaining issues of the divorce. *See, e.g.*, CA 404/70 Evron v. Evron, 25(1) PD 373, 378 [1971] (Isr.). In my opinion, Israeli law identifies three stages in the development of a minor's right to independent status: In the 1960s and 1970s, the determining standard was procedural. In the 1980s, the courts adopted a more substantive model. They sought to identify if decisions concerning the minors were indeed made in their interest, whether or not a separate proceeding was brought on their behalf. *See, e.g.*, CA 289/82 Dauba v. Dauba, 36(4) PD 625, 628 [1982] (Isr.); CA 544/82 Hamami v. Hamami, 38(3) PD 605, 608 [1984] (Isr.). In the last decade the courts again adopted the procedural standard, and in that way broadened a minor's right to independent status. In this third stage, even if it is determined that the decisions made concerning a child are good, the second court will reverse them if they were not made in a separate proceeding on behalf of the minor. *See* HCJ 2898/03 Anonymous v. The Supreme Rabbinical Court, 58(2) PD 550, 563 [2004] (Isr.). The Supreme Court recently decided that the substantive model should be determinative. See HCJ 4407/12 Anonymous v. The Supreme Rabbinical Court (Feb. 7, 2013), Nevo Legal Database (by subscription) (Isr.). In its decision, the Supreme Court considered my extensive research on the subject and accepted the distinctions that I suggested as well as my recommendations.

allowed to initiate a new legal proceeding in a matter that was previously determined by the court, even if there is no material change of circumstances that would otherwise be necessary to justify relitigation.

It is interesting to note that under the Israeli legal system, as opposed to that in the United States, the change that takes place in the status of the minor also impacts those circumstances in which the right to independent status applies. For many years, the presumption that parents might compromise the interest of their children applied exclusively to issues of child support. In all remaining matters, the agreement between the divorcing parents was binding upon the minor.[38] In recent years, however, the concern that parents may compromise the interests of their children has arisen with respect to a broader variety of issues. Thus, the presumption now applies to child custody and visitation[39] as well as to matters of education.[40]

The establishment and broadening of the minor's right to independent status is intended to benefit the minor and to protect his interests. The law must protect minors from anyone who might compromise their interests, even if that person happens to be the parent. This sort of protection is of utmost importance.

III. EXCLUSION OF OTHER INTERESTS IN FAMILY LAW

Judicial decisions must balance different interests. The emphasis on one interest is generally at the expense of another. This part more closely examines the negative impact that the right of a minor's independent status has on other interests.

A. Res Judicata and the Burden of Proof

Among the first interests compromised by the minor's right of independent status are the interests incorporated in the doctrine of *res judicata* and principles concerning finality of judgment. Included among them are prevention of relitigation, *functus officio*,[41] the right of a party not to repeatedly face relitigation, prevention

38 CA 1/81 Nagar v. Nagar, 38(1) PD 365, 387 [1984] (Isr.).

39 HCJ 2898/03 Anonymous v. The Supreme Rabbinical Court, 58(2) PD 550, 563 [2004] (Isr.).

40 HCJ 9539/00 Eitan v. The Supreme Rabbinical Court, 56(1) 125, 133 [2001] (Isr.).

41 CA 9085/00 Shitrit v. Sharvat Brothers Ltd, 57(5) PD 462, 475 [2003] (Isr.).

of burdening the court with relitigation while new claims are waiting to be heard,[42] and other finality considerations.[43]

Certainly, the principle of *res judicata* in family law is more flexible than is customary in other areas of law.[44] The first chapter examines this flexibility with respect to child support, custody, and alimony. In those matters, the court determined that when there is a change in circumstances, the final decision of the court may be modified to suit the new reality. In order to balance the interest of adjusting a payment amount to meet changed circumstances, on one hand, and the interest of the finality of judgment on the other hand, the court requires that the change be a "material change of circumstances."[45]

This balance requires two distinct conditions that are intended to offset and "make up for" the conflict with the principle of the finality of judgment. First, the burden of proving changed circumstances is placed upon the individual initiating the later proceeding and requesting to modify the earlier decision.[46] Second, not every change in circumstances is sufficient. Instead,

---

42 Penelope Pether, *Inequitable Injunctions: The Scandal of Private Judging in the U.S. Courts*, 56 Stan. L. Rev. 1435, 1528 (2004) ("Finally, '[t]he doctrines of res judicata and collateral estoppel are designed to preserve judicial resources by preventing relitigation of issues that had been thoroughly aired in a prior proceeding'" (quoting Jill E. Fisch, *The Vanishing Precedent: Eduardo Meets Vacatur*, 70 Notre Dame L. 325, 340)).

43 *See* Nina Saltzman, Res Judicata in Civil Proceedings 3–12 (Ramot, Univ. of Tel Aviv 1991) (in Hebrew); CA 219/87 Artzi Ltd. v. Shemesh Hadar Ltd., 43(3) PD 489, 497 [1989] (Isr.).

44 Barry B. McGough & Gregory R. Miller, *Domestic Relations*, 56 Mercer L. Rev. 221 (2004) ("The court of appeals, however, held that 'the doctrine of *res judicata* is less strictly applied in divorce and alimony cases, including cases dealing with child support issues'" (citing Dial v. Adkins, 265 Ga. App. 650, 651–52 (2004) (emphasis in original)).

45 *See, e.g.*, Joan G. Wexler, *Rethinking the Modification of Child Custody Decrees*, 94 Yale L.J. 757, 766 (1985); *accord id.* at 779 ("Each of the approaches to modification applications described above represents an attempt to balance competing policy interests. Trying to balance the policies behind the res judicata doctrine on the one hand, and the policies in favor of making the best-advised contemporary determination of the child's welfare on the other, the traditional changed circumstances doctrine holds that not just any changed circumstances, but only substantial ones, should warrant changing custody."); Sally Burnet Sharp, *Modification of Agreement-Based Custody Decrees: Unitary or Dual Standard?* 68 Va. L. Rev. 1263, 1264 n.9 (1982) ("The change of circumstances standard is based on principles of res judicata."); Richard Montes, Harold J. Cohn, & Shelley L. Albaum, *The Changed-Circumstances Rule and the Best Interest of the Child*, 24 Los Angeles Lawyer 12, 12 (2001) ("[O]ne of the purposes of the rule [i.e. changed circumstances] is to recognize the finality of judgments and protect the parties and the child from harmful and needless relitigation of the issues of custody and visitation").

46 The burden for modifying maintenance awards rests with the party seeking modification, and the decision of whether to grant such modification is within the sound discretion of

a material change in circumstances is mandatory and meeting this burden of proof is not an easy task.[47]

In contrast, with respect to the right of the minor to independent status, the conflict with the principle of *res judicata* is not balanced in any way. On the contrary, the burden of proof is placed upon the individual requesting to maintain the previous ruling without change.[48] Only a few days subsequent to a final determination in the matters concerning a couple, one parent may initiate a new claim on behalf of the child, without being required to prove a material or any other change in circumstances.[49]

Therefore, this right of independent status actually reverses the original fundamental presumption. It assumes that the representation of the minor by his parents in the first proceeding was not fitting representation, and thus the minor is allowed to initiate a new proceeding to modify the result.[50] The burden shifts and is placed on the party that objects to initiating a new proceeding.[51] In other words, the burden is borne by the individual wishing to maintain the determination that has already been adjudicated, and not by the party requesting to modify it.

Accordingly, the individual bearing the burden must prove that in the earlier proceeding the representation of the minor was appropriate.[52] This requirement contradicts the natural presumption which assumes that a parent adequately represents his child and faithfully fulfills his duty to protect the minor's interests. Thus by changing the customary premise, the court assumes, instead, that the representation of the child by the parents is inappropriate. Anyone arguing that the parental representation is proper bears the burden of proof.[53] The question of the burden is far more than a theoretical matter.

---

the trial court. *See, e.g.*, Pala v. Loubser, 943 N.E.2d 400, 409 (Ind. Ct. App.) (affirming trial court's termination of spousal maintenance), *transfer denied*, 950 N.E.2d 1212 (Ind. 2011).

47 *See* Wexler, *supra* note 45, at 766; Montes, Cohn, & Albaum, *supra* note 45, at 12.

48 Ruddock v. Ohls, 91 Cal. App. 3d 271, 277 (1979) ("If a judgment determining the existence of the parent-child relationship is to be binding upon the nonparty minor child, respondent has the burden of proving the minor was a party to the action or in some other manner is bound prospectively by the findings and judgment in the parents' marital dissolution action").

49 Famcourt 37181/97 L.Ti v A.Ti (Nov. 26, 2002) Nevo Legal Database (by subscription) (Isr.).

50 HCJ 6103/93 Levi v. The Supreme Rabbinical Court, 48(2) PD 591 [1994] (Isr.).

51 Id.

52 *See Ruddock*, 91 Cal. App. 3d at 277.

53 *See* Jaramillo v. Jaramillo 823 P.2d 299, 307 (N.M. 1991). Placing the burden on the party that wishes to maintain the present situation was of concern to the court in this matter. The

It actually determines, as a matter of policy, who will win in the litigation and who will lose.[54]

B. Contractual Certainty, Rehabilitation, and Motivation to Settle

The right of independent status, which is intended to focus on the interest of the minor, might be used, instead, by one of the parents as a way of avoiding his own obligations. A spouse, who just consented to a range of separation and divorce conditions including matters of joint property, custody, or support, can go back and object to the same agreement. He can thus request it be changed on the grounds that he is not bringing his own claim, but the claim of the minor.[55] The court sometimes defines such claims as fictitious when it becomes clear that the minor does not even know how to express his needs or what he is lacking, and when the initiation of the proceeding is neither the minor's initiative nor his idea.[56]

The presumption of compromising the interests of the minor might therefore be wrongfully taken advantage of by one of the spouses. In a separate proceeding, that spouse could argue that the child had not been properly represented, and thus he might avoid his own obligations under a prior agreement

---

court determined that even though the matter involved minors, it is appropriate to determine a presumption favoring the party that wishes to maintain the existing situation, while the burden of proof should be imposed on the individual requesting the change. The court stated that: "When parents are operating under a joint custody arrangement and one of them seeks to alter the arrangement, it makes perfectly good sense to impose a presumption in favor of the parent who wishes to continue to operate under the joint custody decree and to place on the party wishing to change the decree the burden to produce evidence that the arrangement is no longer workable and needs to be changed."*Id.* The court added and explained that as a rule, placing the burden on one of the parents to justify maintaining the existing situation could result in focusing on the question of whether or not that party met the burden, and the interests of the minor might be hurt. Thus the court stated: "But beyond this presumption in favor of an existing joint custody arrangement, further presumptions for or against the relocating parent and the one who remains behind only frustrate achievement of the ultimate goal of determining the arrangement that will best serve the child's interests" *Id.* at 307. In our matter, the burden in the proceeding is not intended to focus on the lack of trust in the parents but on the question of whether the requested change is in the best interests of the child or not.

54 *Id.* ("In the typical bipolar model of adversary litigation—in which one party's interests are pitted against those of the opposing party—the use of presumptions and the assignment of burdens of proof probably effectuate, in most instances, the relevant policy goals involved in determining who wins and who loses.")

55 *See* D.N. 4/82 Kot v. Kot, 38(3) PD 197, 209 [1984] (Isr.).

56 *See* CA 411/76 Sher v. Sher, 32(1) PD 449, 454 [2003] (Isr.).

with the other spouse. Therefore, the right of the minor to independent status might detrimentally impact the interest of the contract and contractual certainty, making it difficult for the couple to plan their individual futures.[57]

In addition, the duality in the position taken by the court is not easily understood. On one hand, when a parent creates an agreement with his spouse, the court does not trust the parent to protect the interests of the minor. On the other hand, after some time has passed, when a parent brings a separate claim against the other spouse on behalf of the child, such trust is granted.[58] Yet, it is possible that the parent's actual purpose in the new claim is the continuation of the dispute with the other spouse. If the concern is that a parent may be focused on his own interests and not on those of his child, then it is unclear why a proceeding brought prior to the divorce is differentiated from one brought afterwards.[59]

The minor's right to independent status creates a sort of balance of terrors, which threatens the parties and could become an incentive to prevent economic rehabilitation, or at least hide it due to concerns over relitigation. For example, the economic rehabilitation of one spouse could encourage the second spouse to initiate new litigation. A claim could be brought for increased child support from the first spouse due to his improved level of income.

The flexibility of an agreement between the spouses and the possibility of breaching it also negatively impact their motivation to resolve their dispute by agreement. The minor's right to independent status, as noted, places the

57 *See, e.g.*, CA 508/70 Natovich v. Natovitch, 25(1) PD 603, 615 [1971] (Isr.).

58 *See* CA 289/82 Dauva v. Dauva, 36(4) PD 625, 628 [1982] (Isr.).

59 This problematic duality is also expressed in Hunter v. Hunter, 170 Cal. App. 2d 576, 583 (1959) (holding that a parent may not waive reasonably due present and future support on behalf of his or her children, but that a parent may still make a binding agreement about such support). What is the meaning of the validity of an agreement between them if one party is allowed to change it in the name of the minor? What is the difference if a parent is allowed to change the agreement in his own name, or in the name of the minor? In *Van Buskirk v. Todd* for example, we found similar duality: On the one hand the mother is seen as one who acted on behalf of the child and represented his interests. On the other hand, when the minor requests to reopen the proceedings, in contradiction to the agreements that were reached by the mother, the mother's action is ignored. 269 Cal. App. 2d 680, 687 (1969) ("[T]he defendant could not get the case reversed by claiming for the first time on appeal that the child had no standing in court because he did not have a guardian ad litem on the paternity issue. We will presume that the mother acted in the manner of a guardian ad litem, and it is clear that she acted in behalf of the minor consistently with the duties of a guardian ad litem.") It is unclear how the mother is viewed in one proceeding as acting on behalf of the child by obligating the father, while at the same time she is viewed in another proceeding as acting contrary to the child's interests in her relationship with the child.

burden on the individual requesting to preserve the existing agreement so that the party wishing to revise it is in a more advantageous position. This determination thwarts the completion of the agreement.

In addition, one should also consider that maintaining the contract between the spouses ultimately serves the interests of the minor as well. In a home where the parents constantly argue and the atmosphere is filled with hate and bitterness, it is desirable and in the interest of the children that the tension be brought to an end and that the parents divorce.

In other words, there could be situations in which the child is interested in the separation of his parents no less than in his economic well-being.[60] A low level of child support or less than customary visitation does not necessarily mean that the interest of the child has been compromised and that representation by his parents is inappropriate.

From another perspective, the minor's right of independent status serves an additional fundamental interest of protecting the weaker spouse. The first proceeding between the parents takes place before the divorce decree is awarded, while the second proceeding takes place afterwards. Following the divorce, the spouses appear with "equal strength" in a monetary claim. It is not without reason that suits on behalf of minors are sometimes filed only days following the divorce.

During this short period of time, the expenses for the child did not really increase and the prices of commodities did not actually skyrocket. The minor did not suddenly mature and discover that he lacks adequate support. Only one thing has really changed. The parent who initiates the proceeding on behalf of the child is freed from the limitations of the divorce proceedings and is not concerned about a lack of cooperation from his spouse.[61]

---

60 CA 411/76 Sher v. Sher, 32(1) PD 449, 454 [2003] (Isr.).

61 An interesting judgment in New York argues that the "release" itself following a divorce decree constitutes a "change in circumstances." *See* Guillermo v. Guillermo, 43 Misc.2d 763, 773 (1964) ("As soon as the parent's marital freedom is adjudicated, the parent's 'circumstances' thereby *ipso facto* are changed by the new freedom itself. Having been safely separated, divorced or the marriage annulled, the parent for the first time is in a radically 'changed' position—to litigate freely, to strive vigorously for an equitable order of support without fear of refusal by the other parent to co-operate in the separation, divorce, or annulment by consenting to appear, or by declining to controvert the proof. Here in the Family Court, the Judge is for the first time given both sides of the circumstances as contended for by the respective parents, and he can find the facts as they are rather than as a separation agreement and mute parents made them appear to another court.") (emphasis in original).

The civil courts have welcomed relitigation in the name of the minor and have viewed such relitigation as an adjustment to the divorce proceedings. Adjustment is required because there is a gap between the ruling of the rabbinical court and the ruling of the civil court that will be given upon relitigation.[62] For example, the rabbinical courts have regularly determined child support at a lower rate than the civil courts. To that end, the civil courts have even established the minor's right to independent status.

This right of independent status can be used by courts not only to protect the interest of the minor, but to no lesser extent to protect the interest of the weaker spouse as well. Indeed, typically the second proceeding only deals with issues associated with the minor, and not directly with matters between the couple. However, it is no secret that through the issues related to the minor, it is also possible to balance and amend other concerns that are clearly those of the couple. In essence, it is not a matter of separate entities, and there is no absolute differentiation between payments due to the minor and payments due to the custodial parent.

Undoubtedly, the minor's right to independent status and the development of that right is an excellent means of protecting the interest of helpless minors in a legal proceeding. This right is also an excellent tool for safeguarding the interest of the weaker spouse. Together with these important advantages, it is impossible to ignore additional disadvantages and implications of that right that might eventually be harmful to the minor himself. The court-created presumption of parents compromising the interests of their minors conflicts with the legislature's determination of natural guardianship and customary practice in all other fields of law.[63]

In other areas of law, courts do not apply this presumption of parents compromising the interest of their minors. For example, in tort law, minors are routinely represented by their parents. One does not find the argument that the parents are exhausted from the legal proceeding against the wrongdoer and his insurance company. Thus, it is not asserted that signing a settlement agreement on behalf of the minor is not necessarily in the minor's own interest, but may instead be in the interest of his parents.[64]

---

62 Ariel Rosen-Zvi, The Rabbinical Court, the Religious Tradition and the Community- A Very Narrow Bridge, 3 Haifa L. Rev. 173, 178 (1995).

63 *See* CA 404/70 Evron v. Evron, 25(1) PD 373, 378 [1971] (Isr.).

64 *See* Ministry of Justice, the Committee on Children and the Law, Report of the Subcommittee on Education, at 36 (Feb. 2003), *available at* www.justice.gov.il/MOJHeb/HavaadLeZhuyot/YezugNifrad [hereinafter Rotlevy Committee Report] (indicating that

A possible objection to this argument is that tort litigation on behalf of a minor cannot be compared with family court cases. In tort matters, the parents are not disputing each other, while in family law they are in the midst of a controversy. However, a "battle" between the parents can cloud parental judgment. Moreover, in family law, the presumption of neglecting the interest of the minor is relevant even when the parents reach an agreement without going through a conflict.[65] So there is no real difference between family law and all the other areas of law.

In every other field of law, parents are presumed capable of appropriately protecting the interests of their children.[66] Thus, the question that arises is whether in family law the courts did not overly broaden the right of the minor to independent status. It is worthwhile critically reexamining whether legal systems have chosen the correct path. Arguably, that path allows a court of competent jurisdiction to conduct an entire proceeding while knowing that its decisions are not binding and may subsequently be relitigated a few days after the first adjudication. The broadening and establishment of the minor's right to independent status might add to the uncertainty and lack of peace and security that already trouble minors in divorce proceedings. It is not clear whether the important benefit of independent status is indeed greater than its cost.

IV. THREE MODELS FOR BALANCING THE COMPETING INTERESTS

The matters described above may be resolved with an appropriate formula for balancing competing interests including those of the child and his right to independent status, as compared with contractual interests and the finality of judgments. This section examines three legal models for achieving a balance among these factors.

Model A: Consideration of the Interest of the Minor by the Court

The simplest model requires the court to closely examine the interests of the minor when it makes decisions or approves agreements on matters concerning

---

the committee did not examine the independent representation of the minor in the area of torts since it did not see this important and urgent as well. It only has a recommendation for future review regarding other areas only after the issue would be resolved in family law.).

65 CA 363/81 Fayga v. Fayga, 36(3) PD 187, 189 [1982] (Isr.).

66 Capacity and Guardianship Law, 5722—1962, 380 Laws of the State of Israel (LSI) 120, §§ 14–15 (1962) (Isr.) ("The parents are the natural guardians of their minor children. ... The guardianship of the parents includes the obligation and the right to care for the needs of the minor ... and the authority to represent him.")

the minor. This requirement should bring about trust in the court's faithful performance of its duties. The initial assumption is that the court appropriately considers the interests of the minor and thus properly accounts for the child's interests. Whoever wishes to argue otherwise should bear the burden of proof.

The assumption or even the presumption that the court examines the interest of the minor should result in the finality of judgments and thereby encourage couples to reach agreements. The present situation raises certain difficulties when one court allows itself to open an agreement that was previously confirmed by another court. The subsequent court is not a court of appeals, but shares concurrent jurisdiction with the first one. Customarily, courts at the same level of jurisdiction will not intervene in each other's decisions.

However, one must also consider the limited ability of the court to ensure that an agreement submitted for approval is indeed in the best interests of the child. Although the court is able to subpoena witnesses and gather evidence, it does not take upon itself the role of managing a proceeding. Its ability to access evidence is also limited. The court does not seek new information, call upon experts, or even question them:

> [U]nder most states' laws a court must review an agreement to determine whether it is in the child's best interests. ... Despite the appearance of review, however, independent judicial inquiry is difficult because of the inaccessibility of facts that might dictate a different result. The result is the worst of both worlds: parents enter the divorce process with their autonomy to make arrangements for their children officially abridged, and yet arrangements that might truly be detrimental to children are unlikely to be identified.[67]

Despite these objective difficulties, there are instances in which the proceeding between the parents is binding upon the children without requiring further action.[68] Additional litigation, that is separate from the other issues of divorce, may not even be necessary. Similarly, the minor may not need to be added as a party to the proceeding. An "identity of interests" between parent and child is often sufficient to render the proceedings binding upon the child. In other words, when the parent shares common interests with the minor whom he

67 Am. Law Inst., Principles of the Law of Family Dissolution: Analysis and Recommendations 5 (2002).

68 *See, e.g.*, Armstrong v. Armstrong, 15 Cal. 3d 942, 951 (1976).

represents, the legal proceeding is viewed as binding on the minor as well. This is the case even if the minor takes no part in the legal proceeding.

For example, in *Armstrong v. Armstrong,* children whose parents went through divorce proceedings requested an increase in the amount of their support.[69] Their mother brought a claim on their behalf.[70] These proceedings sought a result contradicting a prior proceeding between the parents.[71] Normally, a court assumes the interest of the children may be overshadowed by the interest of the parents and thereby compromised. In this case, however, the interest of the mother was identical to that of the children and therefore her representation of the children was proper. The court determined:

> The doctrinal reach of the *res judicata* bar extends, however, to those persons "in privity with" parties. ... We have previously held that privity exists where the person involved is "... so identified in interest with another that he represents the same legal right." ... In the present case, plaintiffs' mother was entrusted with their care and custody and was a proper representative of their interests. While in similar situations we can conceive of a commingling of interests of parent and child in the negotiation of a marital dissolution agreement to the degree that the future interests of a child are clearly and deliberately subordinated to the present interests and advantages of a parent, the record before us discloses no such circumstances. For this reason, we conclude that plaintiffs are bound by the judgment in the divorce action to which their mother was a party.[72]

Identity of interests is the standard that determines whether a minor is bound by a proceeding in which he was not present.[73] When identity of interests is

69 *See id.* at 945.

70 *See id.* at 945–47.

71 *See id.* at 945–46.

72 *Id.* at 951; *accord* Stevens v. Kelley 57 Cal. App. 2d 318, 323–24 (1943); Murdock v. Eddy 38 Cal. App. 2d 551, 553–54 (1940); Ruddock v. Ohls, 91 Cal. App. 3d 271, 276 (1979) ("Under California law children who are not parties to a divorce action still may be bound by some aspects of a marital dissolution proceeding if the interests of the child are adequately represented by one of the parents").

73 *See* Amstadt v. U.S. Brass Corp., 919 S.W.2d 644, 653 (Tex. 1996) ("To determine whether subsequent plaintiffs are in privity with prior plaintiffs, we examine the interests the parties shared. ... Privity exists if the parties share an identity of interests in the basic legal right that is the subject of litigation.") (citation omitted).

appropriately applied during the initial divorce proceedings, the court's determination is binding upon a subsequent court.[74]

The legal systems should require that the court's confirmation of the agreement between the parties not be a mere rubber stamp, but instead be aimed at ensuring proper and sufficient protection of the interests of the minor. In other words, a clear presumption should be established that the prior court's confirmation incorporates within it the concern for and examination of the needs of the child. Ideally, this presumption should also determine that the legal proceeding is binding on the minor. However, since a court's decision does not presently prevent subsequent proceedings, each case actually remains open, even when the court has confirmed the divorce agreement between the parties.[75]

Today, the confirmation by the court is not considered final because the court acts according to the definitions and the terms determined by law such as "best interests of the child," which can be interpreted with flexibility. Courts have broad discretion and therefore may each view the issues differently, resulting in relitigation with respect to the level of child support, visitations, and so forth. This problem can be resolved or at least limited by determining clearer definitions for identifying the child's best interests. The following section examines such a model.

Model B: Clear Legislative Guidelines

In the state legal systems within the United States prior to the determination of state child support guidelines, the court decisions relied upon vague standards such as "the best interest of the child," and "substantial change in circumstances."[76] Reliance upon these abstract terms was problematic for the

---

74 *See* Yarborough v. Yarborough, 290 U.S. 202, 210 (1933) ("The provision which the Georgia law makes of permanent alimony for the child during minority is a legal incident of the divorce proceeding. As that suit embraces within its scope the disposition and care of minor children, jurisdiction over the parents confers eo ipso jurisdiction over the minor's custody and support. Hence, by the Georgia law, a consent (or other) decree in a divorce suit, fixing permanent alimony for a minor child is binding upon it, although the child was not served with process, was not made a formal party to the suit, and no guardian ad litem was appointed therein").

75 *See, e.g.*, CA 404/70 Evron v. Evron, 25(1) PD 373, 378 [1971] (Isr.).

76 Jeffrey C. Sorenson, *Changing the Changed Circumstances Requirement: A New Standard for Modifying Permanent Custody Orders*, 23 J. Juv. L. 90, 97–99 (2003) (concluding that the best interests of the child should replace the standard of change in circumstances). *But cf.* Jon Elster, *Solomonic Judgment: Against the Best Interest of the Child*, 54 U. Chi. L. Rev. 1, 11–29 (1987).

legal system because courts interpreted the terms differently.[77] This broad judicial discretion resulted in inconsistency when courts awarded economic child support and determined the adequacy of spousal support. Later courts found the earlier court decisions to be erroneous and sought to change them, even if no change in circumstances had occurred.[78] This prevented finality of judgment in family law cases involving decisions regarding children.

Historically, the United States Congress has been concerned about possible harm to minors that are not awarded adequate child support.[79] The determination of low amounts of support places a heavy burden on assistance organizations in the United States.[80] In the mid-1980s, Congress expressed concern "about the adequacy of child support awards."[81] In 1984, Congress conditioned its aid to states and to assistance organizations on the development of clear guidelines for child support.[82]

In 1988, Congress further demanded that these guidelines be given the validity of a presumption in legal proceedings.[83] Thus, a litigant who wished to overcome that presumption had to provide written justification.[84] In light of this requirement, guidelines have been defined in each of the United States.[85] Child support requirements are usually formulated based on estimates of the minimal expenses spent on children in two-parent families.[86]

---

77 *See, e.g.*, Elster, *supra* note 76, at 4–8 (arguing the best interests of the child standard is problematically indeterminate).

78 Hill v. Hill, 620 P.2d 1114, 1119 (Kan. 1980) ("[W]here a custody decree is entered in a default proceeding, and the facts are not substantially developed and presented to the court, the trial court may later, in its discretion, admit and consider evidence as to facts existing at the time of the earlier order, and upon the full presentation of the facts the court may enter any order which could have been made at the initial hearing whether a 'change in circumstances' has since occurred or not").

79 Principles of the Law of Family Dissolution: Analysis and Recommendations, 8 Duke J. Gender L. & Pol'y 1, 2 (2001).

80 In the past, Aid to Families with Dependent Children (AFDS), and today, Temporary Assistance for Needy Families (TANF). *See* Personal Responsibility and Work Opportunity Reconciliation Act of 1996, Pub. L. No. 104–193, 110 Stat. 2105; 42 U.S.C. § 601 (1997).

81 *Principles of the Law of Family Dissolution*, *supra* note 79, at 13.

82 42 U.S.C.A. § 667 (West).

83 Family Support Act of 1988, Pub. L. No. 100–485, § 126, 102 Stat. 2343, 2346 (1988) (codified at 42 U.S.C.A § 667 (West)). Congress passed the Family Support Act (FSA) in 1988 and created the U.S. Commission on Interstate Child Support. The FSA required that by October 1989 each state adopt a child support law using a mathematic formula to establish a support award guideline.

84 *Id.*

85 Principles of the Law of Family Dissolution, *supra* note 79, at 13.

86 *Id.*

The amount of basic child support is calculated as a certain percentage of parental income.[87]

In each of the fifty states within the United States, clear state standards and guidelines have been established for calculating child support and enforcing payment.[88] The establishment of these guidelines resulted in the finality of child support judgments in later disputes.

The system in Australia was also criticized for its inconsistency due to a lack of guidelines.[89] These objections brought about reform in the Child Support (Assessment) Act 1989 (CSA).[90] In order to improve the processes of assessment and payment, the new Australian law removed from the courts the authority to determine the level of economic child support and transferred it to an administrative body that operates according to a structured formula.[91]

The formula allows for easily and quickly determining the level of child support that the non-custodial parent is required to pay.[92] Initially, it was possible to appeal the decision of the administrative body before the courts that exercised broad discretion. Today, the CSA is the entity from which parties can request changes in set formulas.[93] The removal of this authority from the courts narrowed the discretion in the matter and resulted in greater certainty and the finality of judgment.

In Canada, the family law acts vary among the provinces. In the past, the courts also had broad discretion and no real guidelines.[94] Unavoidably, a situation of uncertainty and inconsistency developed with respect to the level of

---

87 *Id.* ("All states now calculate the basic child support obligation as a percentage of parent earnings").

88 *Id.*; Family law is state law, and each state is allowed to create its own laws: *see* Simms v. Simms, 175 U.S. 162, 167 (1899) ("[T]he whole subject of the domestic relations of husband and wife, parent and child, belongs to the laws of the State, and not to the laws of the United States." (citing *In re* Burrus, 136 U.S. 586, 593–94 (1890)); *see also Boddie v. Connecticut*, 401 U.S. 371, 376 (1971).

89 Belinda Fehlberg & Mavis Maclean, Child Support Policy in Australia and the United Kingdom: Changing Priorities but a Similar Tough Deal for Children?, 23 INT'L J.L. POL. & FAM. 1, 3 (2009).

90 *See Child Support (Assessment) Act 1989* (Cth) part 5 (Austl.), *available at* http://www.austlii.edu.au/au/legis/cth/consol_act/csa1989294/.

91 *Id.* at part 5.

92 *Id.*

93 Fehlberg & Maclean, *supra* note 89, at 6–7.

94 Department of Justice Canada, Children Come First: A Report to Parliament Reviewing the Provisions and Operation of the Federal Child Support Guidelines 1 (2002), *available at* http://www.justice.gc.ca/eng/rp-pr/fl-lf/child-enfant/rp/pdf/v1.pdf.

economic child support. This vagueness was detrimental to the willingness of the parents to voluntarily reach agreement regarding the level of support, and it encouraged them to initiate legal proceedings.[95] As a result, Federal Child Support Guidelines were created in Canada as well. The guidelines are designed to ensure certainty, consistency, and restriction of the court's discretion. Especially important to the present matter, they also provide for the finality of judgment.[96]

In contrast, the Israeli legal system does not clearly define the level of the child support obligation. The payment amount is determined according to the personal (religious) law of the individual required to pay the support.[97] Under this law, only the father is obligated to provide the "necessary support" for his children.[98] That term is certainly abstract. Thus, the rabbinic court and the civil court which have parallel jurisdiction with respect to the level of child support, determine significantly different decisions.[99]

On June 5, 2006, the Israeli minister of justice appointed The Committee to Examine the Issue of Child Support in the State of Israel, chaired by Professor Shifman.[100] On September 20, 2012 the committee presented its recommendations.[101] The findings of the committee show that the gap in determination of child support also exists among the judges in the civil court.[102] While the court determines a minimum level of child support, the determination of the maximum level of support is more problematic.[103]

---

95 *Id.*

96 *See* Divorce Act, R.S.C. 1985, c.3 §15 (2nd Supp.) (Can.); *see also* Federal Child Support Guidelines, SOR/97-195 (Can.), *available at* http://www.canlii.org/en/ca/laws/stat/rsc-1985-c-3-2nd-supp/latest/rsc-1985-c-3-2nd-supp.html.

97 *See* Family Law Amendment (Maintenance) Law, 5719—1959, 276 Laws of the State of Israel (LSI) 72, § 2 (1959) (Isr.) ("A person is responsible for spousal support, according to the rules of the personal law applicable to him").

98 *Id.*

99 *Id.*

100 Report of the Committee to Examine the Issue of Child Support in the State of Israel (Shifman Committee), at 106 (Sept. 2012) [hereinafter: Shifman Committee Report].

101 Shifman Committee Report, at 3.

102 Shifman Committee Report, at 25: *see also* Mor Yogev & Ayelet Giladi, *Mom Give Me Equality*, 3 Hearat Din 1, 6 (2006); HCJ 5969/94 Aknin v. The Rabbinical Court (Haifa), 50(1) PD 370, Para. 11 [1996] (Isr.). (acknowledging the fact that different interpretations are given to the level of child support but stating that this is not a desirable conclusion).

103 Famcourt 3400-09-10 Anonymous v Anonymous, (Nevo 29/10/2010) Para 19.

Therefore, the committee recommended the establishment of a formula for child support according to the existing Australian model.[104] This formula will prevent judicial discretion, and hopefully even the need for separate relitigation of a claim on behalf of the minor.

In contrast, under the legal systems both in the states within the United States and in Israel, the issues of custody and visitation remain without any uniform standards and are thus subject to relitigation. From a legal point of view, divorce traditionally required a couple to address grounds for the divorce, property distribution, alimony, child custody, and child support. Today, only those issues associated with children remain open issues in most states. Additionally, while all fifty states in the United States have enacted some form of standardized child support calculation and child support enforcement networks, both child custody and visitation remain often hotly contested issues in divorce proceedings.[105]

Therefore, uniform standards determined through legislation or judicial decisions may bring about finality to these matters. Uniform guidelines will undoubtedly contribute to the finality of judgment, strengthen the principles of *res judicata* and contractual certainty, and prevent misuse of the minor's right to independent status in the dispute between spouses.

Model C: Independent Representation for the Minor

Some legal systems do not allow parents to enter agreements on matters concerning their children. Therefore, while parents may discuss their own matters in connection with divorce agreements, they know in advance that the issues involving their children are not subject to negotiation at all. For example, in Virginia:

> [T]he parents cannot make agreements which will bind courts to decide a custody case one way or the other. The Virginia Supreme Court of Appeals has emphasized this deep-rooted Virginia policy by declaring, "The custody and welfare of children are not the subject of barter."[106]

---

104 Shifman Committee Report *supra* note 102, at 59 ("The bill formulated by the committee is based primarily on the Australian model founded on the assumption that a fixed percentage of the joint parental income is allocated to the needs of their children.")

105 Leite & Clark, *supra* note 1, at 260–61 (citation omitted).

106 Ford v. Ford, 371 U.S. 187, 193 (1962) (quoting Buchanan v. Buchanan, 197 S.E. 426, 434 (1938).

It is worth examining whether a similar model should be adopted in all legal systems so that parents in divorce proceedings will be able to determine only matters affecting themselves such as distribution of family property, but not matters associated with the minor. For this proposal to be enacted, it should be considered in conjunction with the model described below.

It seems that one of the most practical proposals for resolving the concerns discussed above, or at least for preventing their exacerbation, is including the minor in the proceedings between his parents by the appointment of an independent representative for the minor.[107] This modern approach recognizes the need for independent representation of the minor due to the concern that the parents may subordinate the minor's interests in favor of their own. The independent representation for the minor ensures that the process of factual investigation will be protected and that parents will not subsequently relitigate subjects that have already been determined.

Preserving the finality of judgment is of utmost importance and independent representation serves this goal.[108] John Speca and Robert Wehrman analyzed all the cases in the State of Missouri regarding the inherent jurisdiction of the court to appoint temporary representation for a minor. They came to the clear conclusion that children have their own rights and only receive adequate protection in divorce proceedings when they have independent representation.[109] Despite this modern approach, only Wisconsin requires a separate attorney to independently represent a minor in divorce proceedings.[110]

The remaining states grant broad judicial discretion for appointing a guardian ad litem for a minor in a legal proceeding:

> Several other states have adopted the provisions of the Uniform Marriage and Divorce Act, which provide the court with discretionary power to

107 The authority to appoint representation for the minor exists under Israeli law and is expressed in section 29 of the Legal Capacity and Guardianship Law. It requires limiting the natural guardianship of the parents, showing the court a special reason justifying the limitation, and hearing the parents: "If guardianship of one parent was limited, the court may, in addition to the parents, appoint a guardian for the minor for matters to be prescribed by him."

108 S. v. S., 595 S.W.2d 357, 360 (Mo. Ct. App. 1980) ("First, the modern trend of authority recognizes the necessity for independent representation of a child when the parents in a dispute over the custody of the child do not, in any proper sense, protect the best interests of the child").

109 John Speca & Robert L. Wehrman, *Protecting the Rights of Children in Divorce Cases in Missouri*, 38 U. Mo. Kan. City L. Rev. 1, 38–40 (1969).

110 Meyer, *supra* note 2, at 446 (citing Wis. Stat. Ann. § 767.045 (West 1993)).

appoint a guardian ad litem for a minor or dependent child in proceedings for support, custody, and visitation.[111]

As mentioned, several of the states within the United States grant judicial discretion to appoint independent representation for the matters of minors.[112] In certain states within the United States, the appointment of the minor's representative and that representative's responsibilities and duties are broadly determined in legislation[113] including the representative's independent investigation of the evidence.[114] Many scholars have argued that it is not sufficient to rely upon the court to protect the interest of minors, or upon the natural presumption that the parents adequately protect this interest.[115] Instead, these scholars argue that independent representation must be appointed for the minor.[116]

The importance of independent representation is emphasized in the adversary system of law, in which the court relies upon the evidence of the parties and does not gather it by itself.[117] The Australian legal system also defined the principles for appointing independent representation, giving parties a non-exhaustive list of possible arguments for independent representation.[118] In Canada, under the systems of family law in each of the provinces together

---

111 *Id.*

112 Tari Eitzen, A Child's Right to Independent Legal Representation in a Custody Dispute, 19 FAM. L.Q. 53, 67 (1985).

113 *See, e.g.*, Cal. Rules of Court, Rule 5.240 (2014); Uniform Marriage and Divorce Act §310 (1973).

114 2012S.C. Acts 361, § 63-3-830: (A) The responsibilities and duties of a guardian ad litem include ... (1) representing the best interest of the child; (2) conducting an independent, balanced, and impartial investigation to determine the facts relevant to the situation of the child and the family."

115 *See, e.g.*, Robert F. Drinan, *The Rights of Children in Modern Family* Law, 2 J. FAM. L. 101, 107 (1962) (asking whether it would make sense for a court to provide detailed obligations of parents); Robert W. Hansen, *Guardians Ad Litem in Divorce and Custody Cases: Protection of the Child's Interests*, 4 J. FAM. L. 181, 181–82 (1964).

116 Drinan, *id.* at 103. *See generally* Hansen, *id.*

117 Marshall A. Levin, Guardian Ad Litem *in Family Court*, 34 MD. L. REV. 341 (1974) ("[W]ithout meaningful representation of the interests of the child, the adversary system cannot properly effectuate the legal test of what is in the 'best interest' of the child."); In Connecticut, the discussion of this matter has progressed so much that they began considering the questions of post appointment, as for example, if the representing attorney will be granted immunity from claims of professional negligence. *See* Nicole A. Demers, *An Attorney is an Attorney is an Attorney, "Except When That Attorney is also a Guardian Ad Litem: An Analysis of the Connecticut Appellate Court's Decision in* Carrubba v. Moskowitz *Regarding Immunity*, 24 QUINNIPIAC L. REV. 847, 857–63 (2006).

118 Stefureak v. Chambers, [2004] 6 R.F.L. 6th 212, para. 73 (Can.).

with provisions of Federal law, there are still no clear instructions as to when and how to appoint an independent representative. The courts, however, have broad discretion to make such determinations.[119]

Canadian judicial decisions offer three different models for characterizing the nature of independent representation of minors: "the *amicus curiae*, the litigation guardian, and the child advocate."[120]

The third model cited is similar to other approaches that view the independent representation of the minor as the most efficient way to ensure the minor is accorded zealous representation. The proponents of this model emphasize the autonomy of the minor as a client and the importance of his participation as a party to the legal proceeding. They argue that this representation advances the interest of the child because the court does not view the child as an individual requiring protection and consideration, but rather as a person with rights. Thus explains Atwood:

> [T]hose who endorse a child's attorney model emphasize the child's basic right to have his or her wishes presented by a zealous advocate. Proponents emphasize the child client's autonomy and the value to the child and to the court of the child's participation in the proceedings. Under this approach, the child's dignity interests are served when the child has a representative committed to advocating the child's preferences.[121]

This model may balance the concern over possible harm to the child's interests, and result in the finality of judgment. However, while this model seems very tempting, it may potentially burden the legal proceeding. Another attorney joining the dispute between the spouses might take advantage of this weakness, prolong the proceedings, and delay the resolution of the conflict.[122]

---

119 Puszczak v. Puszczak, [2005] 56 Alta. L.R. 4th 225, para 11 (Can.) ABCA 426, para. 11 (Can.) ("The case law in Canada is not highly developed in setting out guidelines to determine when counsel should be appointed in private custody cases and how that should be accomplished").

120 Dormer v. Thomas, [1999] 65 B.C.L.R. 3d 290, para. 44 (Can.).

121 Barbara Ann Atwood, *Representing Children: The Ongoing Search for Clear and Workable Standards*, 19 J. Am. Acad. Matrimonial Law. 183, 194 (2005) (citations omitted).

122 For example, in the case of A.M., an attorney was appointed for the independent representation of a minor. This attorney requested, on behalf of the minor, to bring his own evidence, to cross-examine witnesses, to retain an expert on his behalf, etc. *See* A.M. (Guardian ad litem of) v. K.A.A.M., [2008] N.J. No. 267 ("The child argued that he was granted a role as a fully participating party and sought to call evidence, question witnesses and retain

In addition, the minor's attorney might increase the animosity between the spouses. Lucy McGough argues that adding another attorney to the often already charged atmosphere between the parents could cause an abundance of disagreements, additional lack of clarity regarding the role of the court as a protector of minors, and an increase in the costs of the proceeding.[123] That is the reason, in her opinion, that an attorney is only occasionally appointed to represent the child.[124]

Due to these concerns, McGough argues that the appointment of an attorney for independent representation is not justified in regular circumstances, although it would be correct to grant the court authority to appoint an attorney in exceptional instances where the interests of the parents severely conflict with those of the children.[125] In that context, the appointment of the guardian may be limited only to the specific proceedings (litigation guardian). This "temporary guardian" can also serve as a mediator or arbitrator between the parents and provide recommendations to the court.

McGough suggests not appointing an attorney in this role, since an attorney generally lacks professional training in child development or in family dynamics. She proposes that it would be preferable to appoint professionals in the therapeutic field.[126] It seems that her approach adopts the model used in Canada for appointing an independent representative, a friend of the court (*amicus curiae*).

The Rotlevy Committee also looked into this matter within the Israeli legal system.[127] The committee found that independent representation of a child by

---

experts. The mother agreed with the child. The father objected to the child making applications").

123 Lucy S. McGough, *Protecting Children in Divorce: Lessons from Caroline Norton*, 57 Me. L. Rev. 13, 26 (2005) ("Throwing another lawyer into the fray, however, may not be the solution. The third attorney may compound or even create unnecessary adversarialness in the trial, cause additional confusion about the court's role as the protector of the child, produce delay, and add to the costs of the case. The persuasiveness of these counterarguments explains why separate counsel is rarely appointed for the child").

124 *Id.*

125 *Id.* at 27.

126 *Id.* at 26–27 ("More states authorize the appointment of a guardian ad litem for the child. The guardian need not be an attorney. Aside from needless expense and role confusion, lawyers or guardians typically have no special knowledge of child development or family dynamics … why not appoint a child psychiatrist or child psychologist who can conduct an investigation, interview all parties, analyze the child's best interests, and tell the court how it should decide?") (citations omitted).

127 The Rotlevy Public Committee on Children and the Law, chaired by Judge Saviona Rotlevy, was appointed by the justice minister in Israel on June 27, 1997. This committee was divided into six subcommittees. One of the subcommittees dealt with "Independent

an attorney does not lengthen the proceedings.[128] To the contrary, since the attorney will not be subject to considerations of bureaucracy and budget, the attorney will make sure that the matter will proceed quickly.[129]

The Rotlevy Committee also rejected the concern over additional figures in the life of the child, arguing that it is possible to require the attorney to maintain an ongoing and trustworthy relationship with the child throughout the entire proceeding.[130] Formal measures could also be established to ensure permanent representation.

The Rotlevy Committee determined that clear and defined criteria for the appointment of representation safeguards parental authority.[131] It also determined that from a legal perspective it is preferable that the duty of representation remain with an attorney, and not with a welfare officer or similar official who may be subject to the considerations of welfare offices, policy, budgets, and additional factors that are not always consistent with the best interests of the child.[132]

The Rotlevy Committee further stated that the approach of the welfare officer is through a broad, family perspective that does not focus specifically on the child in the way required by independent representation.[133] The committee members did not discuss how independent representation could influence the other issues of concern raised in this chapter.

Decisions or agreements reached in proceedings in which an independent and separate representative is appointed for the minor should be given the validity of a final judgment. Such matters should not be open to future relitigation based on the claim that the interest of the minor did not receive proper representation.

Some legal systems include assistance units associated with the family court. Therapeutic professionals serve in these units. Their appointment as independent representatives for minors is easy to arrange and may lessen the costs of the proceedings. One may assume that their opinions will be objective.

Representation of Children in Civil Proceedings." The subcommittee's report was submitted to the minister of justice in February of 2003. *See* Rotlevy Committee Report *supra* note 64.

128 *Id.* at 97.

129 *Id.* at 100.

130 *Id.* at 102.

131 *Id.* at 103.

132 *Id.* at 114.

133 *Id.* at 115.

The direct effectiveness of this resource is, of course, adding the minor as a party to the proceedings, ensuring the finality of judgment, and protecting the interests derived from it.

In addition, a decision reached in a proceeding will be more correct when professionals who can recommend solutions from their areas of professional expertise are involved in the process. Statutory entities such as these contribute significantly to proceedings involving minors.[134] Their representation of the minor includes the minor as a party to the proceeding.[135] The decision becomes final and binding on the minor; and the same matter may not be relitigated.[136]

In light of the different models for appointing legal representation for a minor, either the legislator or the court should resolve the remaining uncertainties. The duties, obligations, and limitations of independent representation need to be clearly delineated. One may reason that as long as the roles of the representatives for minors are not defined, the court will refrain from appointing them.

V. CONCLUSION

Different legal systems have expressed concern that parents, who are in the midst of divorce proceedings, may compromise the interests of their children. The increased risk of a conflict of interests between parents and children, coupled with the worsening of the scope and severity of divorce disputes, have strengthened the presumption that parents may compromise the interests of their children. In response to apparent concern for the minor's right to independent status, the courts have allowed relitigation of prior decisions in divorce proceedings and written agreements between spouses, even if they were approved by court.

Including the minors in the proceedings and having the parents declare that they are creating an agreement in the interests of their children, do not make any difference. The burden of proof is borne by the individual wishing

---

134 A.I. v. Ontario (Director, Child and Family Services Act), [2005] 136 CRR (2d) 13, para. 141–42 ("The OCL [Office of the Children's Lawyer] is statutorily mandated to act in the best interests of the children it represents. It is axiomatic, therefore, that a position taken by the OCL is one which the OCL believes to be in the best interests of the child. ... The OCL is frequently an invaluable resource to this court, and I find this case no exception. I found the OCL's involvement to be very helpful").

135 *See, e.g.*, In re A.K. v. Kirchner 620 N.E.2d 572, 580 (Ill. App. Ct. 4th Dist. 1993) ("[The child], however, was a party to the dissolution action here, because [the child] was represented by the guardian *ad litem*").

136 Simcox v. Simcox, 546 N.E.2d 609, 612 (Ill. 1989).

to maintain the previously adjudicated determination and not by the minor requesting to modify it. The right to independent status therefore provides important protection for the interests of the minor.

On the other hand, this right enables courts to reverse earlier judicial decisions, based on the argument that they were detrimental to the minor. The presumption of compromising the interests of the minor and its impact on the possibility of relitigation is detrimental to contractual certainty and finality of judgments. A spouse who has just consented to a range of separation and divorce conditions can object to that agreement and request that the agreement be modified by bringing a claim on behalf of the minor. This sort of relitigation enables one spouse to prolong the ongoing dispute with the other spouse.

It creates an incentive to prevent economic rehabilitation out of concern for possible future relitigation. Such a claim on behalf of the minor also negatively impacts the motivation of a couple to resolve their dispute by agreement. It wastes precious judicial resources and brings about relitigation while other new claims are waiting to be heard for the first time. In addition, the claim misleads the couple that believes the legal proceeding will allow each of them to begin a new path in life. Courts may have gone too far in establishing the right of the minor to independent status given that the right may be an obstacle to the minor himself.

Three models better balance the competing interests. The first model requires the court to comprehensively protect the best interests of the child, and then grants a presumption of validity to the court's determination. The initial assumption should be that the court appropriately considers the interests of the minor, and thus properly accounts for the child's interests. Whoever wishes to argue otherwise should bear the burden of proof. That determination should also serve as binding precedent for a subsequent court.

The second model determines clear legislative guidelines for defining the best interests of the child in order to avoid future relitigation. The establishment of guidelines for child support results in the finality of child support judgments in later disputes. The state legal systems in the United States as well as the legal systems in Australia and Canada adopt this approach. Some of them have even transferred the determination of child support matters to administrative entities, while drastically restricting judicial discretion. These entities implement an established formula based on the objective data of the parents, so that it will be difficult to initiate relitigation by arguing that the interest of the minors was compromised. The Israeli system intends to continue in this direction, although it still relies upon abstract terms in determining child support, a consideration that makes it easier to relitigate on behalf of the minor.

The third model appoints independent representation for the minor. Such representation will add the minor as a party to the proceedings and thereby ensure finality of judgment. Decisions or agreements that are reached in proceedings, in which an independent and separate representative is appointed for the minor, should be given the validity of a final judgment. Such matters should not be open to future relitigation based on the claim that the interest of the minor did not receive proper representation.

These models or a combination of them can be used to create a formula for more appropriately balancing the competing interests and concerns in family law proceedings. Such a system could protect the interests of the minor, while at the same time preserving contractual certainty and the stability of agreements between spouses.

CHAPTER 3

Extramarital Relationships and the Theoretical Rationales for the Joint Property Rules

I. INTRODUCTION

Extramarital relationships are not a new occurrence in married life. At the beginning of the nineteenth century, they were the most common cause of divorce between spouses[1] and today they continue to be widespread.[2] Human history has looked upon this phenomenon severely and imposed harsh punishments on the spouse who is the "wrongdoer":

> Human civilization has long maintained legal consequences for the marital love triangle. We know, for example, that primitive societies punished adultery with severe penalties. It is also well known that Hebraic law specifically proscribes adultery, in the Seventh of its Ten Commandments. ... Classical culture also forbade extramarital affairs.[3]

---

1 Laura Bradford, *The Counterrevolution: A Critique of Recent Proposals to Reform No-Fault Divorce Laws*, 49 Stan. L. Rev. 607, 610 (1997).

2 Studies in the United States show that 40–50 percentof women have extramarital "affairs." *See* Robert R. Bell et al., *A Multivariate Analysis of Female Extramarital Coitus*, 37 J. Marriage & Fam. 375, 380 (1975). Another study reveals that about 70 percent of men under age forty state that they do not negate the possibility that they will be involved in an extramarital affair. Lynn Atwater, The Extramarital Connection: Sex, Intimacy, and Identity 15 (1982). An additional study shows that more than half of the people involved in the study had had an extramarital affair at least once. Constance Ahrons, The Good Divorce: Keeping Your Family Together When Your Marriage Comes Apart 101 (1994).

3 Jeffrey Brian Greenstein, *Sex, Lies and American Tort Law: The Love Triangle in Context*, 5 Geo. J. Gender & L. 723, 724 (2004).

In recent history, the legal system has undergone significant change.[4] This chapter reviews how the law addresses extramarital relationships with respect to the distribution of family property. It examines the theoretical and modern bases for joint property and suggests a new and appropriate model for its distribution. Accordingly, this chapter investigates and examines the dramatic transitions that took place within the legal systems of the United States during the last four decades, starting with the exclusion of fault from divorce and ending with the change in the consideration of fault in property distribution. The chapter also presents the positions of Israeli law and Jewish religious law in these matters. The analysis provides a broad perspective and assists in offering a new model for balancing the values that impact consideration of fault in property distribution.

The discussion of extramarital relationships requires conceptual clarification of the term "fault" in family law. This term is primarily used in tort law, where its meaning is inappropriate or unreasonable behavior. In family law, vagueness surrounds this term. Nevertheless, "fault" can, in principle, be divided into three categories: "economic fault," expressed by inappropriate economic behavior, such as lack of contribution to the family effort, waste of the family's assets, and so forth.; "violent fault," expressed in physical or psychological violence of one spouse towards the other; and, finally, "sexual fault," expressed by inappropriate sexual behavior of one of the spouses, primarily a romantic extramarital relationship. This chapter devotes its discussion to this third category of fault and specifically to extramarital relationships. A portion of the following discussion is also relevant to other behaviors within a marital relationship, but these behaviors might be treated differently than extramarital relationships.[5]

Clearly, the matter raises not only a technical-arithmetic question with respect to the determination of property distribution. It is also influenced by worldviews, values, and societal perceptions of the family unit and the

---

4 Guido Tedeschi, *The Family Crisis and Traditionalists*, *in* LEGAL STUDIES IN MEMORY OF AVRAHAM ROSENTHAL 282 (Guido Tedeschi, ed., 1964).

5 The distinction between the different kinds of fault has much practical significance beyond the analytical differentiation. From the normative foundation of the laws of property between spouses, it follows that the influence of fault should change according to the type of fault. The various types of fault are different from one another on several levels: the types differ in their intensity and severity, they vary in impact on the "innocent" spouse, and they vary in the way in which the laws relate to them, etc. For a broader discussion, *see* Ruth Halperin-Kaddari, *Moral Considerations in Family Law and a Feminist Reading of Family Cases in Israel*, *in* READINGS IN FEMINISM, GENDER AND LAW 651 (Barak-Erez et al. eds., 2007).

appropriate commitment to a relationship. In addition, it is inherently impacted by developments that have taken place in the Western world. Thus, as long as society views marriage as an important public institution, society will allow itself to determine under which circumstances a marriage can be dissolved and the price that will be paid by the person at fault for its dissolution. In contrast, if society views marriage as a private institution, fault for its dissolution will be regarded more leniently. Either way, it is impossible to examine these issues without first understanding the principles of joint family property and their theoretical rationales.

II. PROPERTY DISTRIBUTION AND EXTRAMARITAL RELATIONSHIPS—THE LAWS IN THE UNITED STATES

A. The System of Family Property Distribution

Family law in the United States is included under state law and the independent legislation of each state.[6] In the past, most states distributed the property acquired during a marriage (hereinafter "the family property") according to the traditional principles of common law.[7] Those states treated family property as the separate property of each of the spouses, unless the spouses took steps to transform it into joint property.[8] This system left most of the family property in the hands of the individual who actually purchased and registered it.[9]

In contrast, the system of joint property was established in several states. The joint property regime sets forth the following opposite assumption. All profits accumulated by the spouses during the marriage are family property (also referred to as community property).[10] Each spouse is entitled to one half of such property. In the states that applied this system, joint property is obligatory,

6 *See, e.g.*, Simms v. Simms, 175 U.S. 162, 167 (1899) ("[T]he whole subject of the domestic relations of husband and wife, parent and child, belongs to the laws of [each] state, and not to the laws of the United States"); *see also* Boddie v. Connecticut, 401 U.S. 371, 376 (1971).

7 Am. L. Inst., *Principles of the Law of Family Dissolution: Analysis and Recommendations*, 8 Duke J. Gender L. & Pol'y 1, 20, 19 (2001).

8 *Id.*

9 Support payments (originally called "spousal maintenance" or "spousal support" and later "alimony") were a means of providing monetary assistance that was aimed at compensating the woman for the imbalance in property distribution. *See* Roderic Duncan, *Alimony: What You Need to Know Before Divorce*, NOLO, http://www.nolo.com/legal-encyclopedia/alimony-what-you-need-know-30081.html (last visited Mar. 7, 2015).

10 *See* Am. L. Inst., *supra* note 7, at 20.

so that the value of the property and not the actual ownership is divided in half.[11] These states use alimony as a means of balancing the property division between the spouses when no property is available.[12]

Later, the "common law" states shifted to a property regime that distributes family property according to a different doctrine called equitable distribution. Equitable distribution requires that the court weigh many parameters[13] and attempt to divide family property in a fair and just way that is not necessarily equal.[14] It certainly would be possible that the portion allocated to a mother who was a housewife and gave up her personal career development would be greater than half of the family property, but it could also be less than that.[15]

Five of the "joint property" states followed the common law regime's lead and also adopted the system of equitable distribution rather than equal distribution. The system of equitable distribution is the system prevailing today throughout the United States, except for three states that remain under the system of equal distribution.[16] Under certain circumstances, the system of equitable distribution makes the payment of alimony after a marriage unnecessary.[17]

However, the consensus among equitable distribution states is not very broad. In states that previously employed the system of joint property, joint

11 *See id.* at 20.

12 *See* Adriaen M. Morse Jr., Comment, *Fault: A Viable Means of Re-Injecting Responsibility in Marital Relations*, 30 U. Rich. L. Rev. 605, 642 (1996) ("In view of the lack of property available to most couples for division upon divorce, alimony should become the courts' primary tool in fixing equitable results upon divorce").

13 *See, e.g.*, Unif. Marriage and Divorce Act § 307 [Alt. A], 9A U.L.A. (1973) (including parameters such as "age, health, station, occupation, amount and sources of income, vocational skills, employability, estate, liabilities, and needs of each of the parties, ... and the opportunity of each for future acquisition of capital assets and income"); *see also* Am. L. Inst., *supra* note 7, at 19–24.

14 *See, e.g.*, N.D. Cent. Code Ann. § 14-05-24 (West 2013) ("When a divorce is granted, the court shall make an equitable distribution of the property and debts of the parties").

15 *See, e.g.*, Giammarco v. Giammarco, 959 A.2d 531, 532–34 (R.I. 2008) (affirming the lower court's grant to wife of only 35 percent of the family property, reasoning that she assisted less in acquiring it).

16 Am. L. Inst., *supra* note 7, at 20.

17 Brooke Grossman, Note, *The Evolution of Equitable Distribution in New York*, 62 N.Y.U. Ann. Surv. Am. L. 607, 625 (2007) ("Equitable division of assets acquired during the marriage replaced alimony, the traditional method of support. The purpose of equitable distribution was to 'recognize that when a marriage ends, each of the spouses ... has a stake in and a right to a share of the marital assets accumulated while it endured.'").

property principles still apply during the marriage. In other words, throughout the marriage the spouse in whose name the property is registered is not entitled to sell the property because joint rights exist. In contrast, states that were "common law" states maintain the traditional concept of separation of property during the marriage, up until the time of divorce.[18] These different perspectives bring about different results when determining equitable distribution.

Thus, for example, the system of equitable distribution struggles with how to categorize property registered in the name of one spouse prior to the marriage. States in which the joint property system was formerly in place tend to include such property in the joint property, while the "common law" states tend to view it as separate property.[19] The customary default in the equitable distribution system is equal distribution. This default is more established in states where inherited property or property purchased prior to the marriage is excluded from family property.[20]

For example, California determines equal distribution in every situation, but at the same time specifically excludes separate personal property from family property.[21] In contrast, New York considered revolutionizing its system by transitioning from the separate property regime to the equal distribution regime.[22] In the end, New York reached a compromise and adopted an intermediate solution, the system of equitable distribution.[23] Ten years later, these concepts are virtually indistinguishable.[24]

In most states, the default in the system of equitable distribution is equal distribution. Thus, the primary question is identifying when it is appropriate for a court to distribute property in an *unequal* manner. With respect to the present discussion, this is a question of which behaviors a court is allowed to consider in determining property distribution. Clearly, the answer is not a simple one. Because state laws give broad discretion to the courts, case law varies by state and does not provide clear criteria.

---

18 Am. L. Inst., *supra* note 7.

19 *Id.* at 19–21.

20 *Id.* at 20–21.

21 Cal. Fam. Code §§ 760, 770, 2550 (West 2014).

22 Grossman, *supra* note 17, at 609–14.

23 *Id.*

24 *Id.* at 608 "Although hailed as a radical change, the equitable distribution statute was actually a political compromise between reformers who wanted to establish a system of equal distribution and those who did not want to change the property distribution scheme at all".

Moreover, in the last two decades, additional elements have been considered in the distribution of family property, such as earning capacity, reputation, and personal capital.[25] These elements contributed to changes in delineating property distribution and made the determination of guidelines even more complicated. Certainly, the answers to the question of when it is appropriate to distribute property in an unequal manner are also impacted by how society views the family unit[26] and the roles and commitments of each of the spouses in the family.[27]

B. The No-Fault Divorce Revolution

Before examining how the state laws in the United States address fault in property distribution, this chapter begins with a brief description of the legal issue that precedes and greatly impacts it—considerations of fault in divorce proceedings. For many years, the customary system of divorce gave consideration to the fault of each party. Accordingly, a spouse was entitled to petition for dissolution of the marriage only if the spouse showed that the other spouse was at fault.[28] That fault could be based on an extramarital relationship, desertion, physical cruelty, and more.

A spouse was not entitled to petition for divorce only because he decided that he could no longer get along with or no longer love his spouse.[29] Paradoxically, even if both spouses reached such a conclusion, they were not entitled to file jointly for divorce unless one of them was found to be at fault. These limitations reflected the strong public interest in preserving marriage as a foundation and a basis for societal development.[30] This interest was also expressed

25 *See, e.g.*, Alicia Brokars Kelly, *The Marital Partnership Pretense and Career Assets: The Ascendancy of Self Over the Marital Community*, 81 B.U. L. Rev. 59 (2001).

26 *See* Desnoyers v. Desnoyers, 530 N.Y.S.2d 906, 908 (N.Y. App. Div. 1988) ("[Equitable distribution] was not designed to punish parties for their actions but to treat the marriage as an economic partnership and recognize each party's contribution thereto").

27 Ferguson v. Ferguson, 639 So. 2d 921, 928 (Miss. 1994) (including each spouse's contribution to the harmony and stability of the marriage as factors for equitable division of marital property).

28 Allen Parkman, *Reforming Divorce Reform*, 41 Santa Clara L. Rev. 379, 379 (2001) ("For most of the history of the United States, it was difficult to dissolve a marriage because plaintiffs had to prove that their spouses had committed acts that constituted fault grounds for divorce").

29 Judy Parejko, Stolen Vows: The Illusion of No-Fault Divorce and the Rise of the American Divorce Industry 72 (2002).

30 Jana B. Singer, *The Privatization of Family Law*, 1992 Wis. L. Rev. 1443, 1471 (1992).

in United States Supreme Court decisions such as *Maynard v. Hill.*[31] Narrowing the availability of divorce proceedings and limiting divorce to circumstances based upon fault reflected this interest.[32]

The fault limitation raised a great amount of criticism throughout the United States.[33] Critics argued that the fault requirement causes hostile divorce proceedings, intensifies the animosity between the spouses,[34] encourages false testimony,[35] leads spouses to create a "conspiracy" of fault in order to be granted a judgment for divorce,[36] forces spouses to live together even though there is no meaningful relationship between them, and eventually brings about contempt for the legal process.[37] In addition, sociological studies show that marriages can dissolve as a result of differences between spouses in their approaches to life, differences in their personalities, or other difficulties. Marriages do not necessarily dissolve as a result of one or more behavioral events.[38]

As stated previously, family law is subject to the independent legislation of each state,[39] although various national entities meet from time to time to formulate legislative proposals which are proposed in multiple states. Each state determines whether or not to adopt these proposals in its legislation. For example, the National Conference of Commissioners on Uniform State Laws ("NCCUSL") appointed a committee to formulate a uniform code on matters

31 125 U.S. 190, 211 (1888) ("[Marriage] ... is an institution, in the maintenance of which in its purity the public is deeply interested, for it is the foundation of the family and of society, without which there would be neither civilization nor progress").

32 *See* Brown v. Brown, 281 S.W.2d 492, 498 (Tenn. 1955).

33 Peter Nash Swisher, *The ALI Principles: A Farewell to Fault—But What Remedy for the Egregious Marital Misconduct of an Abusive Spouse?*, 8 Duke J. Gender L. & Pol'y 213, 213 (2001).

34 Lynn D. Wardle, *Divorce Violence and the No-Fault Divorce Culture*, 1994 Utah L. Rev. 741, 741 (1994).

35 Parkman, *supra* note 28, at 384.

36 Michelle L. Evans, Note, *Wrongs Committed During a Marriage: The Child that No Area of the Law Wants to Adopt*, 66 Wash. & Lee L. Rev. 465, 473–74 (2009). Especially well known is the case of a woman who was hired by one hundred husbands to help them create documented instances of adultery in order to ensure their respective divorces. *Id.* at 473.

37 Mary Ann Glendon, The Transformation of Family Law: State, Law, and Family in the United States and Western Europe 191 (1989).

38 Michael Grossberg, *How to Give the Present a Past? Family Law in the United States, 1950–2000*, *in* Cross Currents: Family Law and Policy in the US and England 3, 17–18 (Sanford N. Katz, John Eekelaar & Mavis Maclean eds., 2000).

39 *See, e.g.*, Simms v. Simms, 175 U.S. 162, 167 (1899) ("[T]he whole subject of the domestic relations of husband and wife, parent and child, belongs to the laws of [each] state, and not to the laws of the United States"); *see also* Boddie v. Connecticut, 401 U.S. 371, 376 (1971).

of marriage and divorce.[40] This committee drafted the Uniform Marriage and Divorce Act ("UMDA"), which was approved in 1970.[41]

This uniform code recommended transitioning to a system of no-fault divorce, divorce after a separation period of 180 days, or divorce in the event of difficult differences of opinion.[42] Concurrently, society's view of the family unit transformed and marriage was no longer seen as a single unit with one heart. Instead, it was viewed as a partnership between two individuals, each with his or her own desires and aspirations.[43] The UMDA therefore reflected the view that it should be possible to end a marriage according to the will and initiative of either of the spouses when the marriage no longer fulfilled their needs and ambitions.[44]

The no-fault divorce revolution swept through all the states. California was the first state to legislate the system of no-fault divorce.[45] One after another, states incorporated the recommendations in their legislation, and by 1985 every state had adopted no-fault divorce.[46] From that time on, every spouse has been entitled to file for a divorce judgment, even if the other spouse neither desires a divorce nor is found to be at fault.

The terminology of fault in divorce proceedings was replaced with the terminology of lack of fault. Terms such as "unbridgeable gaps," "incompatibility," "irreparable marital crisis," and "willful separation for a period of time determined by law" became the relevant terms in divorce proceedings. States hoped that the no-fault divorce revolution would make it easier for families in crisis and would expedite the dissolution process. In many instances, no-fault divorce made discussions of fault in divorce proceedings unnecessary.[47]

---

40 *See Marriage and Divorce Act, Model Summary*, NAT'L CONFERENCE OF COMM'RS ON UNIF. STATE LAWS, http://www.uniformlawcommission.com/ActSummary.aspx?title=Marriage and Divorce Act, Model.

41 *Id.*

42 *Id.*

43 Eisenstadt v. Baird, 405 U.S. 438, 453 (1972) ("[T]he marital couple is not an independent entity with a mind and heart of its own, but an association of two individuals each with a separate intellectual and emotional makeup").

44 *See* Bradford, *supra* note 1, at 611.

45 Evans, *supra* note 36, at 474.

46 Karen Turnage Boyd, *The Tale of Two Systems: How Integrated Divorce Laws Can Remedy the Unintended Effects of Pure No-Fault Divorce*, 12 CARDOZO J.L. & GENDER 609, 612 (2006) ("By 1985, all fifty states had some form of no-fault divorce in place").

47 *See* Mark Ellman & Sharon Lohr, *Marriage as Contract, Opportunistic Violence, and Other Bad Arguments for Fault Divorce*, 1997 U. ILL. L. REV. 719, 722–23 (1997); *see also* N.C. GEN. STAT. ANN. §§ 50-5.1, 50-6 (West 2014). *But see* Linda D. Elrod & Timothy B. Walker,

C. The No-Fault Divorce Revolution—The Shattered Dream

About thirty years following the long awaited revolution, everyone was able to see and internalize the contribution that the revolution made to the rise in the divorce rate. This increase in the divorce rate is not surprising since the institution of marriage can be dissolved today upon the sole initiative of either of the spouses, even if the other spouse's behavior was exemplary.[48] The legal limitations that were previously imposed on the spouse who desired to end the marriage were removed and divorce procedures became relatively easy to accomplish. The spouse who desires a divorce does not have to prove that the other spouse is at fault. It is sufficient to state a request to end the marriage.

In comparison, the spouse who desires to continue the marriage, even if the other spouse is at fault, is in a detrimental position no matter how the matter is concluded. On one hand, the committed spouse cannot avoid the dissolution of the marriage at the initiative of the spouse who is at fault. On the other hand, the committed spouse that desires to initiate a divorce cannot argue that the fault of the other spouse is a consideration, because the fault is no longer important.

This revolution, which made it easier to initiate a divorce proceeding, contributed to a lack of stability and certainty within a marriage.[49] The revolution also contributed to the weakening of the social sanctions against divorce. Divorce proceedings did not become more moderate, as those who had demanded and awaited the revolution had hoped. On the contrary, the proceedings following divorce continued to increase and became no less hostile.[50] Moreover, sociological studies demonstrate that economic difficulties, poverty, medical problems, and a high death rate affect divorced spouses at a higher rate than married spouses.[51] Thus, it can be argued that the increase in divorces

---

Family Law in the Fifty States, 27 FAM. L.Q. 515, 661 (1994) ("Thirty states currently retain fault grounds while also affording no-fault alternatives").

48 *See* Wardle, *supra* note 34, at 766.

49 *See* Lynn D. Wardle, *Marriage and Domestic Violence in the United States: New Perspectives about Legal Strategies to Combat Domestic Violence*, 15 ST. THOMAS L. REV. 791, 801–05 (2003).

50 Lynn D. Wardle, *No-Fault Divorce and the Divorce Conundrum*, 1991 B.Y.U. L. REV. 79, 102 (1991). It is also worth noting that approximately 90–95 percent of divorces before the revolution were uncontested. *Id.* at 103.

51 Stephen J. Bahr, *Social Science Research on Family Dissolution: What It Shows and How It Might Be of Interest to Family Law Reformers*, 4 J.L. & FAM. STUD. 5, 8–9 (2002).

following the no-fault divorce revolution has been harmful to the quality of life within this population.[52]

In light of these negative phenomena, many scholars in the United States began criticizing the no-fault divorce revolution and some of them even argue that it has failed.[53] Studies show that half of Americans today do not prefer the changed divorce laws, and would prefer a return to restricting the availability of divorce.[54] Certain states even adopted and legislated a new institution called "covenant marriage" which entitles spouses, at their own initiative, to limit future divorce and allow for it only on the basis of fault.[55]

On the other hand, it is uncertain whether the fault concept prior to the no-fault divorce revolution, which did not enable spouses to divorce, really contributed to well-being in marital life. Scholars continue to deal with this revolution. Some oppose it while others support it.[56] The focus here is to understand the background and changes that took place in divorce proceedings with respect to fault and to analyze the new approaches that followed the removal of fault from divorce proceedings.

D. Fault in Property Distribution—The Laws in the United States

Until 1968, all of the states weighed fault in determining family property distribution, just as they weighed fault in their decisions to grant divorce.[57] With the conclusion of the no-fault divorce revolution, states considered whether to

---

52 *See id.*; *see also* Lynne Marie Kohm, *Does Marriage Make Good Business? Examining the Notion of Employer Endorsement of Marriage*, 25 WHITTIER L. REV. 563, 587 (2004).

53 *See, e.g.*, COUNCIL ON FAMILIES IN AM., INST. FOR AM. VALUES, MARRIAGE IN AMERICA: A REPORT TO THE NATION 1 (1995), *available at* http://www.americanvalues.org/search/item.php?id=24 ("The divorce revolution—the steady displacement of a marriage culture by a culture of divorce and unwed parenthood—has failed. It has created terrible hardships for children, incurred unsupportable social costs, and failed to deliver on its promise of greater adult happiness. The time has come to shift the focus of national attention from divorce to marriage and to rebuild a family culture based on enduring marital relationships").

54 *See* Parkman, *supra* note 28, at 398.

55 The states are Arkansas, Arizona, and Louisiana. *See* ARK. CODE ANN. § 9-11-804 (West 2014); Lynne Marie Kohm, *A Comparative Survey of Covenant Marriage Proposals in the United States*, 12 REGENT U. L. REV. 31, 31–32, 39, 43 (1999–2000).

56 *See* Bradford, *supra* note 1, at 607–8.

57 *See* Arnold v. Arnold, 174 P.2d 674, 676 (Cal. Ct. App. 1946) ("It obviously follows that where the divorce is granted on the more heinous ground of adultery as well as for extreme cruelty the amount awarded to the innocent party should be greater than if granted on the ground of cruelty alone."); *cf.* Lynn D. Wardle, *Beyond Fault and No-Fault in the Reform of Marital Dissolution Law*, *in* RECONCEIVING THE FAMILY 9, 10 (Robin Fretwell Wilson ed.,

broaden the principles of no-fault and to apply them to property distribution as well.[58] Articles 307 and 308 of the UMDA[59] provided that both family property distribution and alimony be determined without considering inappropriate behavior during the marriage. The same was set forth in the Uniform Marital Property Act (hereinafter "UMPA"). In addition to those recommendations are the American Law Institute's Principles of the Law of Family Dissolution (hereinafter: "the ALI Principles").[60]

While the ALI Principles are not legislation, they have significant impact on state legislation.[61] The ALI Principles, which are built upon the UMDA and the UMPA recommendations, attempted to complete the no-fault revolution.[62] They determined that fault should not be considered in the distribution of family property.[63] The rationale at the foundation of these rules is supported by three elements: (a) the uniformity and consistency that were obtained with the no-fault divorce revolution; (b) the fact that the system of compensation through property was intended as compensation only for economic damage, and not as compensation for inappropriate behavior; and (c) the cancellation of immunity from claims between spouses, allowing for a tort claim to be brought against a spouse for inappropriate behavior during the marriage.[64]

As mentioned, most states shifted to the system of equitable distribution. However, states differ in their frames of reference and that impacts the default. States that perceive family property as joint property adopt equal distribution as a default in the equitable distribution system. According to this approach,

---

2006) (indicating that by 1970, a trend had developed "against considering fault in making ... financial awards").

58 Ira Mark Ellman, *The Place of Fault in a Modern Divorce Law*, 28 Ariz. St. L.J. 773, 782 (1996) ("Essentially all the American states moved to laws that allowed divorce on no-fault grounds in the 1970s and early 1980s, and as they did so they made choices about whether to apply the no-fault principle to property and alimony as well. Few have revisited those choices").

59 Unif. Marriage and Divorce Act §§ 307, 308(b), 9A U.L.A. 288–89, 446 (1973).

60 Principles of the Law of Family Dissolution: Analysis and Recommendations, ch. 1, topic 2, I (2002) [hereinafter ALI Principles]; *see also* Ellman, *supra* note 47, at 776.

61 *See* Swisher, *supra* note 33, at 217 ("First, it is important to note that this particular ALI project is not a Restatement of the Law, but instead proposes various 'principles' of family law which 'give greater weight to emerging legal concepts than does a Restatement.'").

62 *See* Katherine Shaw Spaht, *Postmodern Marriage as Seen Through the Lens of the ALI's "Compensatory Payments"*, *in* Reconceiving the Family, *supra* note 57, at 249.

63 ALI Principles, *supra* note 60; *see also* Evans, *supra* note 36, at 479 ("According to the American Law Institute, noneconomic fault—such as adultery, cruelty, or abandonment—is not a legitimate consideration during the divorce proceeding").

64 ALI Principles, *supra* note 60.

rather than transferring property from one spouse to another, the court divides the property between its owners. These states tend not to weigh fault in property distribution:

> As common-law states moved from the traditional title system to the modern system of equitable distribution of marital property, some also internalized the community property view that the spouses jointly own property acquired during marriage through the labor of either of them. Under this view spousal claims on the property at divorce are legal rather than equitable: The court is not transferring assets from the true owner to his or her spouse in recognition of the claimant's compelling equitable claims, but is rather dividing the property between its two joint owners, an exercise in which the marital misconduct of the parties seems largely irrelevant.[65]

In contrast, states that base equitable distribution on the traditional principles of common law do not adopt equal distribution as a default, but rather adopt the separation of property as a default.[66] According to this approach, the court transfers property from one spouse to another when determining property distribution. Those states tend to consider fault during property division:

> There is indeed an apparent overlap between the fifteen states that allow consideration of fault in the allocation of property at divorce and those common law states that have been most resistant generally to moving from the common law marital property system to the marital property idea of joint ownership.[67]

This chapter next examines how these recommendations, together with their various sources and the rationales for the system of family property distribution, actually influenced state laws regarding the consideration of fault in property distribution. In distributing property, all states tend to take into consideration

---

65 Am. L. Inst., *supra* note 7, at 43. This analysis is accepted by Professor Ellman, the chief reporter of the recommendations. Ellman, *supra* note 58, at 783 ("Joint ownership of marital property is nonetheless the divorce law vision of many common law states today, and their adoption of the joint ownership conception at dissolution has apparently encouraged a no-fault approach to its allocation").

66 *See* ALI Principles, *supra* note 60, ch. 1, topic 2, II.

67 *See* Ellman, *supra* note 58, at 783.

economic misconduct that brings about a decrease in family property.[68] However, states differ in how they evaluate fault that does not harm family property, but instead harms family values. Included among the behaviors that are considered "fault" in this context are extramarital relationships, abandonment, and physical and mental cruelty.[69]

Legal scholars in the United States are divided over how to best categorize the states in these matters. Professor Ellman, the chief reporter of the ALI Principles, divides the states into five different categories according to the extent that each state considers fault during the distribution of family property and determination of alimony:

1. Pure no-fault—Twenty states do not consider fault at all in property distribution and determination of alimony. These states adopted the approach of the UMDA.
2. Pure no-fault property, almost pure no-fault alimony—Five states do not consider fault at all in property distribution and almost never consider fault in determination of alimony.
3. Almost pure no-fault—Three states include the slight possibility of weighing fault in property distribution, such as in instances of severe violence or attempted murder.
4. No-fault property, full-fault in alimony—Seven states do not consider fault at all in property distribution but do consider fault in determination of alimony.
5. Full-fault—Fifteen states grant the courts full discretion to consider any inappropriate spousal behavior in determining property distribution and the level of alimony.[70]

Following this analysis, Ellman indicates that twenty-five states reject the concept of fault both in divorce and property distribution proceedings.[71] In his opinion, the remaining states should also adopt this approach.[72] Ellman's

68 *See* Barbara Bennett Woodhouse & Katharine T. Bartlett, *Sex, Lies, and Dissipation: The Discourse of Fault in a No-Fault Era*, 82 Geo. L.J. 2525, 2528 (1994); *see also, e.g.*, Smith v. Smith, 438 S.E.2d 457, 458 (N.C. Ct. App. 1994).

69 Woodhouse & Bartlett, *supra* note 68, at 2532–33, 2538.

70 Ellman, *supra* note 58, at 776, 778–80. This division into five categories was also adopted by the ALI. ALI Principles, *supra* note 60, ch. 1, topic 2, II.

71 *See* Ellman, *supra* note 58, at 782.

72 *Id.* at 776. The ALI endorsed this position. ALI Principles, *supra* note 60.

analysis has been accepted by several courts throughout the United States, and one court even indicated that the majority of state legal systems in the United States prohibit consideration of fault as a factor in property distribution.[73] On the contrary, other scholars continue to argue that the majority of states refuse to weigh fault.[74]

Scholars that criticize Ellman's analysis argue that his description does not reflect reality.[75] Peter Swisher, for example, states that if it is possible to identify a trend, the opposite trend should be endorsed and fault should be considered in property distribution.[76] Swisher specifically disagrees with the analysis reflected in the ALI Principles and notes that most states consider fault in property distribution.[77] Between the extreme positions of Ellman and Swisher are more moderate positions that analyze and categorize the data in a more balanced way. Thus, for example, writes Brett Turner, "[Out of the forty-nine] jurisdictions which permit the trial court to divide marital property equitably, twenty-seven do not permit consideration of fault that has no economic

73 Sparks v. Sparks, 485 N.W.2d 893, 909 (Mich. 1992) (Levin, J., dissenting); *see* Havell v. Islam, 718 N.Y.S.2d 807, 810 (N.Y. Sup. Ct. 2000).

74 *See* Jeannette C. Griffo, *How Fault Remains a Factor in Property Division Upon Divorce: An Analysis of Equitable Distribution in Michigan after* Sparks v. Sparks, 71 U. DET. MERCY L. REV. 421, 450–51 (1994).

75 *See* June R. Carbone, *Economics, Feminism, and the Reinvention of Alimony: A Reply to Ira Ellman*, 43 VAND. L. REV. 1463 (1990); Carl E. Schneider, *Rethinking Alimony: Marital Decisions and Moral Discourse*, 1991 BYU L. REV. 197, 197–98 (1991).

76 Peter Nash Swisher, *Marriage and Some Troubling Issues with No-Fault Divorce*, 17 REGENT U. L. REV. 243, 249 (2004–2005) ("Thus, if there is an arguable majority 'trend' today, it is to retain fault factors in divorce as one of many statutory factors that state courts will still consider in determining spousal support rights, the division of marital property, or both").

77 *Id.* at 258 ("What these commentators largely ignore, however, is that thirty-five years after the so-called no-fault divorce 'revolution,' only a small minority of states—about fifteen—are 'true' no-fault jurisdictions, while a majority of states still retain alternative fault grounds for divorce, and still consider marital fault factors in determining spousal support and the distribution of marital property on divorce. Indeed, forty-two states still continue to evaluate a spouse's noneconomic contributions to the marriage and the well-being of the family, in spite of the [ALI Principles'] arguments to the contrary"). Professor Goldberg analyzes the division of states in a similar way. *See* BARTH H. GOLDBERG, VALUATION OF DIVORCE ASSETS § 1:34 (revised ed. 2005) ("Unfortunately, fault remains a major issue for consideration in many jurisdictions, even though it was presumed that with the passage of the Uniform Property Act its importance would become insignificant. However, this presumption has proved fallacious. In fact, as of 1985 only 17 states have statutes expressly excluding marital fault from the factors to be considered upon dissolution, while sixteen states now permit it to be a factor among others to be considered, and only six remain silent on the subject").

impact."[78] Lynn Wardle has a similar view, "thirty states allow consideration of marital misconduct in both alimony and property disputes."[79]

Part II of this chapter analyzes the aforementioned positions and examines the differences among scholars in categorizing how the states treat fault in the dissolution context. It demonstrates that these differences among the scholars arise not only from their analysis of the factual data but also from their moral views of the family structure and its role in modern society.

It is essential to emphasize that fault remains only one of the factors that is considered in property distribution. Thus, for example, the Michigan Court of Appeals reversed a lower court decision that gave a woman only a quarter of the marital property, when the decision was based on the woman's extramarital relationship.[80] The Michigan Court of Appeals stated that the lower court gave too much weight to fault and failed to consider other factors.[81] In Missouri, a court awarded a woman 63 percent of the property after it became clear that the husband had a child from an extramarital relationship.[82] Similarly, the Court of Appeals of Virginia granted a woman a larger portion of property due to her husband's many years of adultery, although the court considered additional factors.[83]

In contrast, in other states fault that is detrimental to the spousal relationship, such as cruelty, desertion, adultery, or humiliation, is not a relevant consideration in determining the equitable distribution of family property.[84] In those states, inappropriate spousal behavior is not a basis for punishing one spouse or awarding more property to the spouse who was harmed.[85] Swisher

---

78 Brett R. Turner, *The Role of Marital Misconduct in Dividing Property Upon Divorce*, 15 Divorce Litig. 117, 117 (2003), *available at* http://www.divorcesource.com/research/dl/division/03jul117.shtml.

79 *See* Wardle, *supra* note 57, at 15.

80 Sparks v. Sparks, 485 N.W.2d 893, 901–02 (Mich. 1992).

81 *Id.* at 901–3.

82 Huber v. Huber, 682 S.W.2d 493, 495 (Mo. Ct. App. 1984).

83 O'Loughlin v. O'Loughlin, 458 S.E.2d 323, 324–26 (Va. Ct. App. 1995).

84 *See, e.g., In re* Marriage of Muhammad, 108 P.3d 779, 780–81 (Wash. 2005); Warner v. Warner, 807 A.2d 607, 613 (Me. 2002); Hartland v. Hartland, 777 P.2d 636, 641–42 (Alaska 1989); Anderson v. Anderson, 230 S.E.2d 272, 273, 275–76 (Ga. 1976), *superseded by statute*, Divorce and Alimony—Procedures Changed, 1977 Ga. Laws 1253, 1257, *as recognized in* Davidson v. Davidson, 257 S.E.2d 269 (Ga. 1979); Sirek v. Sirek, 693 N.W.2d 896, 900 (Minn. Ct. App. 2005); Thompson v. Thompson, 811 N.E.2d 888, 921–22 (Ind. Ct. App. 2004); *see also* Dvorak v. Dvorak, 693 N.W.2d 646, 652–53 (N.D. 2005); Steiner v. Steiner, 687 N.W.2d 740, 742–43 (Wis. Ct. App. 2004).

85 *See, e.g.,* Grosskopf v. Grosskopf, 677 P.2d 814, 820 (Wyo. 1984) (citing Paul v. Paul, 616 P.2d 707, 715 (Wyo. 1980)); Young v. Young, 609 S.W.2d 758, 762 (Tex. 1980); Read v. Read,

argues that, indeed, in many states the tendency is to ignore fault.[86] Thus, for example, in New York fault was taken into account only in cases that can "shock the conscience of the court."[87] However, the courts in New York agree that an extramarital relationship is not the type of behavior that "shocks the conscious of the court," and therefore should not be considered as a factor in property distribution.[88]

Sometimes courts within the same state disagree as to whether the court should consider extramarital relationships in the property distribution context. Contrary to the New York decision referenced in the previous paragraph, the Virginia Court of Appeals ruled against the consideration of a husband's long extramarital relationship when the affair brought about the dissolution of the marriage, but did not involve economic misconduct.[89] Ultimately, the court affirmed the lower court's decision, granting the husband 65 percent of the family property and explaining that he earned most of it as an orthopedic surgeon.[90]

An additional Virginia court followed this approach and ruled that adultery is not a relevant consideration in property distribution.[91] The same conclusion was reached in West Virginia.[92] Similarly, courts in Florida and North

---

594 P.2d 871, 872 (Utah 1979); Wilberscheid v. Wilberscheid, 252 N.W.2d 76, 81 (Wis. 1977).

86 *See* Swisher, *supra* note 33, at 224–25 ("Therefore, the current judicial trend in many states is that most judges tend to ignore or severely limit the ultimate effect of fault-based statutory factors in divorce, except in serious or egregious circumstances."); *see also* Perlberger v. Perlberger, 626 A.2d 1186, 1195 (Pa. Super. Ct. 1993); Platt v. Platt, 728 S.W.2d 542, 543–44 (Ky. Ct. App. 1987); Tarro v. Tarro, 485 A.2d 558, 561 (R.I. 1984). *But see* Thames v. Thames, 477 N.W.2d 496, 503 (Mich. Ct. App. 1991) (citing Burkey v. Burkey, 471 N.W.2d 631, 634–35 (Mich. Ct. App. 1991)).

87 O'Brien v. O'Brien, 66 N.Y.2d 576, 589–90 (N.Y. 1985) (citing Blickstein v. Blickstein, 472 N.Y.S.2d 110 (N.Y. App. Div. 1984)); Havell v. Islam, 718 N.Y.S.2d 807 (N.Y. Sup. Ct. 2000) (quoting *O'Brien*, 66 N.Y.2d at 589–90).

88 Rosenberg v. Rosenberg, 510 N.Y.S.2d 659, 662 (N.Y. App. Div. 1987); *see also* Nolan v. Nolan, 486 N.Y.S.2d 415 (N.Y. App. Div. 1985).

89 Aster v. Gross, 371 S.E.2d 833, 836 (Va. Ct. App. 1988) ("Circumstances that lead to the dissolution of the marriage but have no effect upon marital property, its value, or otherwise are not relevant ... [and] need not be considered").

90 *Id.* at 835–36.

91 *See* Gamer v. Gamer, 429 S.E.2d 618, 622 (Va. Ct. App. 1993) (citing *Aster*, 371 S.E.2d at 836) (finding that any adultery committed by the husband "had no economic impact upon the parties' property, nor did it affect the value of the marital assets").

92 W. Va. Code Ann. § 48-7-103 (West 2014) (mandating that courts presume equal division of marital property between the parties but allowing alterations to such distribution "without regard to any attribution of fault").

Carolina ruled that adultery should not be considered in property distribution, but should be considered in the determination of alimony.[93]

III. EXTRAMARITAL RELATIONSHIPS AND PROPERTY DISTRIBUTION—THE NORMATIVE VIEW

Part I of this chapter examined the role of fault and specifically extramarital relationships in property distribution regimes. This part discusses the theoretical basis for weighing extramarital relationships in property distribution. Four sections progress step-by-step. The first examines the moral argument, while the second presents a dilemma facing that argument. The third section reviews the impact of a lack of clear guidelines for weighing extramarital relationships in property distribution. Finally, the fourth section discusses which legal field should deal with the fault of spouses.

A. The Moral Argument

As previously stated, the disagreement among scholars in classifying how states consider fault in family property distribution is not only factual but also reflects underlying moral and ideological perspectives. This discussion centers upon the role of the family unit and the weight of moral arguments in family law. On one side of the discussion is Ellman, who argues that most of the states exclude consideration of fault from property distribution.[94] The proposals suggested by Ellman are also incorporated in the ALI Principles.

On the other side of the discussion are the many other scholars who disagree with Ellman. Morse, for example, argues that Ellman does not give credence to the moral aspects, instead favoring only the consideration of the economic aspects.[95] Morse further asserts that the consideration of fault is an

---

93 *See* Tuller v. Tuller, 469 So. 2d 212, 213 (Fla. Dist. Ct. App. 1985) (Cowart, J., dissenting); *cf.* Shoffner v. Shoffner, 371 S.E.2d 749, 751 (N.C. Ct. App. 1988) (reasoning that the court's consideration of one party's "failure to assist in the compilation and valuation of marital property during litigation"—thereby causing the opposing party to incur additional expenses—was "equivalent to the proper consideration of marital misconduct ... related to the economic condition of the marriage as a factor in making the distributive award").

94 *See* Ira Mark Ellman, *The Theory of Alimony*, 77 CAL. L. REV. 1, 23 (1989); Ellman, *supra* note 58, at 807.

95 *See* Morse, *supra* note 12, at 634 (discussing other scholars' views on Ellman's theory).

"excellent tool" both for encouraging appropriate behavior and for deterring inappropriate behavior.[96]

In his opinion, most of society views extramarital relationships as inappropriate behavior. He argues that a financial cost to the individual at fault could disincentivize such behavior.[97] As expressed in his words:

> [F]ault provides an excellent tool to encourage the type of behavior society believes to be appropriate in marriage, and to discourage that behavior which society deems to be inappropriate. It seems that most people would at least agree that engaging in adultery, cruelty, or desertion is not the sort of sharing behavior which marriage should have to endure. In order to provide a disincentive for such behavior, there should be concomitant post-divorce financial consequences for engaging in inappropriate behavior.[98]

Karen Boyd adds that it is morally wrong for an adulterous spouse to retain half of the property.[99] Boyd argues that this result sends a clear message to society that adultery is acceptable behavior, "when a spouse who commits adultery leaves the marriage with half or more of the family's assets, as may occur within the current pure no-fault schemes, an injustice is done. The message is clear—it is acceptable to have an extramarital affair."[100]

Laura Bradford writes that reconsideration of fault in divorce proceedings as well as in property distribution meets the customary expectations of society, "[Reintroducing the fault concept] back into divorce [as well as] into the division of assets and [spousal support] after divorce satisfies the popular expectation that society will reward those who observe their marital vows and commitments."[101]

Lawrence Golden adds that even if one agrees, in theory, that fault should not be considered in property distribution, legislators and judges generally still give consideration to fault and award property accordingly:

---

96 *Id.* at 640–41.
97 *Id.* at 641.
98 *Id.*
99 *See* Boyd, *supra* note 46, at 615.
100 *Id.*
101 Bradford, *supra* note 1, at 621.

> In theory fault or misconduct which is not related to the economic conditions of the parties should not be germane to a division of property. ... Nonetheless, there is a strong feeling among legislators and judges that a "bad person" should not be rewarded, and the strength of this belief sometimes tempers rigorous adherence to abstract principles.[102]

In addition, the weighing of fault in property distribution may lessen the negative results of the no-fault divorce revolution. That revolution has left the weaker spouse exposed to the danger of divorce without being able to prevent it, "As states began to adopt no-fault divorce laws, marriage was transformed from a permanent relationship into a relationship terminable at-will. The reformers had to make some provisions for the economic security of the family members outside of marriage."[103]

Courts have rejected the argument that consideration of fault in divorce is based on religious rationales and thereby unconstitutional.[104] Instead, courts reason that adultery harms individuals of all religions, including those who do not practice religion at all.[105] This argument adds to and strengthens the universal moral position that disapproves of extramarital relationships. Swisher joins this approach and argues that despite the apparent abandonment of fault in the no-fault divorce revolution, much writing about the subject of fault still exists.[106] In his opinion, this continued discussion shows that the moral element is still relevant in the context of family.[107]

Swisher also indicates that legislatures and courts in most states still consider spousal responsibility in the dissolution of a marriage.[108] He argues that the refusal to consider fault comes from a different view of the family and its roles:

> Indeed, if contemporary marriage is viewed today as a shared partnership with important economic *and* noneconomic expectations, then a "true"

---

102 LAWRENCE J. GOLDEN, EQUITABLE DISTRIBUTION OF PROPERTY 255 (1st ed. 1983).

103 Boyd, *supra* note 46, at 620–21.

104 *See, e.g.*, Waite v. Waite, 64 S.W.3d 217, 219 (Tex. Ct. App. 2001); Wikoski v. Wikoski, 513 A.2d 986, 986 (Pa. Super. Ct. 1986)..

105 Arnold H. Loewy, *Morals Legislation and the Establishment Clause*, 55 ALA. L. REV. 159, 166 (2003).

106 *See* Swisher, *supra* note 33, at 220–21.

107 *id.* at 219–21.

108 *Id.* at 220.

> no-fault divorce regime, as proposed in the *Principles*, reduces marriage on dissolution only to impersonal and unrealistic economic calculations, and refuses to consider many important nonmonetary marital contributions to the well-being of the family.[109]

At the same time, extramarital relationships have lost the negative label they have been given in the past. In the name of new values of privacy, autonomy and freedom, the important moral protections of the family were harmed. States that adopted these values implemented a pure approach of no-fault divorce, which imposed a great burden on the "innocent" spouse in property distribution and determination of alimony.[110]

According to Swisher, these legal systems are detrimental to the "innocent" spouse in two ways. First, they prevent that spouse from using the other spouse's moral fault as a basis for fair negotiation, ultimately harming bargaining power.[111] Second, they treat fault and no-fault in the same way, which sends a social message that the marital relationship does not demand commitment.[112]

B. A Dilemma Facing the Moral Argument

In response to the abovementioned writers, Ellman argues that the moral argument relies on the assumption that the cause of a divorce can be determined. However, that cause is not easily identified when the investigation is based on a moral criterion which is neither scientific nor exact. Consider, for example, that some spouses are willing to forgive their partners for extramarital relationships and choose to continue their marriage, while others are not willing to do so. Therefore, when the family unit dissolves following an extramarital relationship, the question to be asked is whether the divorce is the fault of the spouse who engaged in an extramarital relationship or the spouse who could not tolerate it. In other words, is the "cause" of divorce the behavior itself or perhaps the other spouse's intolerance of the behavior?

---

109 *Id.* at 221.

110 *See, e.g.*, Mosbarger v. Mosbarger, 547 So. 2d 188, 189 (Fla. Dist. Ct. App. 1989) (completely adopting the no-fault divorce system to such an extent that it did not consider fault in a case in which the wife attempted to murder her spouse); *In re* Marriage of Cihak, 416 N.E.2d 701, 702 (Ill. App. Ct. 1981) (refusing to consider husband's murder of wife as a factor in property division).

111 *See* Swisher, *supra* note 33, at 222.

112 *See id.* at 221 (citing Morse, *supra* note 12, at 640–41).

Further, couldn't the adultery that eventually brought about divorce be a reaction to a failed relationship, and therefore not the "cause" of divorce? In grappling with these questions, the New Jersey Supreme Court reversed a decision that considered a wife's adulterous relationship in determining property distribution.[113] The court explained that in the complex marriage relationship, one spouse may be acting in response to the actions of the other, so that it is impossible to determine who is at fault in ending the marriage.[114]

Additional questions arise. Should only intentional fault be considered or perhaps unintentional fault as well, such as infertility or mental illness? When one spouse decides to divorce because of the other spouse's illness, which spouse will be considered the wrongdoer? Similarly, how will matters such as the refusal of a spouse to participate in relationship counseling or individual treatment be considered? From another perspective, evidentiary complications may arise. In some instances, identifying the "cause" demands extensive evidence from family members and friends, medical evidence, and third party evidence, all of which can complicate and prolong the divorce proceedings. Inquiry into these issues requires looking at internal family matters such as the intimate relationship between the spouses, thereby infringing on their privacy.

All of these questions raise doubt about the ability of a court to determine the true origin of fault. They show that when a court determines who is at fault for bringing the marriage to an end, the court does not determine the sole cause, but instead evaluates the relative moral failures of both spouses. In actuality, the decision of the court only evaluates who is *more* at fault and not who caused the marriage to end. The complexity of family relationships makes this evaluation difficult. As the affection between parties fades, they are less willing to tolerate each other, making the determination of fault all the more difficult. It is doubtful whether the judicial process is the appropriate tool for investigating the real cause for the separation of spouses.

Furthermore, property distribution according to fault could create an incentive for the harmed spouse to dissolve the marriage in order to hurt the spouse that breached marital trust. In so doing, the harmed spouse might neglect other considerations that should be protected, such as the interest of the children and the preservation of the family unit. In light of these considerations,

---

113 Chalmers v. Chalmers, 320 A.2d 478, 480, 484 (N.J. 1974).

114 *Id.* at 482; *see also* ALI PRINCIPLES, *supra* note 60, ch. 1, topic 2, Reporter's Note a.2.c ("N.J. Stat. Ann. § 2A:34-23.1 governs the distribution of property. Marital misconduct is not among the factors the statute directs the court to consider, although the court is empowered to consider 'any other factor it deems relevant.'").

it is unsurprising that some courts are unwilling to weigh the relative fault while determining property distribution.[115]

Even when a court determines which spouse is more at fault, it is unclear which criteria it uses in doing so. Without clear and defined guidelines, the court places responsibility on behavior that is not a civil wrong. If the behavior that the court punishes is a civil wrong, then tort law provides defined compensation. If not, then the use of the word "cause" is imprecise.

C. A Lack of Guidelines Leads to Judicial Arbitrariness

The ALI Principles also argue that the traditional rules of fault require exceptional reliance on judicial discretion.[116] This reliance on judicial discretion is due to a lack of guidelines regarding the appropriate standard of behavior and its economic consequences.[117] While this problem is relevant to all areas of the law, its significance increases when the topic of discussion is one of morals and values. Thus, the consideration of fault hinders the attainment of greater uniformity and predictability in judicial decisions. These values are fundamental to every legal system:

> The traditional marital-fault rule requires extraordinary reliance on trial-court discretion. Neither the standard of misconduct nor its dollar consequences are much bounded by any rule. While in principle the trial court's decision can be reviewed for "abuse of discretion," reversals are rare. … The traditional fault rule is thus inconsistent with a major theme of these Principles, an effort to improve the consistency and predictability of trial-court decisions.[118]

States that consider fault fail to formulate clear guidelines for the courts. In Missouri, for example, a guideline set by the court in *Burtscher* instructed courts to consider behavior that "throws upon the other party marital burdens

115 Lutz v. Lutz, 485 So. 2d 1174, 1177 (Ala. Civ. App. 1986) (citing Dobbs v. Dobbs, 452 So. 2d 872 (Ala. Civ. App. 1984) ("However, we do not find it necessary for the court to examine each incident of misconduct to determine who was more at fault. If there is testimony of fault from both parties, the trial court does not have to determine the relative fault of the parties when making the property division").

116 ALI Principles, *supra* note 60, ch. 1, topic 2, Reporter's Note a.5.b.

117 *Id.*

118 *Id.*

beyond the norms to be expected in the marital relationship."[119] Despite this guideline, the Missouri Court of Appeals refused to reverse a decision from a lower court that viewed a husband's adultery as morally equivalent to the insistence of the wife to play Bingo four nights a week.[120] Rather than apply the guideline, the court took the wife's behavior into consideration and dismissed the appeal.[121]

The ALI Principles argue further that as long as there is no defined economic harm, consideration of fault grants unlimited judicial discretion. In that respect it exposes the decisions in these matters to the subjective view of each judge.[122]

Swisher agrees with these arguments and explains that they can be extended to all areas of law. There is no way to prevent the involvement of the personal view of the judge, even where clear and uniform standards are applied.[123] Family court judges implement a great deal of judicial discretion. Usually their daily experience guides them to reach fair distribution of family property.[124] It is not a question of unlimited discretion, as legislation in thirty-six states clearly defines which parameters are to be considered when determining property distribution.[125] In addition, the courts are guided and reviewed by the courts of appeals.

Actually, courts encounter inherent problems with the use of even clear guidelines. On one hand, determination of clear guidelines is detrimental to the necessary flexibility of decisions. On the other hand, a lack of clear guidelines leads to gaps in judicial decisions that reflect each judge's personal views about what constitutes fault in a spousal relationship. In the absence of guidelines, the judge is empowered to use family law as a tool for punishing behavior that society has chosen not to criminalize.[126]

---

119 *Burtscher v. Burtscher*, 563 S.W.2d 526, 527 (Mo. Ct. App. 1978) ("[T]he conduct factor becomes important when the conduct of one party to the marriage is such that it throws upon the other party marital burdens beyond the norms to be expected in the marital relationship").

120 *See id.* at 527–28.

121 *Id.* (noting that "[i]t is unnecessary and probably impossible to lay down any precise guidelines for the weight to be given to the conduct factor").

122 *See* Ellman, *supra* note 58, at 790.

123 *See* Swisher, *supra* note 33, at 219–23.

124 *Id.* at 223–24.

125 *Id.* at 224 n.64; *see also* Linda D. Elrod & Robert G. Spector, *A Review of the Year in Family Law: Century Ends with Unresolved Issues*, 33 Fam. L.Q. 865 (2000).

126 *See* Ellman, *supra* note 58, at 787.

Ellman asserts that society still does not deem it proper to punish inappropriate spousal behavior because there is no broad consensus regarding the definition of such behavior.[127] As an additional concern, laws are not gender neutral. In states that take fault into consideration, the legal consequences of a wife's adultery are greater than those of a husband's adultery.[128]

D. Which Field of Law Should Deal with Extramarital Relationships?

If the purpose of the consideration of extramarital relationships in the marital dissolution context is to punish the "guilty" or compensate the victim, then tort law is well-equipped for that purpose. Claims between spouses were originally blocked by rules of spousal immunity. However, in conjunction with the no-fault revolution, states began to recognize tort claims between former spouses:

> The obvious model for such a system is the tort law, which provides compensation for harms and also permits punitive damages in certain circumstances. And indeed, since no-fault's rise in the 1970s, the tort law has changed so that most states now recognize claims between former spouses that were previously excluded by blanket rules of spousal immunity.[129]

Ellman states that the courts tried to avoid the punitive nature of weighing fault by arguing that it is only a matter of monetary compensation for economic damage caused to the spouse by the transition from one economic unit to two separate units.[130] However, this argument is unfounded because the courts that consider fault actually reward good behavior and punish the wrongdoer rather than compensate one spouse for damage caused by the other spouse.[131]

---

127 *See id.*

128 *See, e.g., id.* at 787 n.30 ("Kentucky ([wife's] adultery may reduce alimony award, but [husband's] adultery cannot be the basis for increasing it); ... North Dakota (trial court properly allocated 83 percent of property to [husband] after 19-year marriage, where [wife] guilty of adultery)").

129 *Id.* at 786. In the summary of his article, Ellman concludes that half of the states do not grant alimony on the basis of fault, and more than half do not consider it in determining property distribution. *Id.* at 807. Apparently the reason is that the fault can be dealt with in tort law or in criminal law. *Id.* at 807–08.

130 *Id.* at 788.

131 *See id.*

Furthermore, Ellman's proposal to rely upon tort law is problematic. Experience shows that the number of such claims is very small, and those that result in compensation are even rarer.[132] Couples generally object to continuing divorce proceedings with a tort proceeding for two reasons. The first reason is the complication of the tort proceedings. Second, there is a lack of capital for compensation of the injured party since insurance companies do not cover intentional damage.[133] The addition of a tort claim to a family law proceeding will also raise, among other issues, the question of which procedure should be followed.[134]

Moreover, even when extramarital relationships are a significant factor in spousal separation, there is no defined remedy for either spouse in tort law.[135] An absence of a specific statutory remedy imposes a heavy burden on the spouse who has been harmed and attempts to obtain compensation from the other spouse:

> Neither tort nor criminal law provides an adequate remedy for egregious marital misconduct. ... Finally, the absence of any fault-based statutory relief for egregious marital misconduct may place an almost insurmountable burden on an abused spouse to obtain compensatory relief from an abusive spouse. This serious problem is illustrated in a number of cases in a minority of states that have adopted a "pure" or "true" no-fault regime, where nonfinancial marital fault no longer plays any significant role in determining divorce grounds and defenses, spousal support awards, or the equitable distribution of marital property.[136]

In light of the above, Swisher believes that a state that considers adopting the ALI Principles should at the same time weigh the considerations of fault.[137] In his opinion, this matter should not be dealt with in tort law because family law

---

132 Swisher, *supra* note 33, at 228 (quoting Robert G. Spector, *Marital Torts: The Current Legal Landscape*, 33 Fam. L.Q. 745, 762 (1999)).

133 *Id.* (quoting Spector, *supra* note 132, at 762).

134 *See* Woodhouse & Bartlett, *supra* note 68, at 2566 ("Tort claims raise tricky questions of res judicata and collateral estoppel, the right to a jury trial, overlapping recoveries, and limitations on damages").

135 *See* Evans, *supra* note 36, at 494–95.

136 *See* Swisher, *supra* note 33, at 254.

137 *See id.*

is sufficiently developed to address these types of damages, and there is no need to reinvent laws that already exist.[138]

IV. ISRAELI LAW—EXTRAMARITAL RELATIONSHIPS

A. Extramarital Relationships under a Joint Property Regime

The *Dror* ruling, handed down at the end of the 1970s, serves as the primary basis for excluding the consideration of extramarital relationships from family property distribution in Israel.[139] This case concerned a couple who lived in marital harmony for about three years.[140] The husband argued that their family life started deteriorating when his wife became intimate with other men.[141] Therefore, he argued that joint property rights could neither be established by their marital relationship nor by an implied agreement between the spouses.[142] The Israel Supreme Court rejected this argument:

> Abandoning the house or adultery might create a rift between spouses and in this way terminate the sharing of property, but [the spouses] are not retroactively punished for [these actions] by taking away joint property rights. An explicit rule expressing this idea is found in the United States: CORPUS JURIS SECUNDUM 75 42.[143]

This decision gave no reason why extramarital relationships should not be considered. The reference to the "explicit rule in the United States" is puzzling since the law in the United States is complex and varies from state to state. The minority opinion in the *Dror* case stated that even if the wife was adulterous, her husband forgave her after he found out about the adultery.[144] Though this fact made

---

138 *See* Swisher, *supra* note 33, at 227–28 (citing Ellman, *supra* note 94).

139 CA 264/77 Dror v. Dror 32(1) PD 829, 832 [1978] (Isr.).

140 *Id.*

141 *Id.*

142 *Id.* In some American jurisdictions, however, it is difficult to argue against an argument of fault with the counterargument that the parties continued to live together after the event under discussion. *See, e.g.*, CONN. GEN. STAT. ANN. § 46b-52 (West 2015); Pavel v. Pavel, 495 A.2d 1113, 1114 (1985) (holding that the trial court erred in hearing only evidence related to the final event contributing to the dissolution of the marriage and in suppressing evidence of earlier such events on the basis that the parties had reconciled).

143 *Id.*

144 *Id.*

this case easily distinguishable, later courts relied on this decision. Indeed, this important distinction in the *Dror* decision did not prevent later decisions from relying upon it as binding precedent.[145]

However, with respect to external and personal property owned by one spouse prior to the couple's relationship, one finds an opposite ruling. Extramarital relationships will bring about the exclusion of such property from joint property.[146] Consider, for example, the case of *Salem,* which dealt with common law spouses to whom the joint property rule also generally applies.[147] Mrs. Salem admitted to having an intimate extramarital relationship.[148] The court determined that this relationship did not cancel the joint property rule regarding property acquired during the relationship, but it did not allow for the consideration of external property as joint property.[149]

Another case involving external property is the case of *Anonymous A.*[150] In that case, a couple and their children lived in an apartment that belonged to the husband before the couple met.[151] The rabbinical court[152] ruled that the woman was not entitled to support payments, a portion of the apartment, nor any other residence, because she was a "rebellious wife" who had continuously betrayed her husband.[153]

The woman petitioned the Israel Supreme Court and argued that according to the joint property principles, she was entitled to half of the apartment.[154] In an opinion given by Chief Justice Barak, the Israel Supreme Court dismissed her petition.[155] The court determined that ongoing betrayal undermines the basis for harmony and therefore prevented the application of joint property

---

145 *See, e.g.,* CA 819/94 Levi v. Levi 50(1) PD 300, 304 [1996] (Isr.); HCJ 1135/02 Vazgial v. The Supreme Rabbinical Court 56(1) PD 14, 24 [2002] (Isr.).

146 CA 4385/91 Salem v. Carmi 51(1) PD 337 [1997] (Isr.).

147 *Id.*

148 *Id.*

149 *Id.*

150 HCJ 3995/00 Anonymous v. The Supreme Rabbinical Court 56(6) PD 883, 888 [2002] (Isr.) [hereinafter *Anonymous A*].

151 *Id.*

152 Under Israeli Law, family matters are under the parallel jurisdictions of the civil court and the religious court in which the presiding rabbinic judges are experts in religious law. Ayelet Blecher-Prigat & Benjamin Shmueli, *The Interplay Between Tort Law and Religious Family Law: The Israeli Case,* 26 ARIZ. J. INT'L & COMP. L. 279, 280–81 (2009).

153 *Anonymous A,* 56(6) PD 883.

154 *Id.*

155 *Id.*

principles to external property.[156] However, it did not cancel the joint rights acquired during the marriage.[157]

An additional case for consideration is *Draham*.[158] The abovementioned decisions dealt with whether Israeli law requires the transfer of half the family property to the spouse who is not the registered owner, even though that spouse was disloyal. The courts determined that family property should be transferred, but external property should not. The *Draham* decision, in contrast, dealt with the question of whether to apply the rules of joint property to the external property of the disloyal spouse.[159] In a majority opinion, Justice Dorner determined that the rules of joint property should be applied in their complete scope, including property acquired prior to the marriage.[160] She argued that in harmonious marriages that last for many years, this sort of property usually becomes absorbed into joint property.[161]

It is difficult to avoid the impression that a desire to punish the disloyal spouse affected Justice Dorner since, in this case, the basis for joint external property rested on a very weak rationale. Even spouses living in harmony do not tend to see an external asset acquired by one spouse before marriage as a corporate asset, yet here Justice Dorner stated that an external asset will be shared despite a shaky relationship.

B. Balancing of Resources—The Property Relations Law

In 1973, The Property Relations Law was enacted in Israel.[162] The law was intended to apply to all couples that entered into marriages after 1974.[163] Under this law, the Israeli legislature established the system of delayed sharing. This system creates an absolute separation of property throughout the entire marriage. The property is divided between the spouses only in the event of divorce or upon the death of one spouse.[164] This arrangement is known as the "balancing of resources" in which sharing is obligatory.[165] "Balancing resources" is sharing

156 *Id.*
157 *Id.*
158 CA 1880/95 Draham v. Draham 50(4) PD 865, 876 [1997] (Isr.).
159 *Id.*
160 *Id.*
161 *Id.* at 877.
162 The Spouses Property Relations Law, 5733-1973, 27 LSI 276 (1973) (Isr.).
163 *Id.* § 14.
164 *Id.* §§ 5–6.
165 *Id.*

the value of the property as opposed to ownership rights, and it is delayed until the end of the marriage.[166] This sharing arrangement is implemented by evaluating the property of each spouse.[167]

The spouse who has more property registered in his or her name pays half of the difference in value to the spouse in whose name less property is registered.[168] Section 8(2) of The Property Relations Law provides that if the court finds "special circumstances," it is authorized to determine that the balancing of the property value not be half and half but rather some other proportion.[169]

In the case of *Anonymous B*, the court considered whether extramarital relationships are "special circumstances" justifying a deviation from the "balancing of resources" rule.[170] The rabbinical court held that adultery is included in "special circumstances" and that the wife should not be granted portions of the property that were accumulated in the husband's name.[171] Because issues of property should be resolved according to civil law, the rabbinical court could not base its opinion on punishment under religious law. It therefore provided the following explanation:

> Because of the economic results of divorce due to adultery, the injured spouse will be forced, as a result of the unilateral adulterous behavior, to build another home for himself, to remarry and also to literally purchase another home ... the economic responsibility imposed upon the injured party entitles him to leniency in the balancing of resources to his benefit, whether from rights that were accumulated before the adultery or afterwards.[172]

The wife petitioned the Israel Supreme Court, which relied upon the *Dror* ruling and decided to reverse the decision of the rabbinical court, "The dissolution of every marriage has broad economic impacts. The need to 'build another home' is not unique only to couples whose marriage broke up because of

166 *Id.*
167 *Id.*
168 *Id.*
169 *Id.* § 8(2).
170 HCJ 8928/06 High Court of Justice, Anonymous v. The Supreme Rabbinical Court (Oct. 8, 2008) (Isr.). [hereinafter *Anonymous B*].
171 *Id.*
172 *Id.*

adultery. This is the need of many of the couples whose marriages have come to an end."[173]

Another argument was made by Justice Rivlin in the case of *Anonymous B*:

> One cannot deal with the fault of one of the parties through economic damage in property distribution. It is often difficult to speak in terms of "fault" in this circumstance. The dissolution of marriage is the result of complex circumstances and adultery in itself does not make one of the spouses solely at fault.[174]

It seems that this is the only argument in the Israeli court decisions for not weighing extramarital relationships in property distribution, and it is compelling. This argument also parallels one of the central arguments commonly advanced in the United States, as discussed above and further examined in part IV of this chapter.

C. Jewish Religious Law

The property issues arising from a divorce are civil matters to which religious law should not be applied. However, religious law influences the rabbinical court when issues of property and adultery are brought before it. First, the theoretical basis for the property arrangement in Jewish religious law does not focus on the autonomy of the spouses as individuals.[175] Sharing is not expressed in the property relationship, and there is no joint property regime between spouses.[176] Instead, there is a separation of property along with a relationship of mutual dependence that is created by other rights and obligations.[177] For example, the husband is obligated to provide support for his wife and the wife has an obligation to transfer her income to him.

In Jewish religious law, the consent of the spouses is sufficient to allow for dissolution of marriage.[178] When there is no consent, grounds for divorce are

---

173 *Id.*

174 *Id.* (Rivlin, J., concurring).

175 SC 1/50 Sidis v. Registrar of Jerusalem Execution Office 8 PD 1020, 1130 [1954] (Isr.).

176 *See* Maidi S. Katz, *The Married Woman and Her Expense Account: A Study of the Married Woman's Ownership and Use of Marital Property in Jewish Law*, *in* 13 Jewish L. Ann. 101, 101–09 (Berachyahu Lifshitz ed., 2000).

177 *Id.*

178 Kimberly Scheuerman, *Enforceability of Agreements to Obtain a Religious Divorce*, 23 J. Acad. Matrimonial Law. 425, 427 (2010).

required.[179] Some grounds for divorce are not dependent upon the behavior of the spouse, such as disabilities and illnesses. Others are dependent upon proof of fault such as the inappropriate behavior of the spouse.[180]

There is a correlation between the influence of fault on the divorce laws themselves and its influence on the property relations between spouses. Behavior that causes the destruction of family life leads to economic sanctions against the individual at fault. The treatment of fault is not gender neutral. Asymmetry exists between the consequences of the extramarital relationships of a woman and those of a man.

When the wife is proven to be at fault, her husband is obligated to divorce her.[181] If the court rules for divorce based upon two witnesses, the woman loses her *ketubah* (her financial rights upon divorce under the Jewish marriage document), her alimony, and of course her property that has always been in the sole possession of her husband.[182] In contrast, when a husband is disloyal, the only sanctions are the loss of his wife's handiwork and her income.[183]

V. THE MODERN THEORETICAL RATIONALES FOR JOINT PROPERTY

A. The Joint Property Principles

Aside from the clear ruling in Israeli court decisions that fault is not to be weighed in property distribution, no other explanations are given. This may be due to the delicate and fragile nature of family law in Israel, in which the separation of church and state is not applied and legislation imposes religious norms upon the general secular public. For example, divorce proceedings are determined by religious law, in which fault is a primary consideration. The issue of property is determined by civil law, which differs from religious law in this regard.

Civil courts recognized that extramarital relationships are given significant weight in divorce proceedings, and a particular remedy is provided to the party who was harmed. The courts therefore viewed themselves as exempt from

---

179 Michelle Greenberg-Kobrin, *Civil Enforceability of Religious Prenuptial Agreements*, 32 COLUM. J.L. & SOC. PROBS. 359, 364–66 (1999).

180 *See id.* at 365–66.

181 Irving Breitowitz, *The Plight of the* Agunah*: A Study in* Halacha*, Contract, and the First Amendment*, 51 MD. L. REV. 213, 324 (1992); *Mishneh Torah, Ishut* 24:17; *Shulchan Aruch, Even Haezer* 11:1.

182 *See Mishneh Torah, Ishut* 24:16–18; *Shulchan Aruch, Even Haezer*, 115:5; PDR 8, 354.

183 CA (Jer) 755/05 Anonymous v. Anonymous (Dec. 5, 2005), Nevo Legal Database (by subscription) (Isr.).

compensating for that harm through the property distribution proceeding. In contrast, under the laws in the United States, extramarital relationships are not weighed at all in the divorce proceeding.[184] For that reason it is more appropriate for the state legal systems in the United States to compensate for this fault by weighing extramarital relationships in property distribution.

However, aside from religious considerations, it is worthwhile examining the modern rationales for joint property between spouses as reflected in the Israeli legal system. These rationales are also relevant to the state legal systems in the United States. The rule of joint property in Israel was created by court decisions. At first, it was defined as follows, "When there is no agreement, or when the intent of the parties at the time of the purchase is unclear, the court attributes to them the intention that the property will belong to both of them in equal portions."[185] Sharing is characterized by complete and "equal division" from the beginning of the marital relationship.[186]

At first, the joint property rule was built on two central elements: the existence of a normal marital life (mutual respect, no violence, taking care of each other, etc.); and a joint effort.[187] In later years, the focus transferred from the element of normal marital life to the element of joint effort. With time, this element essentially required that a couple live together under one roof.[188] Ultimately, the joint property rule is a legal tool intended to create an exception to the general property laws and the laws of evidence. Without the joint property tool, spouses would be subject to a separation of property regime.

---

184 *See, e.g.*, Suzanne A. Kim, *The Neutered Parent*, 24 YALE J.L. & FEMINISM 1, 15 (2012) (noting that "concepts of sexual fault no longer formally determine[] the status relationships of men and women in divorce"). *But see* Crawford v. Crawford, No. 259108, 2006 WL 1330321, at *1 (Mich. Ct. App. May 16, 2006) (holding that an extramarital relationship—even if nonsexual in nature—can be the primary reason for a divorce); *In re* Blanchflower, 834 A.2d 1010, 1011–13 (N.H. 2003) (reiterating that adultery is grounds for a fault-based divorce).

185 CA 300/64 Berger v. Dir. of Estate Tax 19(1) PD 240, 245 [1965] (Isr.); MENASHE SHAVA, PERSONAL LAW IN ISRAEL, vol. 1, 191–196 (2001).

186 *See* The Spouses Property Relations Law, 5733-1973, 27 LSI 276 § 3 (1973) (Isr.). This system of property distribution is different from the system of "equitable distribution", which is customary in many of the states in the United States. *See supra* part I; *see also* Shahar Lifshitz, *Past Property, Future Property, and the Philosophy of the Presumption of Joint Property*, 34 HEBREW U. L. REV. 627, 655 (2004).

187 *See* CA 52/80 Shahar v. Fridman 38(1) PD 443, 458 [1984] (Isr.). Under these conditions, the joint property principles may also apply to unmarried spouses who are living together. *See id.*

188 *See* CA 234/80 Gadasi v. Gadasi 36(2) PD 645, 650 [1982] (Isr.).

In early decisions, courts based the joint property rules on a contractual rationale, setting forth an implied agreement between the spouses.[189] Under this implied agreement, spouses intended to share their rights equally.[190] The courts investigated those intentions,[191] and the element of a normal marital life suited the contractual rationale. However, in a strained marital relationship, that rationale could not easily serve as a solid theoretical basis for the joint property rule. Furthermore, the investigation of the spouses' intentions was not a simple task.[192]

It was even more complicated when the "intention attributed to the parties" actually focused on "the intention attributed to the registered owner of the property."[193] In addition, critics argue that the contractual rationale is based on a fiction. The court attributes intentions to the parties based on its evaluations, which are actually a matter of legal policy.[194]

The limitations of the contractual rationale motivated the courts to adopt the proprietary rationale.[195] The investigations by the courts into the intentions of the parties became less frequent.[196] The proprietary rationale led to a focus on the element of joint effort. This focus brought the joint property rule closer to a sort of statutory sharing regime. Eventually, the joint property rule began to reflect the law of trusts or equity.[197] This transition was impacted by the social perception of marriage as a free relationship between two spouses, based on equality and preservation of individual autonomy.[198]

---

189 *See* Shahar, supra note 187.

190 See Berger, supra note 185.

191 The investigation is to determine the intentions of the spouses during the marriage, and not at the time of its dissolution. *See, e.g.,* CA 651/79 Salman v. Salman 36(1) PD 554, 555 [1982] (Isr.).

192 Indeed, in some cases it was argued that it was a fiction. *See, e.g.,* CA 1558/94 Nafisi v. Nafisi 50(3) PD 573, 617 [1996] (Isr.).

193 *See, e.g.,* CA 135/68 Bareli v. Dir. of Estate Tax, Jerusalem, 23(1) PD 393, 398 [1969] (Isr.); CA 529/76 Svirski v. Svirski 31(2) PD 233, 237 [1977] (Isr.).

194 *See, e.g.,* CA 253/65 Briker v. Briker 20(1) PD 589, 597 [1966] (Isr.); CA 77/77 Rahabi v. Rahabi 33(1) PD 729, 734 [1979] (Isr.).

195 *See* Lifshitz, *supra* note 186, at 691 (arguing that this change began in the beginning of the 1980s). For more about the rejection of the contractual rationale as the real rationale for joint property, see ARIEL ROSEN-ZVI, ISRAEL FAMILY LAW: THE SACRED AND THE SECULAR 225, 231 (1990).

196 *See e.g., Nafisi,* 50(3) PD at 605.

197 *See Briker,* 20(1) PD at 595; *see also* HANOCH DAGAN, PROPERTY AT A CROSSROADS 468 (2005).

198 *See* CA 8791/00 Shalem v. Twinco 8–11 (Dec. 13, 2006) (Isr.); CA (Jer) 4623/04 Anonymous v. Anonymous 7–10 (Oct. 8, 2004) (Isr.).

The distinction between the contractual rationale and the proprietary rationale is not a dichotomy.[199] The second rationale did not completely replace the first, and in later decisions one can still find statements relying upon the contractual construction.[200] The transition by the courts between the rationales is not one directional, but swings back and forth.[201] These divergent rationales lead to conflicting results under the joint property rule. Ultimately, the joint property regime became a combination of these two rationales.[202] Consideration of both rationales allowed for the courts to reach proper results.[203]

With the joint property principles, Israeli law adopted the concept of equal distribution. This concept takes an approach opposite to that of the separation of property, which was customary in most of the United States before the no-fault divorce revolution and is still applied under Jewish religious law. In between separation of property and equal distribution is the concept of equitable distribution. The preceding discussion of American law demonstrates the system of equal distribution. This system asserts that family property is joint property from the day that it is acquired and gives less weight to fault in determining property distribution.

In contrast, fault is more relevant under the system of equitable distribution, which views family property as separate property and provides for property sharing only at the end of the marriage. The joint property rule in Israel is based on the concept of equal distribution, making fault ostensibly less relevant. However, the joint property rule in Israel is the result of deeper theoretical bases. Thus, the question of consideration of moral fault needs to be examined in light of these bases.

As stated, the fundamental theory supporting the joint property rule is the contractual rationale. The primary purpose of property arrangements

---

199 *See* Lifshitz, *supra* note 186, at 634 (arguing that the decisions of the 1960s show that the contractual rationale was more dominant then, while in the 1980s the decisions were more suited to the model of the judicial presumption). *But see id.* at 695 n.242 (indicating that the decisions are not always consistent).

200 *See, e.g.*, CA 630/79 Liberman v. Liberman 35(4) PD 359, 368 [1981] (Isr.); CA 663/87 Natan v. Grayner 45(1) PD 104, 109 [1990] (Isr.).

201 *See, e.g.*, CA 75/79 Avrahami v. Yisraeli 34(2) PD 216 [1980] (Isr.).

202 CA 806/93 Hadari v. Hadari 48(3) PD 685, 694 [1994] (Isr.).

203 Thus, for example, this rationale assisted in including business property in joint property. *See* CA 488/89 Nofarber v. Nofarber 44(4) PD 293 [1990] (Isr.). The proprietary rationale also helped to include retirement and pension properties in the joint property. *See* CA 809/90 Lidaei v. Lidaei 46(1) PD 602, 611 [1992] (Isr.).

between spouses is fulfilling the will of the spouses. The law's role is to investigate the presumed intentions of the spouses and to determine property distribution that reflects their will. This approach, based on both economic and psychological logic, assumes that spouses who conduct a "normal" marital life in which each contributes to the family effort would agree on a joint property arrangement.[204] The determination of the nature and content of the joint property arrangement is therefore not a normative process. It is actually a factual one in which the law identifies the distribution that best reflects the couple's presumed intention, even if this distribution does not seem just or fair to the court.

Is the contractual rationale indifferent to an extramarital relationship? It seems that the answer is no. The joint property rule is a factual matter founded on, among other considerations, factual assumptions based on logic and common sense. One may assume that an important factor such as an extramarital relationship would impact not only the content of the property arrangement but also its very existence. The court decisions that adopted the contractual rationale determined that in order to determine an intent to create joint property, the two elements of a normal marital life and joint effort must be fulfilled.[205] The joint effort requirement can be met by active participation in providing family income and carrying out household work.[206]

The existence of an extramarital relationship is ostensibly irrelevant to this requirement. After all, there could be instances in which an adulterous spouse also makes an impeccable contribution to family income or to the household work. However, that is not the case with respect to the requirement for a normal marital life. The logic of this requirement is that the willingness of spouses to create joint property is integral to their marital life. One may assume that the better their marital life, the greater their willingness to create joint property. In contrast, spouses who do not have a normal marital life will not be willing to deepen their commitments by creating an economic joint property relationship separate from their personal one.

---

204 *See* Lifshitz, *supra* note 186, at 655

205 Joshua Weisman, Property Law—Ownership and Partnership, 182 (1997).

206 *See* CA 300/64 Berger v. Dir. of Estate Tax, 19(1) PD 240, 246 [1965] (Isr.) ("The required joint effort is not necessarily financial participation of each of the spouses that comes from income or from his earnings. But even the case in which a wife does not work outside of her home but manages the household and contributes her part to the support of the family including educating the couple's children, may be viewed as an effort on her part no less than the husband's effort who earns an income from work").

The question that arises is whether an extramarital relationship can coexist with a normal marital life, or whether the existence of an extramarital relationship is in itself sufficient to demonstrate that a normal marital life does not exist. A review of case law does not provide a clear answer to this question. When the contractual rationale is the theoretical basis, it seems very difficult to establish full property sharing with the existence of an extramarital relationship. The great majority of people will not agree to share their property with their spouses if they know that their spouses are breaching their trust.

An extramarital relationship could very well be considered a fundamental breach of contract that entitles the injured party to cancel the contract.[207] Therefore, it seems that judges who implement the pure contractual rationale should reexamine the consideration of extramarital relationships. Moreover, the rulings that extramarital relationships exclude external property from joint property add further difficulty to the contractual rationale.

The additional rationale for the joint property rule is the proprietary rationale.[208] In the early 1980s, values from property law, especially the value of labor, began to penetrate the marital property laws and influence their design. This emphasis on labor suggested that property should be given to the person who worked to create it, as a reward for that person's investment in its production. The application of this concept to marital property laws should lead to the implementation of a joint rather than a separate property regime. In the factual-economic reality, both spouses contribute joint efforts to producing and improving family property, so this property should be awarded to each spouse.

The increased significance of the element of "joint effort" and the decreased significance of the element of "normal marital life" are consistent with the labor theory that emphasizes effort in creating and recognizing ownership interest.[209] An additional influence of the labor theory is in broadening the scope of property included in the joint property rule with respect to property acquired during the marriage, and narrowing it with respect to property obtained prior to the marriage, without joint effort.[210]

---

207 *See* Contracts (Remedies for Breach of Contract) Law, 5731 –1970 §§ 6–7 (1970) (Isr.), *available at* http://www.israelinsurancelaw.com/contract-laws/contracts-remedies-for-breach-of-contract-law.html.

208 *See* Rosen-Zvi, *supra* note 195, at 232 ("One cannot also ignore that each element has the ability to influence the legal significance of the other. An extremely atypical marital life could shed a different light on factual circumstances of joint effort").

209 *See* Dagan, *supra* note 197, at 463.

210 *See* Lifshitz, *supra* note 186, at 649, 655.

In addition, the labor theory impacted the transition of the joint property regime from a regime based on consent of the parties to a regime originating in law.[211] The judges supporting the value of the work as the basis for joint property applied the joint property rule even where it was clear that both spouses strictly observed complete separation of their financial matters.[212]

Does the labor theory enable consideration of sexual fault? One's initial reaction may be negative. This theory focuses only on the effort invested by each spouse, without consideration of sexual behavior. However, careful study reveals that the answer is not so simple.

First, according to the labor theory and the argument of reward for work invested, the right of a spouse in joint property is reward for that spouse's contribution in creating the property. A closer look at the term "contribution" can better demonstrate the need for considering sexual fault in the labor theory. It may be argued that the term "contribution" in a broader sense relates not only to the couple's economic relationship but also to the psychological-emotional aspects of the relationship. Creating a supportive environment filled with trust and security also contributes to the creation of property and the production of profits.

Thus, when quantifying the contribution of each of the spouses, one should consider both the direct economic contributions of housework or income, and the contributions to the existence, preservation, prosperity, and development of shared married life based on trust, loyalty, and love. This understanding of the term "contribution" will allow for consideration of sexual fault in determining property distribution.

Second, it has been argued that the recognition of property rights in the fruits of one's labor is based not only on the work invested in producing the property but also on the injustice of transferring it to another person. According to this perception, the recognition of an individual's property rights can be based on values of justice and fairness.[213] Application of these values to the rules of property between spouses leads to the following argument. Both spouses contribute by their efforts to producing property and profits, so it is appropriate and just that they jointly own such property and profits.

---

211 *See* CA 686/85 Maharavi v. Maharavi 40(2) PD 631 [1986] (Isr.).

212 *See* Shahar Lifshitz, *Married Against Their Will? A Liberal Analysis of the Institution of Common Law Spouses*, 25 Tel-Aviv U. L. Rev. 741, 794–96, 825–29 (2002).

213 For a similar argument, see Guy Pesach, *The Theoretical Basis for Recognition of Copyright*, 31 Hebrew U. L. Rev. 359, 399 (2000).

The contribution of the two spouses is what justifies recognition of a joint property regime. Indeed, review of case law from the 1990s demonstrates that the courts based the joint property rule on principles of justice.[214] Understanding the joint property regime through this lens opens a significant door to weighing sexual fault in determining property distribution. According to this approach, just as values of justice were the initial justification for recognizing the spouse's right in joint property, they should also influence the scope and content of this right.

Thus, the spouse's sexual fault should restrict the scope of that spouse's right in joint property, whether by cancelling it entirely, restricting which property is included, or distributing property unequally. In a broader sense, it seems that values of justice allow for weighing this fault while shaping the content of the joint property regime.[215] Therefore, the question that arises is why the court decisions refused to consider sexual fault. The answer is perhaps in the well-known understanding that the meaning of "justice" is somewhat vague and individual judges may have subjective views of justice.

A review of Israeli case law shows that in shaping the contents of the joint property regime, the courts adopted a narrow perception of the word "justice" that relates only to economic fault.[216] However, the vague content of the term "justice" allows for adopting its broader meaning that also considers sexual fault in determining property distribution.[217]

The proprietary rationale is also based on a third value which is the value of equality. From the words of Chief Justice Barak in the *Shalem* case, one can identify two rationales for the value of equality.[218] The first is that the joint property rule expresses recognition of the economic contribution of the homemaker to the family's welfare. In this sense, Chief Justice Barak does not consider equality as an independent value, but as a means of promoting an additional value, the value of reward for effort invested in producing the property.

The second rationale promotes the value of equality as an independent value with contents of its own. This is substantive equality and not formal

---

214 *See* Lifshitz, *supra* note 186, at 699, 702 ("As a result of it, it seemed during this period that the changeover was completed and that the joint property principle was completely based upon the normative values of justice and equality").

215 *See* CA (Jer) 638/04 H.R. v. R.R. (Jan. 23, 2005) (Isr.).

216 *See, e.g.*, FamC 20964/02 Anonymous v. Anonymous 9 (Dec. 28, 2009) (Isr.).

217 *See* Weisman, *supra* note 205, at 181.

218 *See* CA 8791/00 Shalem v. Twinco, 9 (Dec. 13, 2006), Nevo Legal Database (by subscription) (Isr.).

equality.[219] Ostensibly, one might suppose that those who embrace the approach of substantive equality would object to every deviation from equal property distribution based on fault, but that conclusion is not necessarily correct.

The approach of substantive equality applies the Aristotelian principle of equality. According to this principle, equality means treating equals alike and treating those who are different, differently, provided that the differentiation is relevant to the particular circumstances.[220] Thus, in contrast to the approach of formal equality, relating to an individual differently is not necessarily harmful to the value of equality, unless the differentiation is not for relevant reasons. In the context of the present discussion, any unequal property distribution is harmful to the value of substantive equality when it is made for irrelevant reasons.

The questions are how to determine the relevant reason, and whether sexual fault is a relevant reason that justifies a diversion from equal distribution. These questions are not factual questions, but normative ones. Their answers are derived, among other factors, from the attitudes of society with respect to sexual fault. Thus, for example, if it is normatively determined that fault is relevant to property distribution, then the conclusion will be that an unequal property distribution actually fulfills the substantive equality and does not harm it. If, however, it is determined that sexual fault is not a proper consideration in property distribution, then taking it into consideration will be harmful to substantive equality.

The proprietary rationale is thus based on the values of labor, justice, and equality. We have seen that disputes between spouses do not detract from equal distribution and, ostensibly, that should also be the rule regarding an extramarital relationship. However, it is doubtful whether this comparison is suitable. Some matters reach down to the very foundation of the relationship between spouses. Other matters, even if disturbing and challenging to the marital relationship, do not reach its core.

The question is how to categorize extramarital relationships. Does a spouse who conducts an extramarital relationship deserve the exceptional defenses created by case law? When the courts created the rules of joint property, did they envision the disloyal spouse? This doubt is increased by one of the joint property rules. Joint property includes the sharing of obligations and debts,[221]

---

219 *See* Lifshitz, *supra* note 186, at 659.

220 *See* 5 Aristotle, Nicomachean Ethics (W. D. Ross trans. 2009), *available at* http://classics.mit.edu/Aristotle/nicomachaen.5.v.html.

221 *See Shalem*, CA 8791/00; CA 3002/93 Ben Zvi v. Sitin 49(3) PD 5, 7 [1995] (Isr.); *see also* CA 446/69 Levi v. Goldberg 24(1) PD 813, 820 [1970] (Isr.).

except for obligations made in breach of trust (for example, for the purpose of supporting a lover).[222]

Case law reveals that there are different types of obligations. Obligations connected to supporting the family are joint, even if they were created by only one of the spouses. In contrast, obligations that harm the foundation of the marital relationship are not included in joint property. Accordingly, it should be examined whether a greater burden should be placed on the spouse who requests joint property rights after having harmed the foundation of the marital relationship.

This approach should determine that the rationale does not apply to property registered in the name of the spouse who was disloyal when the property was acquired. The adulterous spouse might be the one to argue that there was no intention to create joint property and might even support this argument with the fact that he participated in an extramarital relationship. This situation could reasonably occur when most of the property is registered in the name of the spouse who participated in the extramarital relationship.

Taking fault into consideration might therefore allow him to use his wrongdoing to his own benefit. Under these circumstances, the contractual rationale, based on libertarian thinking and the economic analysis of the law, allows for bringing the claim of estoppel against the spouse at fault, in order to prevent him from raising this argument. The rationale behind the doctrine of estoppel is to protect the innocent spouse's reliance on the representation of the adulterous spouse that the couple has a normal marital life.[223]

The previous paragraphs dealt with the joint property principles and presented thoughts as well as options for considering extramarital relationships in property distribution. These options are more relevant and significant in the second property regime under the Israeli legal system, as set forth in the Property Relations Law. The examination, above, with respect to the state laws in the United States shows that fault is less relevant in a joint property regime than in a property regime of separation. This distinction is to some extent also valid in Israeli law.

The Property Relations Law sets forth a regime of separation of property. During the marriage, each spouse is the owner of his or her own property (as in

---

222 *See Levi*, PD 813, 820.

223 This is the classic estoppel. For further discussion, see Menachem Mautner, *"Creators of Risk" and "Risk Victims": Protection of the Reliance Interest in Israel's New Civil Legislation*, 16 Hebrew U. L. Rev. 92, 112–13 (1987).

the system of equitable distribution), and the distribution between the spouses occurs only when the marriage ends. In this situation, it is more difficult for the spouse who breaches trust to establish joint rights in property registered in the name of the other spouse.

The rationales of the joint property rule are the major considerations in the question of weighing fault, but other factors need to be considered as well. These factors will be discussed in the following two sections.

B. Different Fields of Law and Extramarital Relationships

In the case of *Anonymous C*, Justice Rivlin raised the difficulty of examining emotional relationships from the contractual perspective.[224] In his opinion, there should be no compensation for emotional harm caused by adultery:

> As is well known, the law does not grant a cause of action for emotional harm involved in divorce proceedings. ... Similarly, there is no remedy in our system for someone who suffered emotional harm due to a spouse's adultery. ... Indeed the law does not stop at the entrance to the family home, but the law abstains from trying to settle emotional relationships. ... The deceptive, adulterous spouse, who breaks up a relationship without justification, is perhaps deserving of moral, religious, or social shame, but the person injured by him will have difficulty finding his remedy in law.[225]

Gad Tedeschi notes that the offense of adultery was cancelled in the Israeli legal system with the cancellation of the Ottoman Criminal Law.[226] In contrast, he points out that various countries such as Switzerland and Germany include sanctions for adultery in their criminal laws or tort laws.[227] Tedeschi also indicates that although in the past sanctions were gender-based, today such discrimination would be impermissible.[228] Tedeschi writes that there are no sanctions under Israeli law against the adulterous spouse, except for religious sanctions.[229] In one case, a court concluded that it is impossible to determine that an

224 CA 5258/98 Anonymous v. Anonymous 58(6) PD 209, 226 [1995] (Isr.) [hereinafter *Anonymous* C] (Rivlin, J., dissenting).
225 *Id.* at 233 (citations omitted).
226 Tedeschi, *supra* note 4, at 294.
227 Tedeschi, *supra* note 4, at 295.
228 *Id.* at 302.
229 *Id.* at 318.

extramarital relationship is either contrary to the reasonable norm of behavior or an act of negligence, and therefore the innocent spouse should not be awarded compensation for damages.[230]

In the different states within the United States, one of the considerations for not weighing fault in property distribution is the availability of bringing a claim under tort law or criminal law. In Israeli law, no such availability exists. The need for such a separate claim strengthens the need to weigh fault in property distribution.

C. The Moral Argument—The Approach of Society

In the *Anonymous C* case, which deals with the validity of a married man's promise to marry another woman, Chief Justice Barak stated:

> There is no doubt that preserving the family unit is part of public policy in Israel. ... The interest of society supports stable marriage. ... Nevertheless, throughout the years the perceptions of society have changed with respect to divorce. ... Even the aversion to an extramarital relationship does not reflect the approach of today's society, and the common law marriage principles will prove it.[231]

Justice Procaccia concurred with Chief Justice Barak, "In recent decades, the Western world went through extreme upheavals in basic perceptions of values that are characterized by pluralism in thought and morality together with an increasing recognition of the liberty of the individual to determine his way of life. Those upheavals substantively impact the perceptions of law."[232]

These words contradict the statements of some legal experts in the United States, who argue that even in modern day society the majority of the population is averse to extramarital relationships.[233] These quotations support the notion that the law affects the moral design of society.[234] The consideration or lack of consideration of extramarital relationships in property distribution

230 *See* FamC 21382/01 B.D. v. B.R. (Oct. 5, 2007), Nevo Legal Database (by subscription) (Isr.).

231 CA 5258/98 Anonymous v. Anonymous 58(6) PD 209, 221 [1995] (Isr.).

232 *Id.* at 239 (Procaccia, J., concurring).

233 *See* Morse, *supra* note 12, at 641; *see also supra* part II.A and sources cited therein.

234 *See also* Atwater, *supra* note 2, at 16 ("The proscription of extramarital sex is one of the most ancient and stringent cultural rules regulating family life. In Western civilization, it can be traced back at least to early Hebraic society").

sends a social message. Based on this notion, it seems that today Israeli law tends to be tolerant of an extramarital relationship. However, it is difficult to know which came first. Perhaps case law has evolved and does not reflect the reality in which extramarital relationships will not be considered a breach of trust to be weighed in family property distribution.

D. A Proposal for a New Model—The Dominant Cause Model

This chapter sets forth various considerations for weighing or excluding fault as a factor in property distribution. Among the factors that favor the consideration of fault are: (i) the required coherency with the modern theoretical rationales for the joint property regime. They include the contractual rationale and the proprietary rationale based on labor, justice and equality; (ii) the absence of other fields of law that can provide a remedy for the harm caused by inappropriate spousal behavior and the lack of motivation of the courts to use such cumbersome procedures; (iii) moral considerations; and (iv) the social message. In contrast are the judicial decisions against weighing fault while determining family property distribution.

It seems that the desirable balancing formula is that extramarital relationships be considered in severe circumstances. Such circumstances include those in which extramarital relationships are the cause of the dissolution of the marriage. When the totality of the evidence shows that the extramarital relationship is the dominant cause of the dissolution, and that disregarding the relationship the marriage was stable, then the extramarital relationship should be weighed in property distribution. This is referred to as the dominant cause model. However, when the extramarital relationship is only one difficulty among others already faced in a troubled marriage, then the extramarital relationship should not be weighed in the distribution of property. The consideration of fault in harsh circumstances may better balance the values operating in the state laws of the United States and in the law of Israel.

Some of the approaches in the scholarly literature in the United States argue that due to the emotional impacts of extramarital relationships, such relationships should routinely be weighed in property distribution.[235] In light of the considerations presented above, such approaches should not be accepted. However, the proposed model will provide protection to the spouse who was

---

235 *See, e.g.*, Boyd, *supra* note 46, at 624.

harmed and will grant that spouse a greater portion of the property than he or she would have received in customary distribution.

It also must be emphasized that this model would operate only to protect the spouse who was harmed, and not to that spouse's detriment. The spouse who had an extramarital relationship will not be permitted to argue that there was no intent to share property. On the contrary, the consideration will be whether to grant the spouse who was harmed more than the property to which he or she would have otherwise been entitled in a customary distribution.

There is an additional aspect to this model. The spouse who has an extramarital relationship will not be allowed to claim joint rights in the external property of the other spouse, even if he or she would be able to do so in a customary distribution. Property that did not result from the couple's joint effort will not be included in the shared property. Such will also be the case when the owner of the external property is the individual that had an extramarital relationship. The law does not have to punish that spouse by transferring personal property to the other spouse. Yet it is possible that the spouse who was harmed will be given a greater portion of property acquired by the couple than that spouse would have received under the customary rules of property division.

Implementation of this model might raise questions. The first question is a qualitative one. At what precise point will extramarital relationships be considered severe cases? The second question is quantitative. How should severe extramarital relationships be weighed, and what percentage of property will the individual in such a relationship lose? The third question asks how the dominant cause of the marriage dissolution can be identified. The fourth question is actually derived from the previous three questions. It asks how arbitrary court decisions are when there are no defined tests.[236]

While the responses to these questions remain unclear, the lack of consideration of extramarital relationships also raises significant difficulties. The problematic nature of evaluation does not lessen or nullify the right of the injured spouse. The judicial systems in both Israel and in the states within the United States have recently demonstrated that the courts are not deterred from handling complex questions, provided that an individual's right will not be

236 Thus, for example, the breaking point of the marriage must be determined. From that point on, this sort of behavior will not be considered as having brought the marriage to an end. Clearly, for example, sexual fault after living apart will not be weighed in the same way as sexual fault before the separation. *See, e.g.*, Ferrucci v. Ferrucci, 527 A.2d 1207, 1208 (Conn. App. Ct. 1987); Smith v. Smith, 363 S.E.2d 404, 406, 408 (S.C. Ct. App. 1987).

denied. They have determined that within property distribution, the personal capital, earning capability, and reputation of each of the spouses must also be distributed.[237] The Israel Supreme Court has noted that with time, criteria will be formed to assist the evaluation of intangible property.[238] Such an approach is also appropriate to the present matter.

Nevertheless, there is a distinction between the legal system in Israel and the various state legal systems within the United States. The determination of property distribution looks at the past. The law seeks to distribute the property accumulated by the family in the past and to determine with which property each spouse will leave the marriage. The determination of alimony, in contrast, looks into the future.[239] This distinction may be correct with respect to the state legal systems in the United States. It may help in understanding the asymmetry between those states that consider fault in the determination of property distribution and those that consider fault with respect to alimony.

States that consider fault in property distribution also consider it in determining the amount of alimony.[240] However, even states that do not consider fault in property distribution do consider it in alimony. In that respect they compensate the spouse who was harmed.[241] This mechanism does not exist in the Israeli legal system. Alimony payments are controlled by religious law, under which obligations for support terminate with the marriage.[242] Therefore, the need to consider fault in property distribution is even more essential in Israeli civil law.

VI. CONCLUSION

This chapter reexamines the issue of weighing extramarital relationships in family property distribution, in light of the current and modern theoretical rationales for the joint property principles. The United States is divided on this issue. While some states oppose the consideration of fault in marital dissolution,

---

237 *See* CA (Jer) 4623/04 Anonymous v. Anonymous 16 (Oct. 8, 2004), Nevo Legal Database (by subscription) (Isr.) (illustrating that the Israeli system preceded other systems); Kelly, *supra* note 25, at 69–70.

238 CA (Jer) 4623/04 Anonymous v. Anonymous 19, 22 (Oct. 8, 2004), Nevo Legal Database (by subscription) (Isr.)

239 Carolyn J. Frantz & Hanoch Dagan, *Properties of Marriage*, 104 Colum. L. Rev. 75, 99 (2004).

240 *See supra* note 70 and accompanying text.

241 *Id.*

242 *See supra* part III.C.

others support it.[243] This chapter studies these considerations in detail, presents various scholarly opinions, and sets forth factual data with respect to the various states. This forms a normative basis for a renewed analysis of the issue.

This chapter raises doubts as to whether the exclusion of all consideration of fault, as established in the legal systems in several of the states within the United States and in Israel, is consistent with theoretical rationales for joint property principles. At first the Israeli joint property principles required two elements, a normal marital life and a joint effort.[244] The joint property principles were based upon the contractual rationale.[245] Later, the joint property rule became based upon the proprietary rationale.[246] This rationale is based upon the value of labor. Accordingly, each spouse is entitled to half of the financial worth of the property based on the work that spouse invested in it. Other bases of the proprietary rationale are the values of justice and equality. The value of equality subdivides further into the values of reward for effort in creating property and the independent value of equality.

This chapter demonstrates that a broad interpretation of these bases will lead to the conclusion that fault should be considered in the determination of property distribution. In addition, it is essential to take into account that there is actually no other way to compensate the spouse who has been harmed by an extramarital relationship. Other fields of law do not provide an appropriate channel for this purpose because proceedings are complicated and lack a clearly defined statutory remedy.

In conclusion, this chapter proposes a balancing model referred to as the dominant cause model. According to this model, fault should be considered in property distribution in severe circumstances. Severe circumstances will be defined as occurring when an extramarital relationship was the dominant cause that brought about the end of the marriage. If the marital relationship was unstable anyway, then an extramarital relationship will not be a factor in determining property distribution. Furthermore, external and personal property should remain excluded from joint property, even when they belong to the individual who conducted the extramarital relationship.

The implementation of this model will also present the legal systems with several challenges in evaluating the dominant cause for dissolution of

243 Pamela Laufer-Ukeles, *Reconstructing Fault: The Case for Spousal Torts,* 79 U. CIN. L. REV. 207, 220 (2010).
244 *See supra* notes 185–88 and accompanying text.
245 *See supra* notes 189–94 and accompanying text.
246 *See supra* notes 195–98 and accompanying text.

the marriage. These include the determination of the percentage of property affected by each incident and the concern of arbitrariness. However, the legal systems have already addressed these sorts of challenges in other contexts. In such contexts they require that an individual not be deprived of his or her rights due to difficulties of evaluation. In addition, appropriate protection is given to the spouse harmed by the unique family circumstances. This shift in the legal systems should facilitate reexamination of the consideration of fault in property distribution as well.

CHAPTER 4

Property Sharing Arrangements in Israeli Family Law

I. INTRODUCTION

The arrangement for balancing marital resources in Israel is set forth in the Property Relations between Spouses Law.[1] This arrangement was established to replace the presumption of sharing that had applied until 1973. The presumption determined that all of the spouses' property was jointly owned and shared from the beginning of the marital relationship, and that there was no need to wait until the termination of a marriage in order to share property.[2] The presumption of sharing therefore allowed claims for unregistered rights in family assets, failed to maintain certainty of property ownership and value, and did not protect the interests of third parties.[3]

In contrast, the Property Relations Law creates a separation of property between spouses during their marriage. Sharing begins only upon termination of the marriage. Thus, the spouse who is not a registered property owner according to the Land Registry (hereinafter referred to as an "unregistered spouse") is not entitled to co-ownership, but to half of the property's financial value when the marriage ends and assets are distributed. These two provisions of the law prevent claims for unregistered property rights, maintain certainty with respect to property ownership, and protect the interests of third parties.

The difficulty is that a failure in the structure of the Property Relations Law prevented implementation of the legislature's intent. Distribution of property was made to depend on religious divorce, which according to Jewish law requires the willingness of the parties. Without it, there is no divorce and

---

1 Property Relations between Spouses Law, 5733-1973, 27 LSI 276 (1973) (hereinafter Property Relations Law).

2 *See* CA 300/64 Berger v. Dir. of Estate Tax 19(1) PD 240, 245 [1965].

3 *See* Menashe Shava, Personal Law in Israel 191–96 (2001); Spouses Property Relations Bill, 5729-1969, 849 LSI 333 (1969).

therefore no division of property (financial divorce). The Supreme Court tried to remedy this flaw in the decisions of *Knobler*[4] and *Abu Romi*.[5] Instead based on a flexible application of general property law, it created a new rule that the Property Relations Law allows the presumption of sharing which the law was intended to replace. In addition, the law does not apply to members of Christian denominations whose religious law does not allow for divorce.[6]

Even if the flexible interpretation by the courts of the general property law that re-established the presumption of sharing had been justifiable, it would have been so only before Amendment 4 to the Property Relations Law was enacted in 2008. After the amendment which allowed for property distribution prior to divorce, that is, financial divorce before religious divorce, this construction became no longer justified.

This chapter analyzes and is inspired by comparative law. It proposes a new model, suggesting the return to the basic requirements of the Property Relations Law as designed by the legislature. Included among these basic requirements are the re-establishment of the separation of family assets during a marriage; the application to spouses of the general property laws in the same way that they are applied to unrelated parties; the exclusion from property distribution of assets acquired by one spouse without a joint effort, whether prior to the marriage, by inheritance, or by gift (hereinafter separate property); and restoration of the protection of third parties. This model will provide for protection of property, clarity among creditors, increase in the family's property value, and relief to engaged or married individuals who are concerned about their separate assets.

Part II addresses the normative-theoretical framework and the historical background of the Property Relations Law. The section highlights the challenges created by the presumption of sharing and the solutions the legislature sought to implement in the Property Relations Law. Part III discusses the *Knobler* case and analyzes the different judicial positions that formed the basis for later legal developments. Part IV addresses a series of rulings and describes the gradual development that rendered the Property Relations Law meaningless. Part V analyzes ownership of property by spouses under the law of the United Kingdom; and part VI examines the matter as addressed by the state laws in the

---

4 CA 1915/91 Knobler v. Knobler 49(3) PD 529 [1995].

5 CA 8672/00 Abu Romi v. Abu Romi 56(6) PD 175 [2002].

6 FamC 5794/03 Anonymous vs. Anonymous, Nevo (legal database by subscription), Dec. 2, 2005.

United States. Part VII offers a new model, including changes the Israeli courts must adopt to return to the legislature's original intent in the Property Relations Law and to maintain consistency with comparative law.

II. THE PROPERTY RELATIONS LAW—THE THEORETICAL AND NORMATIVE FRAMEWORK

As mentioned in the previous chapter, during the 1960s Israeli courts began creating a property sharing regime between spouses, which has been referred to as the presumption of sharing.[7] It determined co-ownership by spouses of all assets accumulated during their life together.[8] Sharing is characterized by complete, equal division from the beginning of the marital relationship.[9] At first, the joint property rule was built on two central elements: the existence of normal marital life and joint effort.[10] Ultimately, the joint property rule became a legal tool intended to create an exception to the general property laws and the laws of evidence. The joint property principles were based upon the contractual rationale.[11]

The limitations of the contractual rationale motivated the courts to adopt a proprietary rationale, under which the spouses became co-owners of the property even though it was registered in only one of their names.[12] The proprietary rationale led to a focus on the element of joint effort. Eventually, the joint property rule began to resemble the law of trusts or equity.[13] The distinction

---

7 The presumption of sharing originated in England, see CA 253/65 Bricker v. Bricker. 20(1) PD 589, 598 [1966]. Over time it has gone far from the English jurisprudence; see CA 595/69 Afta v. Afta 25(1) PD 561, 568 [1971].

8 *Berger*, 19(1) PD at 245; CA (Jer) 135/68 Bareli v. Adm'r of Tax Estate 23(1) PD 393, 395 [1969]; SHAVA, *supra* note 3.

9 The equal division system of property distribution is different from the system of equitable distribution customary in many of the states in the United States. *See infra*, part VI; *see also* Shahar Lifshitz, *Past Property, Future Property, and the Philosophy of the Presumption of Joint Property*, 34 HEBREW U. L. REV. 627, 655 (2004).

10 *See supra* notes 185–88, ch. 3, and accompanying text. *See* also CA 52/80 Shahar v. Fridman 38(1) PD 443, 458 [1984]. Under these conditions, the joint property principles may also apply to unmarried spouses who are living together. *Id.*

11 *See supra* notes 189–94, ch. 3, and accompanying text.

12 *See supra* notes 194–98, ch. 3, and accompanying text. *See* Lifshitz, *supra* note 9, at 691 (arguing that this change began in the early 1980s). For more concerning the rejection of the contractual rationale as the real rationale for joint property, see ARIEL ROSEN-ZVI, ISRAEL FAMILY LAW: THE SACRED AND THE SECULAR 225, 231 (1990).

13 *Bricker*, 20(1) PD at 595; *see* HANOCH DAGAN, PROPERTY AT A CROSSROADS 468 (2005).

between the contractual rationale and the proprietary rationale is not a dichotomy. Ultimately, the joint property regime became a combination of these two rationales. Consideration of them both allowed for courts to reach proper results.[14]

As stated, the fundamental theory supporting the joint property rule is the contractual rationale. The primary purpose of property arrangements between spouses is to fulfill the will of the spouses. This approach, based on both economic logic and psychology, assumes that spouses who conduct a normal marital life in which each contributes to the family effort would agree on a joint property arrangement.[15]

The additional rationale for the joint property rule is the proprietary rationale.[16] In the early 1980s, ideas from property law and especially those concerning the value of labor began to influence the interpretation and design of marital property laws.[17] The labor theory affected the transition of the joint property regime from a regime based on consent of the parties to a regime originating in law, supporting the value of work as the basis for joint property. The judges applied the joint property rule even when it was clear that both spouses strictly observed complete separation of their financial matters.[18] The proprietary rationale is also based on another value—the value of equality.[19]

Co-ownership of assets required no formal registration according to the presumption of sharing. Family sharing laws actually overcame general property laws. Under general property laws, an asset does not become shared property due to the shared life of the couple. Property became shared under general property laws only if a transaction was registered in the Land Registry. In contrast, under family sharing laws an asset becomes shared property

---

14 Thus, for example, this rationale assisted in including business property in joint property. *See* CA 488/89 Nofarber v. Nofarber 44(4) PD 293 [1990]. The proprietary rationale also helped to include retirement and pension properties in the joint property. *See* CA 809/90 Lidaei v. Lidaei 46(1) PD 602, 611 [1992].

15 *See* Lifshitz, *supra* note 9, at 655.

16 *See* Ariel Rosen-Zvi, Property Relations between Spouses 232 (1981). ("One cannot also ignore that each element has the ability to influence the legal significance of the other. An extremely atypical marital life could shed a different light on factual circumstances of joint effort.")

17 Dagan, *supra* note 13, at 463.

18 Shahar Lifshitz, *Married Against Their Will? A Liberal Analysis of the Institution of Common Law Spouses*, 25 Tel Aviv U. L. Rev. 741, 794–96, 825–29 (2002).

19 *Shalem*, Nevo, Dec. 13, 2006, at 9.

during the couple's joint life together and without the spouses saying anything about it.[20]

The court determined that sharing is proprietary and immediate during the marriage. Proprietary sharing means that spouses become co-owners of the property even though it is registered in only one of their names. Sometimes sharing was even expanded in case law to include separate property that had belonged to each of the spouses prior to their acquaintance. The sharing does not relate to property that is solely owned by one spouse who is obligated to transfer half of its value to the other spouse. Instead, it relates to joint ownership. Immediate sharing means there is no need for a crisis for co-ownership to arise. It develops as part of the marriage. In practice, the presumption of sharing created rights in family assets, even though these rights are not apparent from the Land Registry.

Such unregistered rights and the resulting uncertainty led to the establishment of the Zussman Committee.[21] The committee recommended an obligatory sharing regime. Accordingly, the spouses' assets are separate during the marriage and each spouse may sell property registered in his or her name without the other's permission. Upon the dissolution of the marriage, a monetary obligation arises between the couple. This is the customary arrangement in most countries, including among them Australia, the United Kingdom, and the United States.

The Israeli Property Relations Law was enacted based on the Zussman Committee recommendations.[22] The statute's introductory remarks indicate that the arrangement adopted by the legislature is a separation of property during the marriage. One spouse in not entitled to any proprietary rights in the other's assets, although the other spouse has a financial obligation towards him or her.[23] This means that spouses apply general property laws that are not affected by family law.

For example, the salary of one spouse that was deposited into a bank account in his or her name belongs only to that spouse as long as they do not divorce. Another example is that a vehicle purchased and registered in the

---

20 This is due to a presumed agreement, but *see* Lifshitz, *supra* note 9, at 655 (arguing that the decisions of the 1960s show that the contractual rationale was more dominant then, while in the 1980s the decisions were more suited to the model of the judicial presumption). But *see id.* at 695 n.242 (indicating that the decisions are not always consistent).

21 Zussman Committee Report, p. 5.

22 *See* Spouses Property Relations Bill, 5729-1969, 849 LSI 333 (1969).

23 For further reading, see Rosen-Zvi, *supra* note 16, at 59–83.

name of one spouse does not belong to the other spouse as long as they do not divorce. The spouse in whose name the vehicle is registered may sell it to a third party without the other spouse's permission.

At the time of the divorce, all property that was registered in the name of one spouse will become shared property, since it was acquired during their joint efforts at the time of the marriage. This is considered a delayed partnership. The legal system aims to balance the couple's property and ensure that each spouse leaves the marriage with equal resources, even though during the marriage each might have owned separate property. This sharing occurs at the time of the divorce and not previously.

The law has another intention in excluding separate assets from property distribution in order to avoid pressuring spouses on the eve of their marriage. Prior to the law, the presumption of sharing had served as a legal basis for including separate assets in shared property.[24] A spouse who entered a marriage with property was concerned that the assets he or she had acquired before the marriage would become marital property. A separate asset could have been left outside of the shared marital property through a written prenuptial agreement.[25]

However, spouses typically refrain from signing such an agreement due to the emotional difficulties involved.[26] In the Property Relations Law, the legislature determined that assets that are not the outcome of a joint effort will remain separate property. The law established an arrangement that attempts to follow the opinion of the majority of the public, and the legislature undoubtedly saw the denial of proprietary sharing as the wish of most of the population.[27]

III. THE *KNOBLER* CASE—A SOLUTION WITH ENDLESS DIFFICULTY

In *Knobler*, the trial court did not apply the Property Relations Law. In that case, two women sought to divorce their husbands and distribute their property, but the court was not authorized by the Property Relations Law to determine that

---

24 Hadari v. Hadari 48(3) PD 685, 694 [1994]; CA 4151/99 Brill v. Brill 55(4) PD 709,716 [2001].

25 *Brill, id.* at 716.

26 *See Knobler, supra* note 4 at 571.

27 *See* Lifshitz, *supra* note 18, at 794–96, 825–29 (arguing that the joint property rule applied even where it was clear that both spouses strictly observed complete separation of their financial matters).

the distribution of property (the financial divorce) would begin before the legal termination of the marriage (the religious divorce).[28] When the law was enacted, religious elements in the legislature were concerned that if the courts ruled on financial divorce before the parties had obtained a religious divorce, one or both spouses could lose motivation to obtain a religious divorce. Thus, they would remain separated without a proper legal divorce,[29] a situation forbidden under Jewish law.

The final version of the law led to the problematic situation that can occur when most of the assets are registered in the name of one spouse who is not interested in allowing the other spouse to enjoy the property distribution. The first spouse might therefore delay the termination of the marriage.[30] Indeed, the trial court in *Knobler* declined to distribute any property because the religious divorce was not final.

Chief Justice Meir Shamgar, President of the Supreme Court of Israel, ruled that there should be simultaneous application of two arrangements with respect to the distribution of the spouses' property: the separation of property under the Property Relations Law and the presumption of sharing (hereinafter referred to together as "simultaneous application"). Simultaneous application revived the Property Relations Law, but at the same time returned to the property sharing arrangement that was applied prior to that law.

Chief Justice Shamgar argued that the *Knobler* trial court was correct in ruling that the foundations of the presumption of sharing had been met with regard to the residential apartment of the parties. Although the apartment had been acquired by the husband before the marriage, the implied agreement between the spouses was that the apartment belonged to both of them in equal shares. The Property Relations Law cannot help the unregistered spouse. Section 5 of this law determines that as long as the couple is in a religious marriage, even if they live separately there is no distribution of their property. Furthermore, according to section 5(a)(1) of the Property Relations Law, separate property is excluded from joint property.

---

28 Such an option was raised in the original bill of Property Relations Law at § 10(4), but was rejected before the law was enacted.

29 *Knobler*, *supra* note 4 at 554; *see also* Shahar Lifshitz, *Family Relationships and Wealth: Challenges and Tasks Following Amendment No. 4 to the Financial Relations Law*, A HUKIM 227 (2009) 227.

30 *See* ROSEN-ZVI, *supra* note 16, at 346–47.

The second justice in the *Knobler* case was Justice Tal.[31] In his opinion the ineffectiveness of the Property Relations Law could not be remedied by bringing back the presumption of sharing because the legislature rejected its application. Justice Tal argued that there was an implied gift between the spouses with regard to their apartment. In his view the acquisition of a gift, unlike an obligation to give a gift, is not required to be in writing.

The third justice, Justice Dorner, concurred with Chief Justice Shamgar that the presumption of sharing should be applied to the parties' apartment.[32]

The fourth justice, Justice Strasberg-Cohen, argued that the arrangement set forth in the Property Relations Law rejects the presumption of sharing.[33] She proposed applying the law prior to religious divorce, so that property distribution could be made after a crisis in the couple's relationship. Thus contrary to the majority of the court, she proposed a broad and flexible interpretation of the general law of gifts, contracts, and property. In her view, the husband should be seen as giving his wife half of the apartment as a gift. She thus concurred with the result reached by Chief Justice Shamgar and Justice Dorner, but not for the same reasons.

Justice Matza was the fifth justice in this decision. In his opinion, the Property Relations Law could not coexist with the presumption of sharing and the ineffectiveness of the law would have to be resolved through legislation.[34] Moreover, he argued that there was no gift and the wife was not entitled to half of the apartment.[35]

Analysis of the *Knobler* case leads to some conclusions that are important for the recommendations that follow. First, the majority opinion is that the presumption of sharing does not apply simultaneously with the Property Relations Law. Second, there is no majority in favor of flexibility in the general law, including the laws of gifts, contracts, and property. Justice Strasberg-Cohen was the only one with this opinion. Third, even if one wanted to argue that the majority of justices supported the simultaneous applicability and flexibility of property law, this judicial development is not what the legislature intended.

---

31 *Knobler, supra* note 4 at 587.

32 *Id.* at 606.

33 *Id.* at 612.

34 *Id.* at 628.

35 See M. A. Ravilo, *The Gift Law, 1968-5728, in* Interpretation of Contract Law 20–21, 78 (1978).

This development resulted from the ineffectiveness of the Property Relations Law because property distribution, or financial divorce, is dependent upon religious divorce. Fourth, the *Knobler* judgment addresses only the relationship between spouses, and not the relationship between spouses and third parties such as creditors. Taking this into consideration, one can further examine how the *Knobler* case later shaped the property relations between spouses in Israel.

IV. THE CASE LAW THAT FOLLOWED THE *KNOBLER* CASE

A. The *Abu Romi* Case—An Obiter Dictum Becomes Precedent

Mr. and Mrs. Abu Romi are Muslims who were married in 1982.[36] The couple had seven minor children who were in the wife's care. They lived with her in the apartment where the couple had lived since their marriage. The apartment was the husband's inheritance, and he was the sole registered owner. The *Abu Romi* trial court applied the Property Relations Law, under which separate property is not included in the distribution of property. The wife appealed to the Supreme Court. Justice Strasberg-Cohen determined that for the purpose of identifying family property ownership, the presumption of sharing should not be applied. Instead there should be a flexible interpretation of general law.[37]

Although section 5(a)(1) of the Property Relations Law states that the assets of the spouses prior to the marriage are separate property, that is only the determination according to family law. In Justice Strasberg-Cohen's opinion, that does not prevent a spouse from claiming rights in separate property based on general law.[38] Then Justice Strasberg-Cohen unnecessarily declared that under general law, specific intent is required and a common household is not sufficient to establish co-ownership of the residential apartment.

The *Abu Romi* judgment, which serves as the foundation for dozens of later rulings, presents three difficulties. First, Justice Strasberg-Cohen erroneously refers to her opinion in *Knobler* as if it had been accepted by the majority. Increased flexibility of the general law was a minority opinion. Indeed, the flexibility of the general law was not the issue in *Abu Romi*. The issue was rather the

---

36 *See Abu Romi*, 56(6) PD 175.

37 *Id.* at 181. She bases her decision on her opinion in *Knobler*, 49(3) PD at 621; *see also* FamC 11560/04 N.B. v. N.M., Nevo, Aug. 8, 2006.

38 *Abu Romi*, 56(6) PD at 182.

applicability of the presumption of sharing. Second, Justice Strasberg-Cohen's statement regarding what the ruling would have been if Mrs. Abu Romi had relied on general law and proved her argument is obiter dictum. Mrs. Abu Romi made no claims for sharing under general law.

Notably, this did not prevent later judgements from relying on *Abu Romi* as a precedent for the sharing of separate property. Third, Justice Strasberg-Cohen tries to emphasize the differentiation between the flexibility of general law and the presumption of sharing, although the two are similar. Indeed, one may doubt how such a narrow distinction can set a binding precedent, since in practice the two really cannot be distinguished.

B. An Asset Registered in the Name of One Spouse Is Held to Be a Shared Asset

Two cases that are referred to as *Anonymous v. Anonymous*, one reported in 2006 and the other in 2007, further interpreted the law of distribution of marital property. The first *Anonymous* case is a challenging one.[39] The couple became married in 1981 and lived in the husband's apartment, which was registered only in his name. After about nineteen years, the husband left the apartment and the couple divorced. The wife claimed half ownership of the apartment. The trial court ruled that despite the Property Relations Law, the wife was entitled to claim her share of the apartment under the general law if she could establish her rights under that law.

Here, however, after the first two years of marriage the couple did not establish a loving or normal family relationship. Therefore, the court dismissed the wife's claim. The wife appealed to the district court. The district court determined that there was a basis for sharing between the spouses since they had tried some fertility treatments and the wife had given part of her monthly salary to the husband. The district court further determined that when one spouse brings an apartment to the marriage and the couple live in it, the first spouse creates a representation to the other that the apartment is joint property unless a different intention is expressed. The court therefore ordered that the apartment would be distributed equally.

The Supreme Court rejected the husband's request for appeal, in accordance with its decision in *Knobler*. The reference to *Knobler* is unclear, as flexible interpretation of property law was only a minority opinion in that case.

---

39 FamC 4951/06 Anonymous v. Anonymous, Nevo, June 14, 2006.

Especially unclear is the reliance on *Abu Romi*, where Justice Strasberg-Cohen's reasoning concerning how the general law should be applied was obiter dictum. Even assuming that the flexibility of the general law doctrine had been previously accepted, the district court's reasoning in *Anonymous* leaves the impression that it relied upon the presumption of sharing, rather than on the general law.

The district court did not determine that the husband intended to share the apartment with his wife or that he promised her half of the apartment, but based its decision on their shared household. Living together is the foundation of the presumption of sharing and not of a specific general law.[40] In addition, in order to prove sharing under general law, the burden of proof is on the applicant who submits the claim for sharing. In *Anonymous*, the burden of proof was on the husband, who wished to prevent the sharing, similar to the burden of proof under the presumption of sharing rather than under the general law.

The second *Anonymous* case demonstrates that although the court addresses general law, it in fact applies the presumption of sharing. The couple were married in 1978.[41] The district court held that the residential apartment was co-owned, although it was registered in the husband's name. In rejecting the appeal, the Supreme Court cited the district court's main reasoning, according to which:

> the couple lived in the apartment for many years, they raised two children there, the wife worked and helped to support the house and the family, and had also invested her own money in renovating the apartment. ... [These facts] all indicate an intent of sharing and including the apartment in the distribution of property.[42]

The Supreme Court added that the husband's argument that he did not intend to create joint ownership in the apartment had not been proven, because he did not explicitly express such an intention for twenty-two years.

Reading these arguments, it seems that the district courts determined the sharing of the separate asset under the presumption of sharing and not under the general law. Their arguments are broad and rely on an assumption that after

---

40 Some courts required a broad evidentiary basis in order to apply the *Knobler* judgment; *e.g.*, FamC 52666-11-10 A.L. v. A.L., Nevo, June 23, 2013.

41 FamC 10734/06 Anonymous v. Anonymous, Nevo, Mar. 14, 2007.

42 *Id.*

many years there is probably an intention of sharing. An assumption of sharing because of a shared household is the foundation of the presumption of sharing. Furthermore, the courts noted that the burden of proof was on the husband who wished to prevent the sharing, and not the wife who sought joint ownership. This allocation of the burden of proof is a commonly accepted feature of the presumption of sharing.

Apparently, the courts have somehow established a norm which states that a separate asset registered in the name of one spouse becomes a shared asset after many years of living together. This norm is contrary to the explicit wording of section 5(a)(1) of the Property Relations Law, and is not in accordance with either the general law or with Supreme Court precedents.

The following interesting pattern emerges from analysis of the judgments. A minority opinion in the *Knobler* case related to flexibility of the general law with respect to separate assets. It was followed by an obiter dictum in *Abu Romi* and they both brought about a binding precedent in the two *Anonymous* judgments. It was determined that a separate asset registered in the name of one spouse can become joint property.

The thin line between implementation of flexible general law (such as the gift law and the general property laws) and application of the presumption of sharing has been completely blurred. This creates a real concern over indirectly bringing back an undue emphasis on the presumption of sharing. This approach of the court continued. In each of the following judgments one can see a further development, when an unregistered spouse's rights prevailed over the claims of the registered spouse's creditors. An alternative interpretation is that from a practical perspective, Chief Justice Shamgar's opinion in *Knobler* became more accepted. It is important to mention that this view was also obiter dictum. It therefore should not have been adopted later as precedent.

C. The *Simchoni* Case—A Separate Asset Registered in the Name of Its Owner and Held by Creditors

Mr. and Mrs. Simchoni were married in 1980.[43] For twenty-six years they lived in an apartment that was registered solely in the husband's name. In 2000, he mortgaged the apartment. Later, the wife requested recognition of her co-ownership of the apartment. The Supreme Court ruled that the wife had

43 CA 11120/07 Simchoni v. Bank Hapoalim Inc., Nevo, Dec. 28, 2009.

invested in the apartment, and therefore a specific intention of shared ownership in the apartment could be assumed.

The question was which of the transactions prevailed: (a) the first one, in which the husband's implied intention of sharing entitled his wife to half the ownership rights in the apartment; or (b) the second one, in which the husband mortgaged all of his rights in the apartment. The court held that the wife's rights, which were prior in time, prevailed unless the husband's transaction with the bank was registered and the bank acted in good faith.[44]

This decision is surprising. Under the regime of the Property Relations Law and in contrast to the presumption of sharing, there is no expectation that the bank would assume that the spouses had a specific intention to share. However, under the Property Relations Law the bank should take into account the rights of both spouses in the family residence, and not only those of the spouse in whose name it is registered.

Although the Supreme Court explicitly stated that *Simchoni* was not determined according to the presumption of sharing, its reasoning suggests otherwise. It based the judgment on the assumption of an intention to share, although the husband did not make an explicit statement that he wished to do so. Sharing a household and investments in the property are the foundations of the presumption of sharing. This decision further blurs the boundary between intention to share under the general law and the presumption of sharing.

D. The *Ben Giat* Case—Reinstatement of the Presumption of Sharing

A new legal rule was set forth in the case of *Ben Giat*.[45] In that judgment, the Supreme Court decision contrasts with the legislature's intention in the Property Relations Law. The couple were married in 1980. In 1982, the husband bought an apartment that was registered only in his name. The first apartment was the husband's separate asset. In 1990, the couple bought a second apartment, located next to the first apartment, and registered it in both their names. The two apartments were combined into one larger apartment.

44 The court based its decision on Land Law § 9 (1969): "If a person undertook an obligation for a real estate transaction and before the transaction was completed by registration, that person made another obligation to another individual for a contradictory transaction, the right of the individual in the first transaction is preferential; but if the second individual acted in good faith and for value and the transaction was registered while he remained in good faith— his right is preferential."

45 CA 7750/10 Ben Giat v. ILD, Nevo, Aug. 11, 2011.

In 1997, the husband mortgaged the first apartment for a loan he received from the Israel Development Corporation (ILD). In May 2001, the couple divorced. The wife filed a lawsuit requesting a declaratory judgment concerning her full rights in the first apartment. The request was based on the presumption of sharing, even though the Property Relations Law was applicable to the couple's marriage.

Justice Amit wrote the majority opinion, ruling that the wife's rights to half of the first apartment must be recognized under the presumption of sharing. In addition, the wife's rights prevailed over the ILD's registered mortgage.[46] In his view, there was a presumption of sharing, even if the Property Relations Law was applicable.[47] Justice Amit discussed the competition between a registered mortgage and the spouse's right in a residential apartment under the presumption of sharing. He ruled that based on the *Ben-Zvi* case[48] and the *Shalem* case,[49] the wife's right prevailed.

Neither of the decisions used as precedent in *Ben Giat* ruled that the presumption of sharing applied to a couple who married after January 1974, when the Property Relations Law was enacted and the presumption of sharing was superseded. The *Ben-Zvi* and *Shalem* cases concern spouses who married before 1974. In addition, although *Ben-Zvi* concerns a separate asset, *Shalem* concerns an asset purchased with the funds of the couple but registered only in the husband's name. Therefore, *Shalem* should not have been used as precedent in *Ben Giat,* which concerned a separate asset.

Proof of sharing between spouses under the presumption of sharing is easier to achieve because it requires less evidence than the idea of sharing under the general law. Nevertheless, since the *Ben Giat* ruling, every company or professional creditor must be concerned. The likelihood of a ruling that property is shared between spouses is greater under the presumption of sharing than it was pursuant to the "specific transaction between spouses" rule under the Property Relations Law.

Ostensibly a creditor is entitled to assume that the Property Relations Law is valid in light of the extensive and continuous case law determining that the presumption of sharing does not apply to spouses who were married after 1974. A creditor is also entitled to assume that the applicable law is as set forth

---

46 *Id.* at 11.

47 *Id.* at 13.

48 CA 3002/92 Ben-Zvi v. Sitin 49(3) PD 5 [1995].

49 *Shalem,* Nevo, Dec. 13, 2006.

in section 5(a)(1) of the Property Relations Law, according to which separate assets are not shared. Therefore, a creditor should not have to be concerned about possible spousal property rights that are not apparent from the Land Registry.

Justice Rubinstein wrote in the minority opinion in *Ben Giat* that the mere existence of a shared household during marriage is not sufficient to establish co-ownership in a residential apartment under the general law. Such a decision indirectly brings back the presumption of sharing. Justice Rubinstein ruled that the creditor's rights prevailed.[50]

Justice Vogelman was the third justice in the *Ben-Giat* case. He faced a fundamental difference of opinion between the other two justices. They disagreed on whether the right to share originates in the presumption of sharing or in the general law. This has far-reaching consequences on issues including (a) the amount of evidence required to prove sharing; (b) whether the obligations of each spouse are shared by both of them; and (c) the degree of responsibility of the creditor. Thus Justice Vogelman should have made a determination, but he chose not to do so. The third justice on a panel bears a great responsibility when the other two disagree with each other.

Although Justice Vogelman explicitly stated that he would not decide between the other two justices, one sees by reading between the lines that he believes the presumption of sharing would apply to spouses who were married after January 1974. This may, therefore, have established a majority in favor of simultaneous application of the presumption of sharing and the Property Relations Law.

In summary, the *Knobler* case preserved the Property Relations Law at the time, allowing a financial divorce without a religious divorce. The difficulty is that the cases that followed *Knobler* relied too heavily upon that decision. As a result, the other provisions of the Property Relations Law and in particular its rationale became irrelevant. Some of the judgments referred to general law and indirectly brought back the presumption of sharing. Some brought back the presumption of sharing more directly.

The result is that contrary to the language of the Property Relations Law, separate property may become community property while the spouses live in a shared household. Rights that are not apparent from the Land Registry have returned. Spouses and creditors have become uncertain in evaluating their rights and the Property Relations Law has become ineffective.

---

50 *Id.* at 14.

E. Family Court Case Law

Some family courts have applied the ruling in the *Knobler* case, which is without simultaneous application of the presumption of sharing and the Property Relations Law.[51] Other courts have required an element in addition to a shared household, in order to prove sharing. For example, when one spouse who was the owner of a separate asset claimed a share of the other spouse's separate asset, sharing was not recognized.[52] In contrast, some courts have ruled in favor of simultaneous application even if a couple were married after 1973.[53]

Other courts that have not specifically ruled out simultaneous application have stated that they would not discuss it because the parties did not make that claim.[54] Some courts have steadily increased the flexibility of the general law, making it similar to the presumption of sharing, without saying so explicitly. They have ruled in favor of sharing separate assets.[55] Some courts have based their decisions primarily on a long duration of a shared, although inharmonious, household. They also determined the sharing of separate assets other than the residential apartment.[56] With no single leading decision, uncertainty remains. The model offered in part VII of this chapter might remedy all of these concerns.

V. THE LAW IN THE UNITED KINGDOM

According to the law in the United Kingdom, marriage or any other form of legally binding relationship has no direct or immediate effect on the property of each of the spouses. Ownership of property remains that of the sole acquirer, unless purchased jointly. United Kingdom property law determines that husband and wife are two separate legal entities for any property-related purpose.[57] Therefore, one spouse does not have any legal right in assets that belong to the other spouse such as pre-matrimonial assets. Marriage does not

51 *E.g.*, CC 1074/95 Nahir v. Nahir PD 32(3) 856; CC (Jer) 1595/96 Montelio v. Montelio, Nevo, Aug. 31, 1998; FamC 110/02 A.B.L. v. H.B.L., Nevo, Sept. 27, 2006; FamC 87173/97 R.F v. R.F, Nevo, June 27, 2007; FamC 32105-05-10 A.G.S. v. S.A.S., Nevo, June 25, 2012.

52 FamC 31324-01-11 A.A. v. R.A, Nevo, May 5, 2015.

53 *E.g.*, FamC 027722/01 N.D. v. N.R., Nevo, Oct. 14, 2007.

54 *E.g.*, FamC 12950/03 D.M. v. R.M., Nevo, Jan. 21, 2008.

55 *E.g.*, FamC 22780/05 H.D. v. Y.D, Nevo, July 11, 2007.

56 *E.g.*, FamC 3591/02 S.C v. H.C, Nevo, Dec. 5, 2007.

57 Law of Property Act,1925, *available at* http://www.legislation.gov.uk/ukpga/Geo5/15-16/20.

establish co-ownership or entitle an individual to any rights in the spouse's assets.[58] However, ownership might change upon the dissolution of a marriage. The financial consequences of divorce in the United Kingdom are regulated in part 2 of the Matrimonial Causes Act (MCA).[59] It essentially determines that property division, referred to as "ancillary relief," is subject to the discretion of the court.

Under Israeli law, the courts were unable to give effect to these economic consequences of divorce because the law requires religious divorce with spousal consent. Such requirements are irrelevant under United Kingdom matrimonial property law, in which marriage and divorce are of a civil nature and therefore may be altered at the court's discretion.[60] However, as in the Israeli Property Relations Law, community of property is also obligatory in the United Kingdom and valid only upon the dissolution of a marriage. Thus the decisions of the courts with respect to division of property are only financial, and do not retroactively create co-ownership.[61] Consequently, the ownership of family assets remains clear during and upon dissolution of the marriage. One spouse cannot bring a claim of right in a separate asset purchased by a third party from the other spouse during the marriage.

Upon divorce, the courts in the United Kingdom have broad discretion for the distribution of property, including reallocation or sale of property, periodic payments, lump sum payments, and pension-sharing orders.[62] This distribution

---

58 Generally, the conduct of the spouses will not affect property ownership status, and will not result in co-ownership. An exception to this rule is found in the Married Women's Property Act 1964, *available at* http://www.legislation.gov.uk/ukpga/1964/19/enacted, which states that property purchased with an allowance provided by the husband to his wife for house maintenance shall be co-owned. *See* Law Commission, *Family Law: Matrimonial Property* 5–7, 1988, https://www.gov.uk/government/uploads/system/uploads/attachment data/ file/ 235805/0009.pdf.

59 Matrimonial Causes Act, 1973, *available at* http://www.legislation.gov.uk/ukpga/1973/18/ contents (hereinafter MCA).

60 *Id.* at pt. 1, § 1(4): "If the court is satisfied on the evidence of any such fact as is mentioned in subsection (2) above [listing the bases for determining irretrievable breakdown of a marriage] it shall ... grant a decree of divorce." Pt. 2, § 23(1) lists decrees that may be granted by the court: "a decree of divorce, a decree of nullity of marriage or a decree of judicial separation"

61 *National Provincial Bank Ltd. v. Ainsworth,* [1965] AC 1175 (H.L.), 1247–48 (appeal taken from England): "Before a right or an interest can be admitted into the category of property, or of a right affecting property, it must be definable, identifiable by third parties, capable in its nature of assumption by third parties, and have some degree of permanence or stability. The wife's right has none of these qualities, it is characterized by the reverse of them."

62 MCA, pt. 2, §§ 21–24.

method has several similarities to Israeli law. For example, sharing of property is obligatory and not proprietary. Second, it is only effective at dissolution of the marriage and unable to occur during the marriage.

United Kingdom law, however, differs from Israeli law in that it does not establish a default rule of equal distribution.[63] Part 2, section 25 of the MCA establishes guidelines that direct judicial discretion, the first of which is the well-being of minor children and the family.[64] The provision does not specify a general principle for distribution. It states that the court's decision shall be based on the overall circumstances including the length of the marriage, the previous standard of living, the ages of the spouses, and their assets.[65] The existence of a prenuptial agreement is considered by the court, but the court is not obliged to enforce it.[66] The law does not define or refer to either community property or property accumulated by one spouse before the marriage.

Until 2000, the policy of the courts in the United Kingdom with respect to division of property was to grant one spouse an amount of the other spouse's assets that was sufficient to meet his or her "reasonable requirements."[67] Furthermore, in 1996 the Court of Appeals rejected the decision that equality should be a guiding principle for division of property.[68] In 2000, in the constitutive ruling of *White v. White*,[69] the House of Lords established the overriding principle of fairness that should guide the courts in dividing property upon divorce.[70] It

---

63 As explained *infra*, note 80 and accompanying text, the British House of Lords first addressed equality as a parameter for distribution in its decision in White v. White, [2001] 1 AC (H.L.) 596 (appeal taken from England), [2000] 2 FLR 981.

64 MCA, pt. 2, § 25: "[The court is] to have regard to all the circumstances of the case, first consideration being given to the welfare while a minor of any child of the family who has not attained the age of eighteen."

65 MCA, pt. 2, 25; for details, *see* Anne Barlow, *Community of Property—The Logical Response to Miller and McFarlane*? 39 BRACTON L. J. 19 (2007).

66 In contrast to Israeli law, which determines that the Property Relations Law is residual to any prenuptial agreement; *see K v K (Ancillary Relief: Prenuptial Agreement)*, [2003] 1 FLR 120.

67 Dart v. Dart, [1996] 2 FLR 286.

68 *Id.*

69 White v. White, [2001] 1 AC (H.L.) 596 (appeal taken from England), [2000] 2 FLR 981.

70 *Id.* at 596: "Everyone would accept that the outcome of these matters, whether by agreement or court order should be fair. More realistically, the outcome ought to be as fair as is possible in all the circumstances. But everyone's life is different. Features which are important when assessing fairness differ in each case. And sometimes different minds can reach different conclusions on what fairness requires. Then fairness, like beauty, lies in the eye of the beholder. ... In consequence, the legislation does not state explicitly what is to be the aim of the courts... Implicitly, the objective must be to achieve a fair outcome."

was further determined that separate (non-matrimonial) assets should remain separate.[71]

"Fairness" is a vague concept, insufficient to provide guidance to the courts. In the 2006 ruling of *Miller v. Miller,* the House of Lords established three guiding rationales for the concept of fairness: needs (of the spouses and their children), compensation (for disadvantages caused by dissolution of the marriage), and sharing.[72]

Accordingly, the court first acts to fulfill all of the needs of the spouses and their dependents, and to provide required compensation. After all needs are satisfied and if the assets exceed the needs of the spouses, the court divides the remaining assets equitably, taking into account the origin of the assets for the benefit of their respective owners. In contrast to Israeli law, equal sharing is not the rule for distribution of property, but only one of its guiding principles.[73]

In *Miller,* the Lords address the term *non-matrimonial property*[74] and state that community (matrimonial) property should be distinguished from separate (non-matrimonial) property. According to *Miller,* the starting point is that premarital assets and gifts or inheritances received during the marriage should not be included in the distribution of property between the spouses at divorce. In contrast, the matrimonial home, even if brought to the marriage by one of the spouses, should be treated as matrimonial property.[75]

---

71 *Id.* at 610: "Property acquired before marriage and inherited property acquired during marriage come from a source wholly external to the marriage. In fairness, where this property still exists, the spouse to whom it was given should be allowed to keep it. Conversely, the other spouse has a weaker claim to such property than he or she may have regarding matrimonial property." For further reading see Jens M. Scherpe, *Comparative Overview of the Treatment of Non-Matrimonial Assets, Indexation and Value Increases,* 25 CHILD & FAM. L.Q. 61, 73 (2013).

72 Miller v. Miller and McFarlane v. McFarlane, [2006] UKHL 24, [2006] 2 AC 618, [2006] 1 FLR 1186 (hereinafter *Miller*; the *MacFarlane* case was an appeal conjoined with *Miller*).

73 *Id.* at 16: "This "equal sharing" principle derives from the basic concept of equality permeating a marriage as understood today. Marriage, it is often said, is a partnership of equals. … [W]hen their partnership ends each is entitled to an equal share of the assets of the partnership, unless there is a good reason to the contrary. Fairness requires no less. But I emphasize the qualifying phrase: "unless there is good reason to the contrary." The yardstick of equality is to be applied as an aid, not a rule.

74 *Id.* at 21–25.

75 *Id.* at 22: "The statute requires the court to have regard to all the circumstances of the case. One of the circumstances is that there is a real difference, a difference of source, between (1) property acquired during the marriage otherwise than by inheritance or gift, sometimes called the marital acquits but more usually the matrimonial property, and (2) other property. The former is the financial product of the parties' common endeavor, the latter is not.

In the *Miller* case, the parties were divorced after a short marriage and the husband had a premarital fortune. The House of Lords ruled that the property exceeded the needs of the couple, and therefore it considered each spouse's contribution to the capital. The husband received 60 percent of the assets and the wife received 40 percent. Thus the court also balanced and shared the non-matrimonial assets between the spouses, although not fully. The impact of this ruling is reflected in the English court judgments during the following years. Separate assets were divided, although unequally distributed.[76]

The *Charman* case[77] was a classic case of a married couple that established a successful business through a joint effort. While the husband took care of "external affairs" concerning the prosperity of the business, the wife was in charge of the "internal affairs" concerning the household and children. The business was successful so that after twenty-eight years of marriage, the family fortune was valued at £131 million. Mrs. Charman demanded 45 percent of the assets. Mr. Charman argued that due to his main contribution to the business establishment, the starting point should not be equal distribution, but that the burden of proof should be on Mrs. Charman to demonstrate her share in the assets.[78]

The appellate court ruled that generally the principle of equal sharing, which is one of the pillars of fairness, applies only with respect to matrimonial assets.[79] However, if the property is insufficient to meet a spouse's needs, no distinction between matrimonial and non-matrimonial assets should be made. All

---

The parties' matrimonial home, even if this was brought into the marriage at the outset by one of the parties, usually has a central place in any marriage. So it should normally be treated as matrimonial property for this purpose." For further reading, see Mary Welstead, *Judicial Reform or an Increase in Discretion—The Decision in Miller V Miller; McFarlane V McFarlane*, 2008 INT'L SURV. FAM. L. 61 (2008).

76 *See* Scherpe, *supra* note 71, at 75, as well as the following rulings: B v B (Ancillary Relief), [2008] EWCA Civ 543; McCartney v Mills McCartney, [2008] EWHC 401 (Fam), [2008] 1 FLR 1508.

77 Charman v. Charman (No 4), [2007] EWCA Civ 503, [2007] 1 FLR 1246.

78 *Id.* at 5–6.

79 *Id.* at 66: "To what property does the sharing principle apply? The answer might well have been that it applies only to matrimonial property, namely the property of the parties generated during the marriage otherwise than by external donation; and the consequence would have been that non-matrimonial property would have fallen for redistribution by reference only to one of the two other principles of need and compensation." See also Joanna Miles, *Charman V Charman (No 4)—Making Sense of Need, Compensation and Equal Sharing After Miller/McFarlane*, 20 CHILD & FAM. Q. 378, 381 (2008).

assets are included in distribution in order to satisfy the needs of the spouses.[80] Classification of matrimonial and non-matrimonial property is required only when the assets exceed the needs.

In the courts in the United Kingdom today, two approaches affect the certainty of spouses regarding non-matrimonial property.[81] The first and more conservative approach strictly adheres to the wording of the MCA, opposes limiting judicial discretion, and therefore avoids classifying property as matrimonial or non-matrimonial. In other words, all of the spouses' assets are taken into consideration in the balancing of resources, and non-matrimonial assets might cause the court to deviate from the determination of equal property distribution.[82]

The second approach provides more guidance for the court's discretion by fundamentally separating non-matrimonial property from the distribution. The starting point according to this approach is that non-matrimonial assets are not included in the division of property between the spouses unless fairness or specific economic needs suggest otherwise.[83] It thus provides greater certainty regarding the distribution of the assets by the court.

In *Jones v. Jones*,[84] an example of the second approach, the court ruled that a non-matrimonial asset should be valued upon the dissolution of the marriage, and therefore the spouse who owned that asset could solely enjoy the profit from the asset during the marriage.[85] The court emphasized that generally there is no reason for equal distribution of separate, non-matrimonial assets that were not acquired through the joint efforts of the spouses.

In February 2014, the Law Commission of England and Wales issued a report calling for clearer regulation of matrimonial relations, in order to provide more certainty, transparency, and uniformity in divorce proceedings.[86] With regard to sharing of non-matrimonial assets, the Commission supported the second approach whereby separate property should be distinguished from

---

80 *Miller*, [2006] UKHL 24, 23; *see* Miles, *supra* note 79, at 8.

81 *See* Scherpe, *supra* note 71, at 75. For further reading see Chandler, *The Law is Now Reasonably Clear: The Courts' Approach to Non-Matrimonial Assets*, [2012] FAM. LAW 163.

82 *E.g.*, Robson v. Robson, [2011] 1 FLR 751.

83 *Id.*; *see* K v. L (Non-Matrimonial Property: Special Contribution), [2011] EWCA Civ 550, [2011] 2 FLR 980.

84 Jones v. Jones, [2011] EWCA 41.

85 The *Jones* court referred to this income as a "springboard effect." The husband's investment prior to the marriage affected his profits after the marriage. *See id.* 38–44.

86 Law Commission, *Matrimonial Property, Needs and Agreements*, 2014, *available at* http://www.lawcom.gov.uk/project/matrimonial-property-needs-and-agreements/.

community property, thus creating legal clarity.[87] The Commission tried to formulate an amendment to include a clear and comprehensive definition of non-matrimonial property.[88]

In addition, the Commission discussed the conditions under which separate property could become community property.[89] Due to differences of opinion, the Commission did not recommend any reform. In its view, since classification of assets is relevant only when assets exceed needs, it is relevant to a minority of cases. The Commission's main recommendation was broader recognition of prenuptial agreements by the courts, enabling spouses to determine the distribution principles.[90]

In conclusion, the law in the United Kingdom is that marriage does not establish co-ownership of property between spouses. During a marriage, the assets of the spouses are separate. Each is entitled to manage his or her separate property[91] and registration may grant ownership rights according to law, very close to the Israeli Property Relations Law. Upon dissolution of a marriage, however, the court is authorized to balance the resources between the spouses while considering the three parameters of needs, compensation, and equality. There are two schools of thought regarding the breadth of the courts' discretion, but in contrast to Israeli law, neither supports a priori equal distribution.

The law does not exclude non-matrimonial assets from the distribution, nor does it give them full protection as property of the spouse who brought them to the marriage. Non-matrimonial assets are not protected from being used to provide for the needs and compensation of the spouses. However, with respect to the third parameter of equal sharing, the court considers the existence of non-matrimonial assets, which usually are not distributed.

VI. THE LAW IN THE UNITED STATES

In the United States, the financial consequences of the dissolution of a marriage are regulated by state legislatures. Most jurisdictions (forty-one states and Washington, D.C.) are common law or separate property states (hereinafter referred to

87 *Id.* at 174.
88 *Id.* at 160–65.
89 *Id.* at 166–72.
90 *Id.* at 160.
91 *Barclays Bank v. O'Brien*, [1993] UKHL 6, [1994] 1 AC 198.

as "separate property states").[92] In these states, there is no automatic joint ownership, and the starting point is that property, whether brought by one spouse to the marriage or purchased during the marriage, belongs to the initial owner or purchaser unless an intention to share it has been explicitly expressed.[93]

Any obligatory sharing is deferred until the marriage is dissolved. A spouse is not granted co-ownership rights in property, but is entitled at most to only half its value. Just distribution is made after the termination of the marriage, similar to the law in England and in contrast to equal distribution under the Property Relations Law in Israel.

In principle, the spouses are free to act as they please regarding their separate property, but legislation or case law have determined restrictions, primarily in order to protect the other spouse's rights in the matrimonial home. Thus the consent of both spouses may be required for transfer or pledge of their residence.[94] The law in some states also provides some protection to a spouse from execution on the common residential home by creditors.[95]

The nine remaining states, including among them Arizona, California, Nevada, and Texas, are community property states. The starting point in these states contrasts with that of the separate property states and is similar to the presumption of sharing, which was the proprietary arrangement in Israel before enactment of the Property Relations Law. In these states, community of property is immediate from the acquisition of the asset or the creation of sharing, with regard to property accumulated during marriage. Sharing is reflected in joint management of the property. Each spouse has the right to manage and perform transactions in joint assets, while important transactions as specified by

92 Emily Osborn, *Treatment of Unearned Separate Property at Divorce in Common Law Property Jurisdictions*, 1990 Wis. L. Rev. 903, 909 (1990).

93 *E.g.*, New York: N.Y. Dom. Rel. Law § 236. For more information see American Law Institute, *Principles of the Law of Family Dissolution: Analysis and Recommendations*, 8 Duke J. Gender L. 1 (2001) (hereinafter ALI Report). (The common law treated property owned by the spouses during the marriage as the individual property of one of them unless, as to a particular piece of property, the spouses had acted to create joint ownership. The title in which property was held was critical.)

94 See Mary Ann Glendon, The Transformation of Family Law: State, Law, and Family in the United States and Western Europe 130 (1989): "Even though both spouses are in principle free to deal with their property as they wish, their powers are somewhat restricted in many states by statutes and case law doctrines developed to protect the other spouse's rights to a share in inheritance and by Homestead laws which require the consent of both spouses to conveyances and encumbrances of the land on which the family home is located."

95 *Id.* at 130: "Homestead laws also assure a spouse a certain amount of protection, which varies from state to state, from execution on the matrimonial home by creditors."

law require the approval of both spouses.[96] In contrast, separate assets acquired prior to the marriage or received during the marriage (such as inheritances or gifts) remain solely owned by the recipient spouse.[97]

This dichotomy between the two regimes is less significant today than in the past,[98] since at the time of the termination of a marriage the court in all jurisdictions is authorized to divide the couple's assets, in whole or in part.[99] Division of property is made under the doctrine of equitable distribution.[100] Each state has established by law the criteria considered by the court at the time of distribution, but in all states distribution is made in a fair and sensible way, according to the court's discretion, and not necessarily equally.[101]

The goal of distribution is to meet the economic needs of the parties and reduce the payment of alimony by dividing the community property. Courts are also entitled to order the payment of maintenance for rehabilitation or compensation for needs that cannot be met by the division of assets. The courts usually prefer to rely on prenuptial agreements, if any, as long as these are in accordance with applicable law.[102]

---

96 *Id.* at 123: "[E]ither spouse acting alone, may deal with community property, joinder of both spouses being required only for certain important transactions, such as purchase, conveyance, or encumbrance of community real estate."

97 *Id.* at 142.

98 Unif. Marital Prop. Act, Prefatory Note (1998, as amended): "Common law states have been moving closer and closer to the sharing concept in both divorce and probate legislation, and the Uniform Marital Property Act builds on the direction of that movement."

99 *E.g.*, Colorado: Colo. Rev. Stat. § 46-1-13, and Washington, D.C.: D.C. Code § 16-910. For more information about the differences between states see J. Thomas Oldham, *Changes in the Economic Consequences of Divorces, 1958–2008*, 42 Fam. L.Q. 419 (2008).

100 Oldham, *id.* at 429: "This sharp dichotomy between common law and community property traditions no longer prevails in the United States. All the common-law states now allow the divorce court to distribute the spouse's property between them on a basis other than common-law principles of ownership, under a doctrine known generally as "equitable distribution." Five of the eight community property states also instruct their divorce courts to divide the community property between the spouses "equitably" (rather than "equally"). Equitable distribution is therefore the dominant rule today, followed everywhere but in the three "equal division" community property states."

101 Exceptions to the equitable distribution rule are California, Louisiana, and New Mexico, which apply a principle of equal division. ALI Report, *supra* note 93, at 20.

102 *See* Raymond C. O'Brien, *Integrating Marital Property into a Spouse's Elective Share*, 59 Cath. U. L. Rev. 617, 687 (2009): "At divorce, there are similarities between community-property and separate-property states. First, both community and separate-property states seek to meet the economic expectations of the parties at dissolution through existing community (marital) assets, thus curtailing ongoing support obligations. Second, a court may order support to enable rehabilitation of one of the parties or, if rehabilitation

As mentioned above, the difference between the two groups of states is at the starting point of separation or sharing of assets, which influences the nature of the equitable distribution. For example, in community property states, equitable distribution is also made in the event of the death of one spouse, while in common law states equitable distribution is made only upon dissolution of marriage. Another difference is in the method of distribution, including the questions of whether the starting point is an equal division and which assets are within the community distribution "pool."[103] In community property states, there is a strict policy of equal distribution, but also a careful distinction regarding the separation of separate assets.[104]

With respect to the assets found in the distribution pool, in most states the basic principle distinguishes between community property which is included in the distribution pool, and separate assets which are not.[105] This is similar to the

---

is impossible, to compensate that party for what a division of existing marital assets cannot provide. The latter procedure is referred to as reimbursement. Third, private contracting to fix the rights of adult parties through prenuptial or postnuptial agreements is preferred, but the contracts must be executed in accordance with statutory guidelines."

103 *See* ALI Report, *supra* note 93, at 20: "In community property states, the concept of joint ownership is pervasive, applicable not only at dissolution but also at death and during the intact marriage. The common law states, in contrast, generally retain their traditional separate ownership principles in all matters other than the system of equitable distribution they apply at divorce. These different starting points in the basic underlying concepts of ownership may yield differences in the application of equitable distribution rules that are similar in form. The two most critical features of any law of equitable distribution are its rules for identifying which spousal-owned property is within the pool available to the divorce court to allocate on equitable grounds, and its default or presumptive allocation rule. The trend in equitable division states has favored a presumption, whether formal or in practice, that an equitable division of property is an equal division, but not all states follow this pattern, and its strength varies among those that do. Such differences in the default allocation rule are sometimes related to differences in the definition of property available for allocation."

104 *Id. E.g.*, in Ruggles v. Ruggles, 860 P.2d 182, 185 (N.M. 1993), the New Mexico Supreme Court set forth the following guiding principles for distribution in community property states: First, "each spouse ... has a present, vested, one-half interest in the spouses' community property." Second, upon dissolution of a marriage, the court has a duty to divide the community property equally. Third, to promote equality of ownership at divorce, each spouse should receive "complete and immediate control over his or her share of the community property in order to ease the transition of the parties after dissolution." For more information see O'Brien, *supra* note 102, at 689.

105 O'Brien, *id.* at 688: "[C]ommunity-property standards are increasingly *predominant* in divorces occurring in separate property states." For more information see J. Thomas Oldham, Divorce, Separation and the Distribution of Property §5.03, Determining What Is "Marital Property" (2016). (Distinction between premarital acquisitions and gifts or inheritances belonging to one spouse and acquisitions during marriage due to effort has

laws in England and Israel. Generally, in both separate and community property states, separate assets (mostly premarital assets, gifts, and inheritances) do not become shared assets for the determination of proprietary rights or for the purpose of distribution, regardless of the length of the marriage.[106]

In order for a separate asset to become community property an action is required, such as registration of the property in the name of both spouses, transfer of funds into a joint account, or a written contract defining the nature of the assets.[107] Nevertheless, this issue is not uniformly regulated and different states have established different laws concerning how separate property might become common property.[108] Separate property can become community property, inter alia, if it is absorbed into the community property by a transfer, sale, or guarantee.[109] Registration is not conclusive for the classification of property as community or separate,[110] and the length of time the property is held jointly affects its classification as common or separate.[111]

In sum, similar to the present law in Israel, most states within the United States require something extra in order to share a separate asset. A shared household alone will not suffice, contrary to the presumption of sharing which was the arrangement in Israel prior to the Property Relations Law.

---

been accepted as the guiding principle for how property should be dealt with upon divorce by a majority of U.S. separate property states. Separate property is not to be divided; marital property is shared.)

106 An interesting exception to this rule is the State of Washington, in which the law provides that a separate asset may be taken into account in the distribution after divorce, "In a proceeding for dissolution ... the court shall, without regard to misconduct, make such disposition of the property and the liabilities of the parties, either community or separate as shall appear just and equitable." WASH. REV. CODE ANN. § 26.09.080. For more information, see J. Thomas Oldham, *Should Separate Property Gradually Become Community Property as a Marriage Continues?* 72 LA. L. REV. 127 (2012).

107 Oldham, *id.* at 133: "If a party wants to share ownership of separate property with a spouse, a few avenues are already available. The owning spouse could add the other's name to the account or convey a 50 percent interest to the spouse. Alternatively, if the property consists of liquid assets, the assets could gradually be commingled with marital funds. In addition, the parties could sign a written agreement to change the character of the property."

108 For further reading, see Osborn, *supra* note 92, at 915.

109 *E.g.*, Gersten v. Gersten, 219 P.3d 309, 316 (Ariz. Ct. App. 2009), where the court ruled that unemployment benefits, severance earning capacity, and medical expenses resulting from the state are community property, as well as assets acquired by them. *See* Joan M. Krauskopf, *Classifying Marital and Separate Property—Combinations and Increase in Value of Separate Property*, 89 W. VA. L. REV. 997, 1000 (1987).

110 Borghi v. Gilroy, 219 P.3d 932, 937 (Wash. 2009).

111 *In re* Marriage of Wojcik, 838 N.E.2d 282, 292–93 (Ill. App. Ct. 2005); O'Brien, *supra* note 102, at 77.

In 1983, the Uniform Law Commission formulated the Marital Property Act which proposed adopting the approach of community property states nationwide, thus creating greater uniformity in the distribution of property.[112] This act includes clauses for the protection of third parties. For example, when a bona fide buyer purchases from one of the spouses an asset that was obtained through the joint efforts of both spouses, the other spouse has no cause of action (even if there was joint ownership).[113] However, in order to protect the spouse, gifts of community property by one spouse are void if their value exceeds $500.[114] It should be noted that the act did not have great success, and was adopted only in Wisconsin.

Several additional suggestions have been made with the goal of maintaining fairness while increasing certainty, so that under certain conditions a separate asset could become community property. For example, the American Law Institute suggested that if divorce occurs after a specified period of marriage, all property (whether separate or joint) will be part of the distribution pool. This would apply even without proof of specific intent of sharing such as that which is required under the Israeli law.[115] Another proposal is to determine whether an asset given as an inheritance or gift is a shared or separate asset by comparing

---

112 Unif. Marital Prop. Act § 4 (1998, as amended).

113 *Id.*, explanatory note to § 5: "Third parties will deal with the spouse or spouses who manage and control, and that in turn depends on which spouse "holds" marital property. When one who satisfies the bona fide purchaser requirements deals with a spouse who has management and control rights under section 5, the transaction is free from the claim of the other spouse. *Bona fide purchaser* means a purchaser of property for value who: (i) has not knowingly been a party to fraud or illegality affecting the interest of the spouses or other parties to the transaction; (ii) does not have notice of an adverse claim by a spouse; and (iii) has acted in the transaction in good faith.

114 *Id.* § 6: "Gifts of Marital Property to Third Persons (a) A spouse acting alone may give to a third person marital property that the spouse has the right to manage and control only if the value of the marital property given to the third person does not aggregate more than [$500] in a calendar year, or a larger amount if, when made, the gift is reasonable in amount considering the economic position of the spouses. Any other gift of marital property to a third person is subject to subsection (b) unless both spouses act together in making the gift. (b) If a gift of marital property by a spouse does not comply with subsection (a), the other spouse may bring an action to recover the property or a compensatory judgment in place of the property, to the extent of the noncompliance."

115 ALI Report, *supra* note 93, § 4.12: "The drafters argue that after many years of marriage, spouses "typically do not think of their separate-property assets as separate," and "the longer the marriage the more likely it is that the spouses will have made decisions about their employment or the use of their marital assets that are premises in part on ... expectations [of having access to] the separate property of both spouses." For more information, and criticism of the proposal, see J. Thomas Oldham, *supra* note 106, at 128.

the length of marriage when the gift or inheritance was received to the age of the recipient at that time.[116] These proposals have not yet been accepted.

In summary, in most states within the United States the starting point is separation of property, whereby each spouse has rights to manage his or her property during the marriage. This is similar to the Israeli Property Relations Law, but not to the presumption of sharing which according to some is still relevant. In a minority of states within the United States, immediate sharing of property takes place during the marriage, while separate assets remain external.

In all states, upon the dissolution of a marriage, the court balances the spouses' assets according to the principle of equitable distribution. As part of that division of property, the court determines which assets are community property and how they are distributed. Separate assets are usually not included in the shared property. The conditions under which a separate asset becomes joint are somewhat inconsistent and ambiguous. A specific action is often required for an asset to become shared, and a shared household will not suffice. Over the years, a number of proposals have been made to determine distinct phases of the transition. However, these proposals have not yet been accepted.

Mary Ann Glendon summarizes the current law in England and the United States:

> In sum, then, an English or American property owner does not ordinarily gain or lose ownership rights upon marriage and is relatively free to deal with his or her own property during marriage, but he or she does become subject to a system of legal rules that promote sharing of property when the marriage comes to an end.[117]

VII. A NEW MODEL IN LIGHT OF AMENDMENT 4

A. Amendment 4—A Significant Change

The ineffectiveness of the Property Relations Law resulted from the lack of jurisdiction of the court to grant financial divorce prior to religious divorce.

---

116 *E.g.*, if a person age fifty-two receives a gift after eight years of marriage, 8/52 percent of the gift will be shared; *see* Carolyn J. Frantz & Hanoch Dagan, *Properties of Marriage*, 104 COLUM. L. REV. 75, 118 (2004).

117 MARY ANN GLENDON, *supra* note 94, at 131 (1989).

This inability led to all the legal constructions developed in the *Knobler* case and continued thereafter in the long series of rulings described in part IV, above. The resulting uncertainty of property rights brought the Israeli legal system back to where it had been before the Property Relations Law was enacted. The law quickly became ineffective and the legislature has since drafted several bills in an effort to improve the legislation.[118]

In 2007, a draft amendment was published.[119] The proposed amendment's explanatory notes set forth the sad history of the law, and perhaps also of the relations between religion and state in Israel.

In 2008, Amendment 4 was wisely added to the Property Relations Law.[120] The goal of the amendment was to allow for financial divorce to be made before religious divorce. Section 5(a) was added, providing that:

> (a) Each spouse shall have the right to equal distribution of resources even before the termination of the marriage if a year has passed since one of these procedures was initiated: (a) a procedure for dissolving a marriage; (b) a claim for the distribution of property ... or if ... the couple live separately, even if under one roof for a period of at least nine months.

Amendment 4 resulted in a significant change in Israel. In addition to bringing back the possible distribution of property before religious divorce, it remedied the issues described above. Furthermore, members of Christian denominations whose religious law does not allow for divorce also have the chance to distribute their property. The legal development made in the *Knobler* case and the cases that followed was a result of the ineffective law. Careful reading of the *Knobler* case reveals that without the difficulties brought about by the Property Relations Law, the judges would have avoided those legal developments.

The following remarks of Justice Cohen were made with respect to the creation of the presumption of sharing. However, they are also appropriate with regard to maintaining the presumption of sharing between spouses who were married after 1973, and the flexible interpretation of the general law:

118 *See, e.g.*, Spouses Property Relations Bill, 5747-1987, 1821, at 196.

119 Spouses Property Relations Bill (Amendment 4) (proceeding balancing of resources), 5767-2007, 163, at 240.

120 Spouses Property Relations Law (Amendment 4) 5768-2008, 2186 LSI 18 (Nov. 12, 2008).

> Legislation by case law may give satisfaction for a feeling of justice in a particular case, but it may interfere with the property laws and the obligations laws, creating a situation of uncertainty, and ultimately lead to unjust results in other cases.[121]

B. A Desirable Normative Arrangement in Light of Amendment 4

Surprisingly, Israeli law after Amendment 4 continues as it did before. In the rulings presented above that were made after the amendment, the family courts ignore the amendment so that it is ineffective. The courts used case law to overcome the difficulties of the law prior to the amendment and have already developed legal constructions to achieve what they consider to be desirable results without the amendment. Perhaps one may cautiously suggest that the amendment might interfere with the ruling. If the Property Relations Law had not been amended, it would have been addressed as irrelevant, lost its binding force, and enabled the judges to use the flexible general law with their absolute discretion.

Following the amendment, the courts should have recognized the binding provisions set forth in the law. In practice, these provisions might conflict with a judge's own sense of justice in a specific case. An irrelevant law might be preferable for the judges to the amended law, which is vibrant and influential, and in particular sets boundaries on judicial discretion.

The case law that bends the Property Relations Law indirectly brings back the presumption of sharing. Paradoxically, despite Amendment 4, the presumption of sharing came back into direct focus and with a variety of problems. The state legal systems within the United States and the legal system in the United Kingdom also lack certainty, but it seems that the legal situation in Israel is more problematic.

In the new model, the case law following Amendment 4 should differ from the previous case law in three main aspects. First, the simultaneous application of the separation of property under the Property Relations Law and the presumption of sharing must be cancelled. The era of legal construction came to an end with Amendment 4. It is impossible and undesirable to maintain the presumption of sharing due to its negative results. The proprietary separation found in the Property Relations Law must be restored.

121 *Afta*, 25(1) PD at 572.

Second, the flexible general property law that, in practice, indirectly brings back the presumption of sharing must be eliminated. The distinction between these two doctrines is academic and very fine. Nevertheless, as the general law becomes more flexible, one practically achieves full proprietary sharing between the spouses. This creates rights that are not apparent in family asset registrations. As a result, creditors cannot rely on the Land Registry. Elimination of the presumption of sharing will bring certainty of rights to family property.

The third change relates to property obtained by the spouses before their marriage. Many spouses enter marriage today with assets they acquired before they met their spouses. Upon the dissolution of marriage, they may discover that over the years their separate assets have become community property without any action or intent on their part. While the presumption of sharing should be applicable only to a couple married before January 1974, the case law described above further applied it to spouses that were married later. A spouse who wishes to avoid sharing an asset must declare so explicitly.[122] It is easy to understand the devastating implications of such a statement on the eve of a marriage. An alternative, which isn't much more feasible, is entering a prenuptial agreement.

As mentioned above, the enactment of section 5(a)(1) of the Property Relations Law which determines that a separate asset will not be shared, was consistent with the opinion of the majority of the public. The explanatory notes to the Property Relations Law primarily address creditors. Yet it appears that the legislature also attempted to avoid placing a burden on spouses by having them declare their separate assets on the eve of their marriage.

One can assume that most spouses who own separate assets do not want them to become shared property. However, those individuals would certainly prefer not to have to make that statement to a betrothed or spouse, but to have the legislature regulate the matter. The difficulty was that the ineffectiveness of the Property Relations Law also made section 5(a)(1) ineffective and the courts ruled that the separate property of one spouse could become shared property through flexible application of the general law. Amendment 4 of the Property Relations Law remedies this difficulty by providing that separate property remains separate.

The foundation of the three changes suggested above is the application of the general property laws as if the spouses were unrelated with regard to premarital property. It seems that this was also the original intention of the

122 *Hadari*, 48(3) PD 685.

legislature.[123] Accordingly, a third party that relied on the Land Registry in purchasing an asset from a registered spouse should be protected from a claim for rights not apparent from the asset registration and later brought by an unregistered spouse.

Undoubtedly, in extreme cases where spouses live together in a separately owned asset for many years, such a comprehensive statement might lead to an unjust result. This matter has also been of concern in the state legal systems within the United States and in the legal system in the United Kingdom. Justice Rubinstein suggests that if the couple decided to share property, they must register the joint ownership in the Land Registry.[124] It is uncertain how realistic this advice is, because spouses often avoid explicitly determining whether to share property purchased before their marriage. This challenge leads to the discussion in the following section.

C. The Normative Arrangement Concerning the Residential Apartment

Professor Rosen-Zvi believes that with respect to the residence of the couple, the general property laws should be applied as if the spouses were unrelated. If they wish the residence to be shared property, a contract should be made, but family law should not create such rights ex nihilo.[125] His comments were not accepted by the courts. They hold that the residential home in which the couple lived for many years and invested their time and money should be joint property owned by both spouses, even if it was the separate property of one of them prior to the marriage.[126] The courts seek to prevent a spouse who is not a registered owner from becoming homeless.

Therefore, the suggested new model takes a middle path between the position of Professor Rosen-Zvi and that of the courts before Amendment 4. One might especially disagree with the conclusion in *Abu Romi*, that a lesser standard of proof is required to establish joint ownership of the residential apartment.[127] Although this new model requires further clarification, preliminary justification for it may be found in examining the underlying principle. The

---

123 Rosen-Zvi, *supra* note 16, at 307.

124 *Ben Giat*, Nevo, Aug. 11, 2011, at 16.

125 Rosen-Zvi, *supra* note 16, at 192–93.

126 *See supra* part IV.A; *see also* Menachem Mautner, *"Risk Creators" and "Risks Encounters"—The Protection of One Who Relies on the Representation of the Others in the New Civil Legislation*, 16 MISHPATIM 92 (1986).

127 *See Abu Romi*, 56(6) PD at 183.

language accompanying the need to establish the right of an unregistered spouse used the term "residential apartment." This term implies that if the court does not assist the unregistered spouse, he or she might become homeless.

However, this term is somewhat misleading. Even if an unregistered spouse is given a claim of right in the residence, it is only a right to half ownership of the property. A registered spouse intends to transfer, if at all, only one half of his or her separate property. In any event, an apartment will be put on sale when creditors own the other half of the rights. They are entitled to demand dissolution of the sharing of the apartment under section 37 of the Land Law. Thus, even if the right of a spouse is a proprietary right as determined by case law, that right is only obligatory, because logically the property will be sold.[128]

Pursuant to this model, the spouse's right in the residential home should be a matter of the law of obligations and not of property. An unregistered spouse will have a right in the residential apartment notwithstanding the provision of section 5(a)(1) of the Property Relations Law. However, the right must be an obligation both towards the other spouse and a creditor, not a fifty-fifty ownership decision but an interest under section 8(2) of the Property Relations Law. Under certain circumstances, that section allows for judicial discretion in determining that the balance of resources will not be in two equal parts, but according to a different proportion determined by the court. In other words, general property law should apply to the residential apartment, and the unregistered spouse will not acquire the apartment.

This is the default. Nevertheless, in exceptional cases, primarily when the house has been a shared residence for many years, the court should grant that the unregistered spouse has an enforceable claim against the registered spouse. This decision should not involve a categorical fifty-fifty division. Such a categorical decision would be contrary to the legislative intent of section 5(a)(1) of the Property Relations Law, which completely removes separate property from the property that is shared. It would also be inconsistent with the legal systems in the states within the United States and in the United Kingdom.

128 *See* Land Law § 40a, "Dissolution through sale." *See also* Property Relations Law § 6A, "Sale of the residential apartment of the spouses" (Amendment 4) 5769-2008: "If the court determines that for the purpose of balancing the resources it is necessary to sell the apartment in which the spouses live or their minor children and the custodial spouse live, the court will not order that it be sold as long as it does not determine that for the minor children of the spouses and the custodial spouse other living accommodations are found that are suited to their needs."

An advantage of using section 8(2) of the Property Relations Law is the protection of third parties. A third party that acquired an asset while relying on the Land Registry would not be concerned with rights that are not apparent in the registration. Separate property would remain separate. The proprietary rights of a registered owner would again be certain.

This model can be improved on one other level. As stated, the family residence would usually be sold. However, based on a similar arrangement in section 40a of the Land Law with regard to the couple's children, case law could determine that the family residence would be regulated under special law. Accordingly, it would not be sold until a suitable housing arrangement would be found for the unregistered spouse.[129]

VIII. CONCLUSION

The Property Relations Law became irrelevant and ineffective soon after it was enacted. The time for beginning property distribution, the financial divorce, was to be the same as that of the religious divorce. Since religious divorce depends solely on the will of the spouses, no authority was given to the court to distribute even those assets acquired in a joint effort. In the mid-1990s, after a delay of about twenty years, the Supreme Court assisted the spouses in the *Knobler* case by adopting the presumption of sharing and a flexible interpretation of general property law. The court stated that it is possible to determine the division of property before a divorce. In addition, a spouse's separate asset could become a joint asset without any explicit intention or contract.

This judgment and all the cases that followed it contradicted the intent of the legislature. These decisions made the general law flexible and brought back the central focus on proprietary sharing—the presumption of sharing. As a result, the concern returned regarding rights that are not apparent from property registration. Proprietary certainty was once again lost and the value of family assets decreased. Creditors and credit institutions faced uncertainty.

This chapter argues that Amendment 4 to the Property Relations Law was intended to restore the original intention of the legislature. The goal of the amendment was to nullify the judicial constructions made in the *Knobler* case. Nevertheless, the courts have ignored the amendment and managed without it.[130] Paradoxically, when the amendment was enacted it became

---

129 *Id.* Property Relations Law § 6A.

130 *See, e.g., Simchoni*, Nevo, Dec. 28, 2009; *Ben Giat*, Nevo, Aug. 11, 2011.

irrelevant as well and did not bring about an effective change in the Property Relations Law.

This chapter, inspired by state legal systems in the United States and the system in the United Kingdom, suggests a new model that fully adopts the pure intention of the legal provisions: deferred obligatory sharing as to the relations between spouses and creditors, rather than proprietary sharing with a spouse who is not a registered owner. It includes three changes in the current case law: (a) cancellation of the presumption of sharing, so that it will not be applied simultaneously with the Property Relations Law; (b) elimination of flexible interpretation of the general law; and (c) a renewed determination that a separate asset will remain separate.

These changes will promote certainty and stability regarding family property. Creditors and spouses will not be concerned with sharing separate assets. The model also relates to the residence. Protection of a residence of many years can be achieved using section 8(2) of the Property Relations Law, financial compensation, and an extension of the arrangement in section 40a of the Land Law by finding a housing solution for the unregistered spouse. These methods will bring new life to Amendment 4 and its legal rules. These arrangements are inspired and supported by the state legal systems in the United States and the system in the United Kingdom.

CHAPTER 5

Recognition of Foreign Civil Marriages

I. INTRODUCTION

When the State of Israel was established in 1948, it decided to adopt some of the legislation enacted by the British government which had ruled the country prior to its independence. One such example is The Palestine Order in Council, 1922–1947. Article 51 states that "Matters of personal status mean suits regarding marriage or divorce, alimony, maintenance, guardianship ..."[1]

Article 47 sets forth:

> The Civil Courts shall further have jurisdiction ... in matters of personal status as defined in Article 51 of persons in Palestine. Such jurisdiction shall be exercised in conformity with any law, ordinances or regulations that may hereafter be applied or enacted and subject thereto according to the personal law applicable.[2]

This Order in Council has not since been annulled. The law in matters of personal status is personal law that varies depending upon the individual. Personal status law is not territorial and it is not identical for every person in Israel. The courts have also determined that the applicable personal law is that of the religion of the litigant, not of his citizenship or his residency.[3] Thus the law of the church applies to Christians;[4] Jewish law is the applicable law for Jews; Sharia

---

1 Article 51 of The Palestine Order in Council, 1922 also referred to as King's Order in Council in III Laws of Palestine, 2569.

2 Article 47 of The Palestine Order in Council, 1922, III Laws of Palestine, 2580.

3 CA 26/51 *Kotik v. Wallfson*, 5 PD 1341 (1951) (Isr.).

4 Regarding the different Christian communities in Israel, see the following Israel Ministry of Foreign Affairs website. There are ten Christian denominations that as "recognized" communities are granted jurisdiction in matters of personal status: Y. Eldar, Focus on Israel: The Christian Communities of Israel, Israel Ministry of Foreign Affairs (May 1, 2014), available at <http://www.mfa.gov.il/mfa/aboutisrael/people/pages/focus%20on%20israel%20%20the%20christian%20communities%20of%20isr.aspx>.

law applies to Muslims; and the Druze religious law is applicable for the Druze people. These are the four major religions in Israel, and the only religions that are legally recognized.

Five years after Israel's establishment, section 2 of the Rabbinical Courts Jurisdiction (Marriage and Divorce) Law 1953 set forth more explicitly: "Marriage and divorce of Jews in Israel will take place according to Jewish religious law."[5] This means that Israel has no separation of religion and state in matters of personal status. The entities responsible for marriages are the religious institutions themselves. Spouses belonging to the same religion are subject to its exclusive authority, both in their marriage and in their divorce.[6] Marriage prohibited by religion cannot take place in Israel. For example, a non-Jew cannot marry a Jew.

In the United States and in European countries where there is a separation of church and state, rulings and decisions can be determined by the civil courts rather than by religion. However, in Israel the applicable law in family matters is religious personal law. Thus prohibited marriages such as a marriage between spouses only one of whom is Jewish, or a marriage between same-sex spouses, should not be recognized. Surprisingly, and inconsistent with religious personal law, the courts have allowed their civil perspective to shape their decisions to recognize legal protections and rights for those couples.

Concurrent with the authority given to religions over the institution of marriage and the prohibition of marriage between certain individuals, the Israeli courts, in contrast to the legislature, began developing alternatives to religiously sanctioned marriage. Among these alternatives are private marriage,[7] civil marriage,[8] and common law marriage.[9] Of course, nobody referred to them as such,

---

5 Rabbinical Courts Jurisdiction (Marriage and Divorce) Law, 5713–1953, § 2, 165 LSI 72 (1953) (Isr.).

6 Rabbinical Courts Jurisdiction (Marriage and Divorce) Law, 5713–1953, § 1, sets forth: "Matters of marriage and divorce of Jews in Israel, being nationals or residents of the Sate, shall be under the exclusive jurisdiction of rabbinical courts." See https://www.knesset.gov.il/review/ReviewPage2.aspx?kns=2&lng=3.

7 See, *e.g.*, HCJ 51/69 *Rodnizki v. The Supreme Rabbinical Court*, 24(1) PD 704 (1969) (Isr.); HCJ 80/63 *Gorfinkel v. The Supreme Rabbinical Court*, 17 PD 2048 (1963) (Isr.).

8 CA 8256/99 *Anonymous v. Anonymous*, 58(2) PD 213 (2003) (Isr.) (Regulating the civil support between spouses married abroad in a civil ceremony); HCJ 2232/03 *Anonymous v. The High Rabbinical Court*, (Nov. 21, 2006), Nevo Legal Database (by subscription, In Hebrew) (Isr.) (Regularizing the status of spouses who were married abroad in a civil ceremony and states that they are married under the laws of the nations of the world).

9 See, *e.g.*, CA 52/80 *Sha'ar v. Friedman*, 38(1) PD 443 (1980) (Isr.); CA 4385/91 *Salem v. Carmi*, 51(1) PD 337 (1991) (Isr.).

blurring the distinction between these alternatives and religious marriage that all became included under the umbrella term "marriage." Everything was done under the cloak of specific solutions to the plight of privacy and humanity. However, these specific solutions have created an entire area of civil law in Israel that in certain respects is even more developed than in countries in which civil law applies. This chapter analyzes the development of this civil law with regard to civil marriage.

Another way that prohibited marriage has found recognition in Israel is through the Population Registry. People who are not permitted or have no desire to marry according to religious law may choose to marry abroad. Upon returning to Israel, they are then registered in the Population Registry as married.[10] How is this registration consistent with the law stating that only religious law determines marriage? Article 3 of the Population Registry Law, 1965 provides that, "Registration ... will be prima facie evidence of the correctness of registration except for the details of nationality, religion, marital status, and spouse's name."[11] As a result, registration of such details appears to be of no effect.

As a matter of fact, this acts to avoid disputes concerning ideology, fundamental principles, and religion upon the arrival of new immigrants to the country. Figuratively speaking, such matters are not under discussion "at the border." The provision in Article 3 has helped Israeli law or perhaps stated more precisely, the Israeli nation, to avoid potential ideological arguments in relation to the registration of marriages forbidden by religion such as marriages between spouses only one of whom is Jewish.[12] The argument is that registration does not in any case provide prima facie evidence of the marriage.[13] However, this provision of law[14] has also resulted in the registration of certain matters which most certainly fell outside the scope of what was intended by the legislature.[15]

---

10 Article 17 of the Population Registry Law 1965 states that every resident must in fact register any changes in status within thirty days.

11 Population Registry Law, 5725–1965, 270 Laws of the State of Israel (LSI) 85, § 3 (1965) (Isr.).

12 HCJ 143/62 *Schlesinger v. The Minister of the Interior*, 17 PD 225 (1963) (Isr.).

13 *Id.* at 249.

14 Population Registry Law, 5725–1965 § 3, 270 LSI 85 (1965) (Isr.).

15 See, *e.g.*, HCJ 264/87 *Shas Movement v. Director of the Population Administration*, 43(2) PD 723 (1987) (Isr.) (It was determined that the registry clerk is required to register the conversion of a person on the basis of a document attesting to conversion by a Jewish community in a foreign country. This ruling applies even if the clerk believes that the conversion process is not valid according to religious law in Israel); HCJ 2888/92 *Goldstein v. The*

This chapter focuses on the registration and validity of marriages performed abroad and prohibited by the laws of the State of Israel. It is written in a gradual manner. The first part addresses the issue of registration of marriage between a man and a woman, only one of whom is Jewish. The second part deals with the more complex question of the validity of civil marriage in Israel, beyond the question of registration. It is divided into three subsequent sections. The first concerns the simpler case in which a couple were residents of a foreign country when they married there. The second section deals with the case in which a couple who were residents of Israel travelled to a foreign country with the sole purpose of marrying. The third section examines a dramatic precedent in the last decade that recognized civil marriage entered into in a foreign country.

The third part provides history and background of the recognition of same-sex couples in Israel. The fourth part takes an additional step further and considers the registration of same-sex marriages that take place in a foreign country. This form of marriage is more difficult to recognize than that of a marriage between a man and a woman, in which only one spouse is Jewish.

II. THE *SCHLESINGER* CASE—A MARRIAGE BETWEEN A JEW AND A NON-JEW

The most fundamental ruling with regard to registration of a prohibited marriage that was entered into in a foreign country was decided in the *Schlesinger* case. In Cyprus, a Christian woman who was a citizen of Belgium married a Jewish resident and citizen of Israel. She requested registration of her marriage in the Population Registry of the State of Israel. The registry clerk refused to register them. He asserted that under the laws of the State of Israel the couple were not married and he was therefore exempt from registering them. She appealed to the Supreme Court to instruct the registry clerk to register them as a married couple.

Minister of the Interior, 50(5) PD 89 (1987) (Isr.) (The Supreme Court ordered the registration of a marriage held at the Brazilian Embassy in Israel despite the fact that foreign ambassadors lack the authority to conduct marriage ceremonies in Israel); HCJ 5070/95 *Na'amat v. The Minister of the Interior*, 56(2) PD 721 (1995) (Isr.) (The Supreme Court ordered the registration of individuals who underwent a Reform conversion in Israel or in Jewish communities in foreign countries, even though Reform conversions performed in Israel are not valid).

As stated above, the applicable law in family matters is the religious personal law, according to which this marriage is not valid.[16] However, under Article 64(ii) of The Palestine Order in Council which was incorporated into Israeli law, and according to the relevant private international law, the validity of the marriage of a foreigner should be determined by his own national law.[17] Since the woman is Belgian, her status should be determined by Belgian law, under which there is nothing wrong with a marriage between a Christian and a Jew. In contrast, the status of Mr. Schlesinger is to be determined by the laws of the State of Israel. Therefore, under his law he is unmarried and single, while under Belgian law the woman is married to him.

Justice Zilberg argued in a dissenting opinion that, while indeed it is absurd for a woman to be married to a man who is single, in this "fragmented and divided area, full of contrasts and contradictions within private international law, such wondrous creatures also exist."[18] In his opinion, under religious family law in Israel the couple is not married and that does not contradict the views of the general Israeli public. Due to the conflict with Israeli public policy, he determined that the marriage is invalid for both partners, and therefore the registry clerk has no duty to register their invalid marriage.[19]

The majority opinion determined otherwise. Justice Zussman relied upon the guidelines for registry clerks, according to which a citizen who appears before an administrative authority is presumed to speak truthfully. The registry clerk does not have the authority or tools to check the truth of the citizen's statement, and thus the clerk must register what the citizen asks him to register. In his opinion, the Population Registry is neither evidence nor proof of anything.[20]

In his view, when the registry clerk is presented with prima facie evidence such as a marriage certificate from Cyprus, he must register it. Otherwise, he would be intervening in an area beyond his administrative authority.[21] The registry clerk is not a judge and does not rule on matters, but only registers them.[22]

16 Babylon Talmud, Marriage (*Kidushin*) 68.

17 Article 64(ii) of The Palestine Order in Council, 1922, states: "The personal law shall be the law of the nationality of the foreigner concerned unless that law imports the law of his domicile, in which case the latter shall be applied."

18 *Schlesinger, supra* note 12 at 233.

19 *Id.* at 238.

20 In 1965, an amendment to the Population Registry Law determined in section 3 that certain information regarding personal status does not constitute prima facie evidence of its correctness, as explained in the Introduction.

21 *Schlesinger, supra* note 12, at 249.

22 *Id.* at 246.

If there were any need for a legal determination, then the clerk would moreover have to be an expert in the rules of private international law and conflict of laws, which are among the most complicated rules of jurisprudence.[23]

Justice Zussman argued that the registry clerk is not authorized to determine the validity of the marriage.[24] He also ruled that the registry clerk collects statistical material as to whether or not a wedding ceremony took place. The clerk may refuse to register it only if there is an "obvious inaccuracy."[25] An example of a document that is obviously incorrect is a foreign public document indicating that an adult is five years old.[26] Certainly, the registry clerk would not be compelled to enter such information into the registry.

Justice Zussman commented on a principle which is of fundamental importance in Israel with regard to the recognition of foreign legal actions:

> Any country that wants to live together in the family of nations must for that purpose relinquish the implementation of some of its rules when a foreign element arises and intervenes in a legal action ... and we, just as we demand that other nations recognize Israeli law, we do not rule out a transaction only because the applicable foreign law is different from ours. To the extent that the rules of conflict of laws refer us to foreign law, the Israeli law steps back ... and only when foreign law will be contrary to the sense of justice and morality of the Israeli public will we have to invalidate it. ... The fact that Jewish religious law invalidates intermarriage (between individuals only one of whom is Jewish) does not necessarily lead to the conclusion that when determining a matter according to foreign law, we will invalidate the marriage because it is an intermarriage.[27]

The court further stated that neither English law nor the state laws within the United States rule out the validity of a marriage because the couple went to a foreign country where they were married in a ceremony that could not be performed in their own country.[28]

---

23 *Id.* at 251.
24 *Id.* at 251.
25 *Id.* at 243.
26 This example is explicitly cited in the judgment. See *id.* at 243.
27 *Id.* at 256.
28 *McDonald v. McDonald* (1936), 58 P (2D) 163, 104 *A.L.R.* 1290; *Simonin v. Mallac* (1860), 2 L.T. 327, 330.

The significance of the *Schlesinger* ruling is that if spouses who are residents of Israel (i) were married in a civil ceremony in a foreign country as provided by its laws; and (ii) submitted certification of that marriage; they will be registered in the Population Registry as "married," even if they are not actually married under Israeli law.

Many judges and scholars have criticized the *Schlesinger* decision.[29] Some saw it as turning a blind eye.[30] Justice Englard once wrote:

> If it is only a matter of statistics that lack substantive meaning, why are there continued struggles over registration? ... The truth is, of course, that the symbol here is of the essence, and without a certain worldview there is no determination in the question of registration in the Population Registry, and there are no statistics.[31]

III. THE VALIDITY OF CIVIL MARRIAGE

A. The *Skornik* Case—The Validity of a Marriage with Regard to Maintenance

The question of civil marriage registration was decided in the *Schlesinger* case, but the more important question is whether a civil marriage performed abroad may be deemed valid under Israeli law, for example for the purposes of maintenance.

The leading judgment on the matter is the *Skornik* case. The case dealt with a Jewish couple who were residents of a foreign country (Poland) when they married in a civil ceremony. Only afterwards did they immigrate to and become citizens of Israel.[32] The wife then filed a claim in Israel against her husband for maintenance. Her husband claimed they were not married, because a civil ceremony does not comply with marriage under religious law. In addition, they did not ever intend a religious marriage, even though it would have been possible in Poland.

The district court held that under Jewish religious law applicable in Israel, where they then resided, they should not be considered married. However,

---

29 M. Shava, Registration and recognition of a foreign adoption order within lesbian family, 1 Kiryat Ono L. Rev. 103, 132 (2001).

30 HCJ 5070/95 *Na'amat v. The Minister of the Interior*, 56(2) PD 764 (1995) (Isr.).

31 *Id.* at 757.

32 CA 191/51 *Skornik v. Skornik*, 8 PD 141, 179 (1951) (Isr.).

according to the principles of English private international law that were adopted in Israel, the applicable law is Polish law, which is the law of their place of residence at the time of their marriage. Therefore they were to be regarded as married.

The Supreme Court agreed and added:

> The question of the validity of the status that a person acquired for himself is determined by the law applicable to the person at the time he acquired that status, and he does not lose it with a change in his residence or his nationality, when he becomes subject to another law.[33]

The court further stated:

> There is a conflict between secular civil law which has an effect limited by national borders, and therefore recognizes and applies another law in relation to the status of a person before he resided in the country—as compared with religious law that does not know borders and restrictions and applies to a person from his birth until his death without any relevance to the place or time in which an event happened.[34]

The court held that in this conflict of laws regarding spouses who were residents of a foreign country when they married in a civil ceremony, the personal law in Israel will be subordinated to the rules of private international law, and their status will be determined as a married couple. If the law applicable to the spouses at the time of the marriage recognizes the validity of the marriage, the Israeli civil law will recognize it.[35] Maintenance is thus required by the personal law of Israel. This in effect combines religious law (maintenance) with civil law (the marriage status).

Justice Agranat added in the majority opinion that the obligation of maintenance is so universally accepted that the wife, who acquired her marital status under a foreign law, should not be required to prove that maintenance is granted by that system. Even if the court were to say that she did indeed have to identify the relevant foreign law, it is reasonable to assume that the foreign

---

33 *Id.* at 150.
34 *Id.* at 158.
35 *Id.* at 167.

law is like the domestic law and thereby recognizes the right of a wife to receive maintenance from her husband.[36]

Professor Shava states in his book:

> From the time that the parties acquired the status of being married under their national law, every change in their personal rights that will afterwards take place due to a change in their citizenship, will not deprive them of their status of married people.[37]

B. Three Approaches for Examining the Validity of a Marriage

The more difficult question is the validity of a civil marriage performed in a foreign country between Israeli residents. In such circumstances, the couple decided not to marry according to religious law in the religious institutions of the state. They chose instead to travel abroad, marry there, and return to Israel with an official foreign marriage certificate. Israeli case law includes three main approaches to this question.

According to one approach, in examining the validity of a marriage that includes a foreign element, one should refer to the English rules of private international law,[38] adopted into Israeli law through Article 46 of The Palestine Order in Council, 1922. With regard to the validity of the form of the marriage (referred to as formal validity), the applicable law is the law of the location in which the marriage was performed (*lex loci celebrationis*). With regard to the legal capacity of the parties to marry (referred to as essential validity), the applicable law is the law of the domicile at the time of entering the marriage (*lex domicilii*) or the law of the location where the parties intend to live when they are married. This approach is hereinafter referred to as the "English approach."[39]

Therefore, the validity of a civil marriage between Jews who are residents of Israel and have the legal capacity to marry each other according to their Jewish personal law will be examined according to the law of the location in which the marriage took place. Assuming that a civil wedding ceremony is a valid form of marriage where the marriage took place, such marriage will also be recognized under Israeli law. However, if the couple lacks the legal capacity to marry under Israeli law, the foreign marriage will not be recognized as valid, although

36 *Id.* at 172.

37 M. Shava, *The Personal Law in Israel* (Vol. 1, 4th edn., 2001), 80.

38 *Skornik, supra* note 32, at 179.

39 Dicey & Morris, *Conflict of Laws* (13th edn., 2000), 651, 675.

the couple will be registered as married according to the *Schlesinger* decision referred to above.

The second approach rejects the applicability of the English rules of private international law that distinguish between content and form in favor of the personal law. With respect to residents and citizens of Israel, the validity of the marriage will be decided by applying the personal laws of the couple at the time of entering into the marriage, even if the marriage involves a foreign element.[40] Therefore, if religious law does not recognize the marriage, then it is completely invalid under Israeli law. This is indeed the approach of Justice Zilberg in the dissenting opinion in the *Schlesinger* case (hereinafter also referred to as the approach of Professor Shava).

The third and most liberal is the approach taken in the United States. The questions of both legal capacity and form are examined according to the location of the marriage ceremony.[41] Thus, a marriage in Cyprus between a Jewish man and a non-Jewish woman is valid in Israel because it is valid where the ceremony was performed. In contrast, in both the English approach and the approach of Professor Shava, such a marriage is not valid in Israel.

C. The *Anonymous* Case—The English Approach

A determination was not made among these approaches for decades. However, in 2006 the High Rabbinical Court of Israel ruled on the issue for the first time. In the *Anonymous* case, Jewish spouses who were citizens and residents of Israel married in a civil ceremony in Cyprus.[42] Upon their return to Israel, and on the basis of the Cypriot marriage certificate, they were registered in the Population Registry as married.

At a later time, the husband filed for divorce in the religious court and it was determined that the couple had never actually been married. Their registration in the Population Registry as a married couple was deemed not to constitute proof of the validity of their marriage, as stated above. The husband insisted on receiving an additional statement permitting him to marry someone else, as an unmarried individual. This statement was necessary because even if he was not religiously married, he was still registered as married from the civil perspective. If he married another woman he would violate the law against bigamy

40 M. Shava *supra* note 29, at 554.
41 *Schlesinger*, *supra* note 12, at 253.
42 *Anonymous* 2232/03, *supra* note 8.

in the Penal Law.[43] In a surprising step, the rabbinical court annulled the civil marriage. The wife appealed to the High Rabbinical Court, arguing that a religious court does not have the authority to annul a civil marriage performed in a foreign country.

The High Rabbinical Court set a precedent that "from the perspective of civil law, the parties entered a civil marriage, and they are considered a married couple all over the world, including in Israel."[44] The High Rabbinical Court further stated that rabbinical courts have the exclusive jurisdiction to dissolve a marriage. However, a court cannot annul it since it should be recognized by Israeli law as valid. Nevertheless, the court did not grant the marriage the same status as a marriage performed in accordance with the requirements of Jewish religious law. The wife appealed to the Supreme Court.

The Supreme Court adopted the determination of the High Rabbinical Court and stated further:

> Recognition of the validity of the marriage can be concluded from the rules of private international law, which constitute an integral part of Israeli law and were adopted in the past from the English law. Accordingly, when a marriage includes a foreign element, it must be taken into consideration. Private international law supersedes any municipal law which is purely internal.[45] Hence the validity of a marriage entered into by a Jewish couple outside of Israel, even if both spouses were at the time residents and citizens of Israel, will be determined while taking into consideration the rules of conflict of laws generally accepted in Israel. Accordingly, the marriage is valid in form (foreign law) and in substance (Jewish law), and is therefore valid in Israel.[46]

The Supreme Court added that this result would adequately reflect the nature of modern Israeli society. Thousands of Jews who are citizens and residents of Israel seek to enter into civil marriages outside of Israel. The willingness to recognize the validity of personal status acquired by Jews under foreign law and not in conflict with public policy in Israel is reinforced by the significance of the right to marriage and family life. The court ultimately accepted the English

43 Penal Law, 5737–1977 § 178, 1246 LSI 62 (1977) (Isr.).

44 Appeal, High Rabbinical Court 4276/63 *H.S. v. H.Y.*, (Feb. 5, 2003), Nevo Legal Database (by subscription, In Hebrew) (Isr.).

45 *Skornik, supra* note 32 at 179.

46 *Anonymous* 2232/03, *supra* note 8 at section 26.

approach, which remains the prevailing approach in Israel with regard to the validity of civil marriage.

However, the rabbinical court emphasizes that it does not view the spouses as a fully married couple under Jewish law, but rather regards their marriage as a "marriage of the nations of the world." Thus the marriage is not intrinsically invalid. Spouses are thus not permitted to remarry others without dissolution of prior marriage. Dissolution takes place through a divorce judgment, as is common in civil law in many countries. The judgment for divorce is a divorce in every respect—without requiring a *Get* (divorce certificate) as is necessary under Jewish law.[47]

The grounds for divorce will not be determined under the law of the location where the civil marriage ceremony took place (a foreign country). In the opinion of the Supreme Court, the rules of private international law require the recognition of foreign personal status, but they do not require recognition of all manifestations of the same status under foreign law. Therefore, if the lives of the couple are centered in Israel, there is no fault in applying the views of Israeli society concerning the right to divorce.[48] Thus, the appropriate ground for divorce is that of irreconcilable differences.[49]

The rabbinical court further ruled that recognition of marriage denotes partial recognition, only extending to the "external aspect" of the marriage which concerns the prohibition of marriage to a third party as long as the marriage is not dissolved. However, recognition does not extend to the "internal aspect" of marriage dealing with the mutual obligations between the spouses.

Thus the marriage does not create obligations of maintenance and property division between the spouses. The Supreme Court rejected this divided position and therefore determined that the exclusive jurisdiction concerning maintenance and property division belongs to the civil courts rather than their religious counterparts. The applicable law is civil law rather than Jewish religious law. This differs from the actual divorce proceedings in which the rabbinical court has exclusive jurisdiction.[50]

It is important to note that although this determination is indeed a tremendous innovation in Israeli law, it relates only to spouses who have the legal capacity to marry. There is still no ruling concerning the validity of prohibited

---

47 *H.S. supra* note 44 at 8.

48 *Anonymous* 2232/03, *supra* note 8, at section 35.

49 *Id.* at section 36.

50 *Id.* at section 31.

civil marriage, such as a marriage between a Jewish man and a non-Jewish woman, or a same-sex marriage. In these cases, the three different approaches remain as described above.

IV. THE *BEN ARI* CASE—REGISTRATION OF SAME-SEX CIVIL MARRIAGE

The next chapter describes the background and further clarifies the difficulty and innovation with respect to the recognition of civil marriages of same-sex couples who are residents of Israel. A marriage between same-sex couples and even sexual relations between them are absolutely prohibited according to religious law. Nevertheless, the civil courts in Israel have circumvented the religious law and developed recognition of the rights of same-sex couples. The legislature in Israel has taken some action with regard to same-sex couples. Nevertheless, the small handful of amendments made to Israeli law have not aimed to recognize same-sex couples or grant rights to such couples, but rather to prevent injury or penalty. Thus far the discussion in Israel has dealt with economic and financial rights, such as inheritance, social rights in the workplace, and so forth, as discussed in the next chapter.

However, registration of civil marriage is a public policy decision that in some sense is more controversial and more a matter of principle, as further examined in this section. The most significant decision of the Supreme Court of Israel on this issue is the *Ben Ari* case.[51] The case deals with five petitions by five different same-sex male couples. Though the individual spouses were all Israeli citizens, they were married in civil marriage ceremonies in Canada and subsequently requested to be registered as married couples in Israel's Population Registry. Their request was denied.

In order to understand the discussion in this matter, it is necessary to refer to the *Schlesinger* case, in which the court ruled that the registry clerk is not authorized to determine the validity of a marriage.[52] In *Schlesinger* the court also ruled that the registry clerk collects statistical material as to whether or not a wedding ceremony took place. The clerk may refuse to register a marriage only if there is an "obvious inaccuracy."[53]

---

51 HCJ 3045/05 *Ben Ari v. Director of the Population Administration,* (Nov. 21, 2006), Nevo Legal Database (by subscription) (Isr.).

52 *Schlesinger supra* note 12, at 251.

53 *Id.* at 243.

The state's argument in the *Ben Ari* case was that the term "married" in the registry means marriages that are consistent with the basic legal template under Israeli law regarding marriage. This format only referred to marriage between a man and a woman. Chief Justice Barak wrote the majority opinion rejecting the state's argument:

> The question brought before us is not an application to recognize a marriage of a same-sex couple performed outside of Israel. When this question will arise, it will be examined according to our usual rules of private international law. The only question brought before us is the question of registration—registration rather than recognition—of marriage of same-sex couples performed in a foreign country. The approach of the state that we should reject the petitions because the marriages entered into by the petitioners are not a recognized "legal template" in Israel is an approach that requests to take a position on the question of status. It is an approach that requests the court take a position on a controversial social question.[54]

Chief Justice Barak explained further that an "obvious inaccuracy," as referred to in the *Schlesinger* case, represents factual inaccuracy.[55] In contrast, the court determined that the state had incorrectly argued that the term referred to inaccuracy with respect to the law.[56] Chief Justice Barak added that it was neither a question of whether same-sex couples can marry in a civil ceremony in Israel, nor a question of whether they are married. These questions should be left to the legislature. The only question which is relevant before the court is whether the registry clerk must register the marriage performed in a foreign state.[57] Chief Justice Barak gave an instruction to register it. Five judges agreed with him.

It is difficult to accept the position of Chief Justice Barak that it is not the minister who should determine the ministry's policy. In a properly functioning democratic system, the minister is chosen as the representative of the people and is responsible for determining policy. Indeed, the right to establish new policy exists every time a new minister is elected. This is the essence of democracy and the essence of the concept of the rule of the people. The role of a judge is not to say, "The legislature is silent, so I will lead the change." The silence of

54 *Ben Ari supra* note 51 at section 22.

55 *Id.* at section 21.

56 *Id.* at section 21.

57 *Id.* at section 22.

the legislature says something. It might say that there is no need to change the law and that the current situation is desired.

Justice Rubinstein, who sat in the "religious justice seat,"[58] argued in the minority opinion that the Population Registry is not only a statistical registry but also a social and public symbol.[59] It is the "gateway" to Israeli legal reality.[60] He explained that this court must give its opinion, even regarding the question of how far it distances itself from social consensus.[61] Justice Rubinstein cites passages from two books written by Justice Barak:

> The judge must consider the degree of social consensus with social values and the legal norms derived from them. It is desirable to avoid choosing an option that sharply opposes the fundamental perceptions of the public. ... The reason for this approach lies in democratic considerations, the considerations of separation of powers and the need to ensure public trust in the judicial system. ...[62] A judge does not have to be the flag bearer of new social consensuses. He must give expression to fundamental values recognized in his society rather than create them.[63]

Justice Rubinstein referred to these citations and said that one should examine these matters not only from the perspective of individual justice but also from the perspective of a broad common denominator which extends as much as possible among the parts of a divided Israeli society, while avoiding extremes. An issue regarding a public symbol in Israel should justifiably be determined by the legislature. The registration is an official approval of the state to create a family unit, which is recognized by only a small minority of the countries in the world.[64] Therefore, Justice Rubinstein suggests that the petitions should be rejected.

It is important to mention that in December 2006, Justice Rubinstein wrote in his opinion that only six among 192 states recognize same-sex marriage, and

---

58 The State of Israel has a procedure which states that among fourteen Supreme Court justices it is important to have at least one religious judge. This is not set forth in provisions of law, but determined in accordance with internal guidelines.

59 *Ben Ari supra* note 51, at section 9 in Justice Rubinstein's opinion.

60 Indeed the religious parties in Israel are competing for the leadership of the ministry in charge of the Population Registry.

61 *Ben Ari, supra* note 51, at section 16.

62 A. Barak, *Judicial Discretion* (1987), 289.

63 A. Barak, *The Judge in a Democracy* (2004), 47.

64 *Ben Ari, supra* note 51, at section 10 in the opinion of Justice Rubinstein.

therefore the State of Israel should not lead this trend, especially as a country that defines itself as a Jewish and democratic state. However, following the *Obergefell* decision,[65] this is undoubtedly no longer a strong argument.

Chief Justice Barak does not want to address or determine the questions of whether a same-sex marriage is a family unit and whether it is valid in Israel. He only makes a determination regarding the authority of the registry clerk and whether he should register each of the couples as married. All the parties agree that each of the marriage certificates submitted to the registry clerk is valid and legal in Canada; the marriages are valid in Canada; and all the information detailed in each certificate is correct. Therefore, the registry clerk must reg-ister the parties as married couples in the Israel Population Registry and this is the new ruling in Israel.

V. CONCLUSION

In Israel, where there is no separation of religion and state, marriage is governed exclusively by religion. It is therefore against all expectations to have witnessed there the recognition of prohibited marriage, such as (i) the marriage of same-sex couples that contrasts with marriage in all recognized religions in Israel; (ii) the marriage between spouses only one of whom is Jewish; or indeed (iii) any marriage entered into in a foreign country and not permitted under Israeli law. The conflict is between religious law which is not limited by the borders of a country and does not recognize the rules of private international law, and civil law which desires to become part of the family of nations. Civil law seeks to respect legal actions taken under foreign law, even if contrary to local state law.

Nevertheless, Israeli law as interpreted in the decisions of the Supreme Court has overwhelmingly recognized the rights of couples married in civil ceremonies outside of Israel. This process began with the registration in Israel of a marriage between a Jewish woman and a non-Jewish man (the *Schlesinger* case), and with the recognition of standard spousal obligations. Included among such obligations are property division and maintenance with respect to a couple married abroad before becoming citizens and residents of Israel (the *Skornik* case). Such recognition is part of the development of Israeli civil law rather than

65 *Obergefell v. Hodges*, 135 S.Ct. 2584 (2015). This Supreme Court decision set a precedent in ruling that the Constitution of the United States requires same-sex marriage. Therefore all fifty states within the United States are obliged to allow it.

religious law. This civil law is designed to respond to the dynamics of life and the personal distress of individual partners.

The question which poses greater difficulty than that of registration concerns the validity of civil marriage between Israeli residents who travelled to a foreign country, entered into a marriage under its laws, and returned to Israel. Israeli case law includes three main approaches to this question: the English approach, the approach of Professor Shava, and the approach in the United States. However, in 2006 the rabbinical court unexpectedly recognized the validity of such civil marriages, albeit stating that they do not yield property rights. This was sufficient for the Supreme Court to then recognize foreign civil marriages with respect to all aspects of the domestic law, including property rights.

However, this decision applies only to marriage permitted under Jewish religious law. It does not relate to prohibited marriages performed in a foreign country. With respect to such marriages, religious law very much conflicts with private international law. In the *Ben Ari* case, the Supreme Court ruled that the registry clerk should register the marriages of same-sex couples performed in a foreign country. While it seems not to have fully addressed the issue, the court explained that the question of registration is not one of status but rather only an administrative question concerning the authority of the registry clerk. Although the court did not determine the validity of the marriage, it *de facto* preferred private international law over personal religious law.

Some critics argue that the law in Israel, whereby marriage is determined only by an individual's religious personal law, has now become meaningless. The decisions described above reflect the constant prevailing tensions regarding Israel not only as a Jewish state but also as a democratic state. Although the Basic Laws stipulate that Israel is both, in practice these values conflict and often collide. This is clearly reflected in the issue of civil marriages performed in a foreign country and prohibited by religious personal law.

CHAPTER 6

The Issue of Document Disclosure in General Court and in Family Court

I. INTRODUCTION

In 1995 the Family Court Law established family courts in Israel.[1] The law determined that various family matters, previously under the separate jurisdictions of different courts, would all be brought before one judicial authority.[2] Together with the establishment of the family courts, the need arose to determine their applicable procedures. The rules of procedure that apply to general proceedings were not fitting for sensitive family disputes. Therefore, a unique section of family court procedures was incorporated into the general rules of procedure in order to address the special needs of the family dispute.

This chapter analyzes the tension between the general rules of procedure and those of the family court, especially with regard to mandatory disclosure. The chapter deals with the application of the general mandatory disclosure procedures in the family court. For that purpose, the chapter is divided into four sections. The first section critically examines the justification of the provision of law that enables family courts to deviate from the general rules of procedure. That section argues that the family courts tend to utilize this provision, even when local doctrines are available for resolving the question before the court.

The second section presents the problematic nature of that provision and its interpretation by the courts of appeal with respect to the document disclosure process. A family court procedural rule denies family courts the authority to grant orders for document disclosure and inspection, and to impose sanctions such as the striking of pleadings for noncompliance.[3] The family courts

1 Family Courts Law, 5755—1995, 1537 LSI 393 (1995) (Isr.).

2 *Id.*

3 Civil Law Procedure Regulations, 1984, KT 5744, r. 258 (Isr.).

could have used the provision of law releasing them from procedure in order to overcome this procedural rule. However, the interpretation of that provision by the appeals courts prevents the family courts from doing so.

The third section analyzes the reaction of the family court to this interpretation that restricts the court with respect to document disclosure. It further examines the response of the family court and argues that it actually circumvents the decisions of the appeals courts. The fourth section considers the situation in several legal systems throughout the world. In light of those systems, the chapter presents a solution that not only allows for more efficient mandatory disclosure procedures in the family court but also contributes to legislative harmony. It provides a model for how legislation could improve the present situation.

The family court rule, which prevents the family court from issuing an order for document disclosure and inspection and from imposing sanctions on a party that fails to disclose his documents, could cause injustice and substantial harm to certain spouses. One spouse, who trusts the other to manage their family business, could find himself with a very significant procedural disadvantage. During the marriage, whether consciously or due to a lack of awareness, such a spouse might avoid preserving documents, recording financial activities, and so forth. With the outbreak of a controversy he might find himself helpless due to inaccessibility of documents and a lack of knowledge as to the extent of the family assets.

In contrast, the spouse who manages the family finances and business might have a very significant procedural advantage. It is doubtful whether this arrangement is consistent with the purpose of establishing the family court. It is also uncertain if the solutions created by the family courts are procedurally appropriate. What is, therefore, the fitting and desirable solution regarding document disclosure? This chapter considers these subjects.

The restrictive family court procedural rule prevents the courts from ascertaining the truth for efficient and just conflict resolution. It is also inconsistent with the family court's purpose of achieving speedy and effective dispute resolution with the consent of the parties. When one party is unable to see the documents of the other party, he strongly maintains his position, is unwilling to compromise, and refuses to personally come to terms with a judicial decision given on the basis of an incomplete picture.

The chapter argues that the family courts should be granted even broader authority for issuing document disclosure orders than is customary in the general courts. Such authority could also prevent suspicions and concerns between married spouses with respect to the preservation of documents. They will be assured that the legal system will protect them should the need arise. This suggestion is also inspired by other legal systems around the world.

II. THE UNIQUE NATURE OF THE FAMILY COURT

A. Establishment of the Family Court—Historical Background

Every family dispute that comes before the court reveals that there is a deeper problem within the family. Thus, a specific decision regarding a particular point of controversy is not sufficient, but more comprehensive treatment is required. The centralization of all of a family's own matters before one judge makes the system more efficient, avoids duplication of procedures and judicial decisions, allows for a more systematic and clearly structured solution, shortens the proceedings, and thus brings about better solutions. The family court is an inseparable part of the general court system. Nevertheless, the law authorizes the minister of justice to determine unique procedures applicable exclusively in the family court.[4] Accordingly, the minister of justice "inserted" special family court procedures within the general rules of procedure.[5]

These specific rules are based on the following principles applicable to every family dispute. The family system is dynamic and requires immediate solutions, while a delay in issuing a decision could cause irreparable harm. The decisions should be based upon updated and reliable information. It is also desirable to completely utilize the possibilities for dispute resolution prior to initiating court proceedings.[6]

The special nature of the family dispute should shape the family court procedures. This nature should influence the procedural approach through which the rules will be implemented and interpreted during the court proceedings.

---

4 The Supreme Court of Florida also established a committee in 1992 that will recommend unique family court rules, different from those of the general courts. *See* Michael L. Hastings & George S. Reynolds III., *The New Family Law Rules — What You Must Know*, 70 FLA. B.J. 2, 14 (1996) (stating that the Florida Supreme Courts decided to create separate procedural rules for family courts apart from the civil court rules).

5 Civil Law Procedure Regulations, 1984, KT 5744 (Isr.).

6 These are the customary purposes of the different legal systems in establishing the family court. *See* Norman J. Davis, *A Reference Guide to the New Family Court Rules*, ARIZ. ATT'Y, Feb. 2006, 42, 42 ("The new family court rules were designed to reduce the harm to families and children that is inherent in civil litigation, to more closely fit the needs of families in conflict, to simplify and reduce unnecessary delays in court proceedings, and to bring a less adversarial and more problem-solving approach to family disputes").

In order to examine the appropriate procedural approach in family court, one must view from a broader perspective the current procedural approaches in general legal proceedings worldwide.

The adversary system that is customary in the United States and Israel is based on the perception that the proceeding should be managed by the disputing parties.[7] This system is founded on clear and uniform rules created for the purpose of limiting and reducing the intervention of the judge. It assumes that these conditions will provide the court with a broader exposure of the facts.[8]

In contrast, the inquisitorial system that is typical of the Continental legal systems in Europe, asserts that the better way to discover the truth is by enabling the court to manage the proceeding.[9] That system allows broader judicial intervention in directing the proceeding.[10] Beginning in the 1990s, inquisitorial elements were introduced into the legal system in Israel, thus weakening its classic adversarial foundations.

The fundamental rationale guiding the application of the procedural rules in the general courts focuses on disclosing the truth, setting forth the disputed issues and their substance, clarifying them, and deciding upon them.[11] In contrast, the fundamental rationale in the family court focuses on family and not on "disputing parties."[12] The spouses will continue dealing with each other, not only during the legal proceeding but also and primarily thereafter.

The fundamental purpose of the family court is not clarifying the issues, but attaining a comprehensive, speedy, and efficient resolution achieved as

---

7 *Compare* John H. Langbein, *The German Advantage in Civil Procedure*, 52 U. Chi. L. Rev. 823, 823 (1985) (describing and criticizing our systems as "lawyer-dominated"), *with* John C. Reitz, *Why We Probably Cannot Adopt the German Advantage in Civil Procedure*, 75 Iowa L. Rev. 987, 987–88 (1989–1990) (arguing with Langbein's belief that we should adopt the German system).

8 *See* Richard Eggleston, *What is Wrong with the Adversary System?*, 49 Austl. L.J. 428, 431 (1975) (displaying the assumption that proponents of the adversary system believe the lawyer-based system improves the fact-finding process).

9 *See id.* at 428–31 (expressing the view that the European system better arrives at the truth); Arthur R. Miller, *The Adversary System: Dinosaur or Phoenix*, 69 Minn. L. Rev. 1, 1 (1984) (emphasizing the lack of efficiency in the American system compared to foreign systems); Thomas Fleiner, Common Law and Continental Law: Two Legal Systems, 21 (2005) (stating that the Continental system began and is more common in Europe).

10 *See* Eggleston, *supra* note 8, at 428–29 (demonstrating the larger role of the court in the proceeding).

11 *Id.* at 429–31 (discussing the basic principles of an adversarial system, while comparing its effectiveness with other systems).

12 Davis, *supra* note 6, at 46–47.

much as possible with the consent of the parties.[13] An agreed upon solution is essential for dealing with the emotional aspect of these disputes, especially because these are relationships continuing far beyond the legal proceedings. It seems that the nature of the family dispute and this purpose of the family court are inconsistent with the classic adversary system.[14] The unique nature of the family dispute seems to require greater intervention by the court, not only in gathering the evidence but also in directing the proceeding.[15]

B. The Release from Procedural Rules—Analysis and Review

The legislator provided the family court with an additional important provision that releases it from the procedural rules. Section 8(a) of the Family Court Law sets forth:

> 8(a). In every matter of evidence law and procedure, where no other provision applies, according to this law, the court will act in the way that it sees best for implementation of justice.[16]

The rationale at the basis of this provision (hereinafter also referred to as the "release from rules of procedure") is very consistent with the rationale for

---

13 In different legal systems, these purposes appear as part of the legislation. *See* Supreme Court Family Rules, B.C. Reg. 169/09 (Can.) ("(1) The object of these Supreme Court Family Rules is to (a) help parties resolve legal issues in a family law case fairly and in a way that will (i) take into account the impact that the conduct of the family law case may have on a child, and (ii) minimize conflict and promote cooperation between the parties, and (b) secure the just, speedy and inexpensive determination of every family law case on its merits.")

14 The legislature in California also views it this way, as is set forth in the California Family Code. *See* CAL. FAM. CODE § 2100(b) (West 2004) ("Sound public policy further favors the reduction of the adversarial nature of marital dissolution and the attendant costs by fostering full disclosure and cooperative discovery").

15 *See* Langbein, *supra* note 7, at 830 ("From the standpoint of comparative civil procedure, the most important consequence of having judges direct fact-gathering in this episodic fashion is that German procedure functions without the sequence rules to which we are accustomed in the Anglo-American procedural world. The implications for procedural economy are large. The very concepts of "plaintiff's case" and "defendant's case" are unknown. In our system those concepts function as traffic rules for the partisan presentation of evidence to a passive and ignorant trier. By contrast, in German procedure the court ranges over the entire case, constantly looking for the jugular — for the issue of law or fact that might dispose of the case. Free of constraints that arise from party presentation of evidence, the court investigates the dispute in the fashion most likely to narrow the inquiry").

16 Family Courts Law, 5755 –1995, 1537 LSI 393 (1995) (Isr.).

establishing the family court, as described above. In order to reach a speedy and just determination as required in a family dispute, the judge needs to be released from the restraints of rules of procedure and evidence law.

The general rules of procedure are based on norms that are intended for uniformity and certainty in the legal proceeding.[17] Those purposes make the rules of procedure rigid. A lack of flexibility could result, for example, in essential evidence not being brought before the judge for consideration. This concern becomes greater in the family dispute characterized by a lack of documentation, a lack of records, and an unwillingness of relatives or other potential witnesses to be a part of the family dispute. Thus the release from rules of procedure could enable the judge to intervene in the proceeding and to overcome hurdles that might arise from uniform and rigid use of the general rules of procedure.

However, the release from rules of procedure could have problematic implications within the formal environment of procedure. This authority was not granted to the general courts. Nevertheless, a general court may clearly also find that following the general procedural rules is not always "the way that it sees best for implementation of justice." The following are several criticisms of the argument that procedural flexibility is required in family matters.

First, it is doubtful whether this release from rules of procedure is still fitting following the broadened scope of "family matters." A dispute among "family members" presently includes not only spouses and their children but also a wider range of family members. Such family members do not necessarily maintain relationships as close as those between the spouses themselves or between the spouses and their children. The extended family does not need this exceptional flexibility in rules of procedure.

Second, the criterion for release from rules of procedure is "implementation of justice." This is a term taken from the substantive law.[18] It has a flexible surface and belongs to the realm of "standards," rather than the realm of

---

17 Kathleen M. Sullivan, *The Supreme Court 1991 Term, Foreword: The Justices of Rules and Standards*, 106 HARV. L. REV. 22, 57–58 (1992–1993) (discussing that rules, once formulated, allow minimal discretion); Louis Kaplow, *Rules Versus Standard: An Economic Analysis*, 42 DUKE L.J. 557, 596–97 (1992) (explaining that individuals prefer rules to standards due to their predictable nature); Mary Ann Glendon, *Fixed Rules and Discretion in Contemporary Family Law and Succession Law*, 60 TUL. L. REV. 1165, 1166 (1985–1986) (explaining that code revision requires the predictability and reasonable certainty of rules along with the flexibility of discretion); Carl E. Schneider, *Discretion, Rules, and Law: Child Custody and the UMDA's Best-Interest Standard*, 89 MICH. L. REV. 2215, 2249–50 (1990–1991) (discussing the advantages of rules).

18 Family Courts Law, 5755 –1995, 1537 LSI 393 (1995) (Isr.).

"rules."[19] Its incorporation into the environment of procedure, that by its very nature is an environment of rules, could cause significant tension. Moreover, legal proceedings in general and family proceedings in particular are characterized as a zero-sum game.[20] Justice for one party is not justice for the other. "The implementation of justice" remains in the subjective discretion of the judge from case to case.

The ability to deviate from procedure and to act without clear rules will result in inconsistent application of the law. It is detrimental to the expectation interest of the parties, the advance planning of their legal steps, certainty, and more. It may be harmful to values that are at the basis of the civil procedure, as reflected in the opinion of Professor Goldstein:

> There is no doubt that one of the cardinal values of a procedural system is to insure a certain, sure and predictable process on which the parties can rely. That is, the rules should be clear so that a party knows what is expected of him, and they should be certain and predictable so that if person acts in accordance with them he need not fear that his case will be lost on procedural grounds.[21]

It is difficult to say whether the court utilizes the release from rules of procedure too often. However, it is impossible to ignore its use, even when a conventional alternative is available from the natural environment of procedural rules. It seems that such use appears to serve as a shield for the family courts from intervention by the appeals courts. See, for example, the case of *Anonymous* in which the family court could have resolved the issue by implementing local doctrines through regular rules of procedure. Yet the court surprisingly saw fit to also base its decision on the exceptional release from rules of procedure.[22]

It appears that the court's perception that views a digression from the general procedural rules as the main road to follow is what caused it to unnecessarily use this exceptional release. The court adopts an open-ended norm instead

---

19 *See* Sullivan, *supra* note 17, at 57–59 (distinguishing between the two).

20 Lucy S. McGough, *Protecting Children in Divorce: Lessons from Caroline Norton*, 57 Me. L. Rev. 13, 28 (2005) ("Finally, in most lawsuits, litigation is a zero-sum game: one party wins, the other party loses").

21 Stephen Goldstein, *The Influences of Constitutional Principles on Civil Procedure in Israel*, 17 Isr. L. Rev. 467, 481 (1982).

22 File No. 5044/00 Family Court (TA), H.P. v. S.C. (Jul. 09, 2000), Nevo Legal Database (by subscription) (Isr.).

of clear local doctrines that are part of and more natural in the procedural environment. This is detrimental to the natural and formal environment of procedure that seeks to preserve uniform rules.

To clarify, the present argument is not that this release from rules of procedure should not be used or that it is unnecessary for family law to include such a procedural norm. However, its use should be reserved for exceptional cases after all other options have been exhausted.[23] Only in this way will the desired uniformity of family court procedural rules be preserved and the parties able to direct their actions while relying upon this uniformity.

III. DOCUMENT DISCLOSURE

A. Document Disclosure in the General Courts

The guiding principle in the general rules of procedure is that each party has the right to inspect documents in the possession of the other party. The parties need to be allowed to "play with open cards so that one of them will not surprise his opponent during the legal proceeding with unexpected evidence."[24] The mandatory disclosure procedures were intended to simplify the proceedings, lessen the need to bring evidence, and allow each of the parties to be prepared for the legal proceeding while also relying upon documents held by the opposing party.[25]

The general rules of procedure determine that the process of document disclosure will take place prior to the pre-trial, even without intervention by the court, in order to allow at this stage for the formulation of the questions in dispute.[26] This format for disclosure reflects a classic adversary system, in which the parties themselves address each other to request documents and they decide whether to involve the court at all.

Under the general Rules of Civil Procedure, the court may issue an order instructing the parties to disclose in an affidavit the documents in his possession

---

23 For example, it would be possible to add that this rule will only be used for special reasons set forth in writing, so that its appropriate implementation would be clear. This addition is included whenever the legislator desires to limit the use of a provision.

24 File No. 001384/05 Family Court (Hadera), MR v. MA (Sept. 19, 2005), Nevo Legal Database (by subscription) (Isr.); File No. 2221/98 Family Court (TA), R.L v. H.L. (Jan. 1, 2001), Nevo Legal Database (by subscription) (Isr.).

25 File No. 15094/99 Family Court (TA), RL v. TL (Jan. 9, 2001), Nevo Legal Database (by subscription) (Isr.).

26 *Id.*

that are relevant to the dispute.[27] The request of the party seeking disclosure could be directed towards documents that his opponent might present in court that are to his detriment—"harmful documents." His request might be directed towards documents that the opponent would not wish to present in court because their content might support the party requesting disclosure—"helpful documents."[28] This is the general disclosure order, and it includes all the documents concerning the matter in dispute.[29]

Aside from the general order for disclosure, a party may request an order for disclosure of a specified document.[30] In other words, a party may demand that his opponent disclose whether he has a specified document in his possession. Moreover, the demand for document disclosure is a demand for a detailed list of documents in the possession of the party but is not a disclosure of their content. Therefore, the demand for document disclosure is usually a preliminary demand prior to the demand for document inspection.

The sanctions for noncompliance with orders for document disclosure and inspection are determined in the general Rules of Civil Procedure.[31] A party who does not disclose a document will not be allowed to present it as evidence on his behalf, except with the permission of the court.

A more severe sanction determines that if that party is the plaintiff, his Statement of Claim will be stricken.[32] If that party is the defendant, his Statement of Defense will be stricken and the court can issue a judgment in the absence of a defense.[33] Such a judgment will usually accept the plaintiff's arguments. The court avoids these severe steps as much as possible, unless it is convinced that a party willfully refuses to fulfill his obligation.[34]

From a more in-depth perspective, when one party demands that the other disclose a document and does not receive a response, he is entitled to

---

27 Civil Law Procedure Regulations, 1984, KT 5744, 25 (Isr.)

28 Civil Law Procedure Regulations, 1984, KT 5744, 25–26 (Isr.).

29 Civil Law Procedure Regulations, 1984, KT 5744, 25 (Isr.).

30 *Id.*

31 Civil Law Procedure Regulations, 1984, KT 5744, 25–27 (Isr.).

32 Civil Law Procedure Regulations, 1984, KT 5744, 27 (Isr.).

33 *Id.*

34 *Id.* at 25, 27; see also Michael Karayanni, *Pre-Trial Discovery in Civil Israel: Trends*, 35 HEBREW U. L. REV. 559, 565 (2008) (regarding the distinction between the two rules.) Karayanni argues that the sanction in Rule 122 is too severe and the courts avoid utilizing it. Therefore it is doubtful to what extent it can urge a party to present his documents. In contrast, Rule 114A, added at a later date, is more accessible and useful to the court, and therefore it can better serve this purpose. *Id.*

the remedy preventing the non-disclosing party from presenting the document as evidence. If the document harms the individual requesting disclosure, this remedy certainly serves his interest. If, however, the document is helpful for the party seeking disclosure, this remedy harms him because he is denied the document disclosure in which he is interested. The latter therefore requires implementing the more severe sanction of the striking of pleadings.[35]

B. Document Disclosure in Family Court

With the legislation of the Family Court Law and the relevant family court procedures, an additional format was established for mandatory document disclosure in the family courts. This format is consistent with the general principle that the disclosure procedure in family court should take place with greater transparency than in a general civil proceeding.[36] Thus, the disclosure process includes some elements of the inquisitorial system. The process is not left to the voluntary initiative of the parties. Document disclosure and inspection already take place with the submission of pleadings.

The disclosure, the inspection, and the submission of documents are combined into one stage and their timing moved forward to the submission of pleadings.[37] Both the plaintiff and the defendant are required to attach documents to their pleadings.[38] In addition, the pleadings in family matters are verified by an affidavit that also serves as an affidavit of direct examination.[39] A form including specified detailed information needs to be attached to a file in which an action was brought between spouses.[40]

Clearly, the family court rules seek to make the family court proceeding especially transparent and open, and to impose upon the parties increased duties of providing information. Attaching all the documents to the pleadings is desirable and correct, primarily in family court, in light of its purpose of resolving disputes speedily and efficiently. Due to the rules of mandatory

35 Civil Law Procedure Regulations, 1984, KT 5744, 27 (Isr.).

36 *See* File No. 005044/00 Family Court (TA), F v. S.H. (July 9, 2000), Nevo Legal Database (by subscription) (Isr.).

37 File No. 2221/98 *supra* note 24.

38 *Id.*

39 Civil Law Procedure Regulations, 1984, KT 5744 (Isr.).

40 Civil Law Procedure Regulations, 1984, KT 5744 (Isr.) (detailing the information that must be declared, including: details regarding the residential apartment, data on violence in the family, data on other files on family matters, and connection with therapeutic entities).

early disclosure, the court receives the "complete" file before the pre-trial session.[41]

This enables the court at an early stage to better consider how to manage the file and its procedures, and how to suggest a more accurate settlement proposal. Mandatory early disclosure may help the parties to reach an agreed upon solution, or at least to come to terms with the decisions of the court. As long as the documents are disclosed, the parties are more aware of their legal situation and less entrenched in their initial positions.

However, and surprisingly so, the process of document disclosure in family matters is narrower than the similar process in general civil proceedings. In the latter, the disclosure relates to every document "relevant to an issue in the case."[42] This expression was interpreted by the court as including both "harmful documents" that may work against the interest of the party requesting disclosure and "helpful documents" with content that may assist the party requesting disclosure.[43] In contrast, the duty of disclosure in family matters applies only to documents upon which the pleadings rely,[44] and does not appear to apply to documents that may be detrimental to the individual submitting a pleading. This issue raises the next question for consideration.

C. Does General Document Disclosure Apply in Family Court?

A family court rule determines that the general rules of procedure regarding document disclosure will not apply to family proceedings.[45] In other words, a party is not allowed to request a document disclosure order, a disclosure order for a specified document, or an order for document inspection. This particular rule seems to conflict with the purposes of the family court. The family court is supposed to be provided with a comprehensive and full picture.

---

41 File No. 2221/98, *supra* note 24.

42 Civil Law Procedure Regulations, 1984, KT 5744, 25 (Isr.).

43 *See* CA 27/91 Kabalo v. K. Simon Metal Works Ltd., 49(1) PD 450 [1991] (Isr.) (discussing the correct interpretation of the disclosure requirement).

44 In contrast, in the Australian legal system as I will discuss further below, the mandatory disclosure applies to all the relevant documents. *See Family Law Rules 2004* (Cth) r 13.07 (Austl.) ("The duty of disclosure applies to each document that: (a) is or has been in the possession, or under the control, of the party disclosing the document; and (b) is relevant to an issue in the case").

45 File No. 001384/05 Family Court (Hadera), MR v. MA (Sept. 19, 2005), Nevo Legal Database (by subscription) (Isr.).

One explanation of the rule may be found in the words of the court in the *Boteh* case.[46] The court states that perhaps the legislator wanted to avoid complication of proceedings and to contribute to their efficiency.[47] A Statement of Claim in family matters is subject to factual clarification that is not complex, and it demands a speedy decision. The mechanism of document disclosure set forth in the general rules of procedure might burden and slow down the proceedings.

The court also explains that, "In this branch of the law, the documents are more personal and the duty of disclosure is more harmful to the privacy of the litigant. The balance among the considerations is therefore conducted differently."[48] It is not clear how this last reason justifies not applying the process of document disclosure in family court. After all, the proceeding is closed to the public and the documents are made available only to the spouses and the judge.[49]

The family court rule excluding document disclosure and inspection brought before the Supreme Court the tension existing between disclosure in general courts and disclosure in the family courts. In the *Boteh* case, a woman petitioned the family court for an inheritance order following the death of her husband.[50] His brothers objected to issuing the order and argued that the deceased had left a will.[51] The parties agreed that the woman would submit all the documents in her possession for inspection only by the court, and that the court would determine whether they included documents concerning a will.[52] When the court saw that the matter involved hundreds of documents, it turned the documents into an "Affidavit of Document Discovery" and instructed the woman to submit all the documents directly to the brothers. The woman appealed that decision.[53]

The Supreme Court ruled that the general document disclosure rules should not be implemented when there is a specific rule determining that they will not apply in claims regarding family matters.[54] The court added that

46 CA 994/99 Boteh v. Boteh (Feb. 3, 2000), Nevo Legal Database (by subscription) (Isr.).

47 *Id.*

48 *Id.* at 20–21.

49 Courts Law (Consolidated Version), 5744–1984, 1123 LSI 198, § 68(e) (1984) (Isr.).

50 File No. 2466/00 Supreme Court (Jerusalem), *Boteh v. Boteh* (Nov. 19, 2000), Nevo Legal Database (by subscription) (Isr.).

51 *Id.*

52 *Id.*

53 *Id.*

54 *Id.*

the release from rules of procedure is relevant only when there is no conflicting rule in the specific family court procedural rules.[55] As long as there is an express provision in the family court procedural rules, the court cannot deviate from it.[56] The court determined that preserving the unique and exclusive family court rules will bring about the implementation of justice and that they should not be disregarded.[57]

In other words, when the family court acts in accordance with the general procedural rules, it may deviate from them by way of the provision for release from rules of procedure. However, when a unique and exclusive procedural rule was determined especially for the family court, the regulator had already weighed and balanced the considerations of justice. The court does not have the discretion to deviate from this balance.

The family courts are therefore bound to the special procedure that does not allow them to issue an order for document disclosure. Certainly the desirable procedural uniformity is thus preserved. However, it would be possible to argue that this is the extreme case in which it was appropriate to use the release from rules of procedure that was intended precisely for such circumstances.

A lack of documents harms the ability to resolve the dispute, and hence is detrimental to a fundamental purpose of the family court. Without the documents and without the ability to order their disclosure, each party remains steadfast in his own position and refuses to agree to a proposed compromise, or at least to come to terms with the court's decision. Each party might naturally think that the opposing party has documents that are helpful to him, and that their disclosure could have brought about a different decision. This situation may have negative impacts on the quality of the continuing relationships between the divorced spouses themselves and between the spouses and their children.

This issue impacts the spouses even before a crisis breaks out, and even when no crisis is visible on the horizon. From the time that it becomes well known that the one spouse who trusts the other to handle their finances will be disadvantaged during a dispute, such a spouse will be encouraged to no longer trust the other. The rule restricting document disclosure in family court could cause an atmosphere of tension and suspicion even in the life of a normative

55 *Id.*
56 *Id.*
57 *Id.*

family. The legal system in every society has an important interest that spouses will trust each other and live in harmony and not in suspicion. For that purpose, the system must provide desirable solutions during a crisis situation.

The solutions need to be in the form of effective orders, so that each spouse will know that even if he trusts the other and does not prepare himself during his normative life for a future legal proceeding, the legal system will protect his interests should it become necessary.

The matter is not unique to a dispute between spouses but fitting for any family dispute. The dispute between spouses, however, is more sensitive and usually exposes a deeper imbalance between their strengths. The following section examines how the family courts have dealt with this limitation.

IV. THE RESPONSE OF THE FAMILY COURT—A CRITICAL REVIEW

The *Boteh* ruling restricts the family court with respect to document disclosure. This ruling determines that the family courts are not able to order specified document disclosure or inspection, or to strike pleadings.[58] Hence, this ruling brought the family court closer to the adversary system, even more than is customary in the general courts.[59] The parties attach their documents according to their own discretion, and the court is unable to intervene in the matter, to demand disclosure of an additional document, or even to implement any additional sanction.[60]

This extreme stringency seems surprising in light of the maximum transparency intended in the family court. If one of the sides does not fulfill the duty of mandatory disclosure at all, or if he fulfills his duty by attaching only those documents upon which his pleading relies, the opposing party will be disadvantaged.

---

58 *Id.*

59 The mandatory early disclosure changed the procedure in other legal systems as well. For example, in the Canadian legal system, following the legislation of the mandatory disclosure, the right to pre-trial interrogation by the party was eliminated and conditioned on the permission of the court. At the same time, the weight of the court in gathering evidence increased and brought it closer to the inquisitorial legal system. *See* D.A. Rollie Thompson, *The Evolution of Modern Canadian Family Law Procedure: The End of the Adversary System? Or Just the End of the Trial?*, 41 FAM. CT. REV. 155, 173 (2003). The author argues that it was harmful to one of the primary justifications for the adversary system that sees an advantage in the active participation of the parties in the proceeding in their appearance before the court. The mandatory disclosure through documents narrowed the extent of their court appearances. *Id.*

60 File No. 2466/00 Supreme Court (Jerusalem), Trust v. Trust (Feb. 3, 2000), Nevo Legal Database (by subscription) (Isr.).

In addition, Professor Karayanni argues that a change has recently taken place in the guiding perception.[61] He explains that the purpose of document disclosure today is not based on the conflictual approach.[62] The conflictual approach asserts that the purpose of document discovery is to refine the issues in dispute between the parties.[63] Instead, the purpose of document disclosure is based on the normative approach (which is close to the inquisitorial system).[64] The normative approach asserts that the purpose of document discovery is the discovery of the truth.[65] These words were said regarding the general rules of procedure, but they are all the more correct in the family court. The discovery of the truth is not the purpose for which the family court was established, but it is a necessary means for fulfilling that purpose. It seems difficult to reach a speedy and efficient solution without the comprehensive picture of the documents.

The court's inability either to issue a disclosure order or to impose an incentivizing sanction could result in the refusal of a party to attach harmful documents to his pleading. He could even refuse to submit them to the opposing party during the proceeding. As long as a spouse knows that the court has neither the authority to issue an order for document disclosure, nor the authority to apply any sanction, he might have no motivation to disclose his documents in the mandatory disclosure proceedings. Several family courts created original constructions in order to circumvent the Supreme Court ruling. The following sections examine this issue.

A. The "Pre-Trial" Rules as Authority for Document Disclosure

The family courts developed two constructions in order to adopt certain portions of the general document disclosure process. The first construction argues that the court may utilize the rules granting judicial authority in a pre-trial.[66] The court is authorized, among other judicial actions, to make a decision "concerning document disclosure and inspection."[67] Accordingly, at least as one

61 Karayanni, *supra* note 34, at 563.

62 *Id.*

63 *Id.*

64 *Id.*

65 *Id.*

66 File No. 12631/00 Family Court (TA), Bombach v. Bombach (Dec. 14, 2001), Nevo Legal Database (by subscription) (Isr.).

67 *Id.*

court asserts, the court may issue orders with regard to everything concerning mandatory disclosure and inspection of relevant documents.[68] An additional court ruled that the judicial authority to order document disclosure in a pre-trial is an additional authority, separate from the regular practice of document disclosure.[69]

These two courts found the construction insufficient and therefore developed another construction enabling the court to adopt portions of the general document disclosure process. The second construction argues that the rule excluding the general document disclosure process is intended only to exclude "technical provisions," such as a preliminary request from a party, waiting for his response, and so forth.[70] It is not, however, intended to exclude the "general provisions" for issuing a disclosure order.[71]

An additional decision provides a third construction for adopting portions of the general document disclosure process. It is, however, limited to issues of property distribution. The court ordered document disclosure and explained as follows:

> In my opinion the authority given to the court for the purpose of preserving the property rights of the wife, also includes within it the authority to order late document disclosure. In this case the plaintiff requests disclosure and inspection of documents including essential information concerning the scope of the couple's future rights, and therefore, the issuing of an order concerning the production of the documents is taking measures required for preserving the potential rights of the spouse, in accordance with the Property Relations Law.[72]

These constructions for adopting certain portions of the general document disclosure process were not limited to issuing orders for disclosure of a specified document. They were broadened to also adopt the sanctions provided in the general process, as further explained in the following section.

---

68 *Id.*

69 *Id.*

70 File No. 3070/02 Family Court (Hadera), M.R. v. M.A. (Sept. 19, 2005), Nevo Legal Database (by subscription) (Isr.).

71 File No. 001384/05 Family Court (Hadera), M.R. v. M.A. (Sept. 19, 2005), Nevo Legal Database (by subscription) (Isr.).

72 File No. 3342/97 Family Court (Jerusalem), V. v. A. (May 31, 2005), Nevo Legal Database (by subscription) (Isr.). Sec 17.

B. The Sanction for Noncompliance with Document Disclosure Orders

Rule 114A of the Rules of Civil Procedure sets forth:

> If a party fails to reveal a document that must be revealed under regulation 112, or does not respond to a demand under regulation 114, he shall not have the right to submit that document as evidence on his behalf in that action, unless the Court so permitted after being convinced that the party had reasonable justification for his refusal; having permitted the document's submission, the Court may make any order on costs and other matters.[73]

A party who did not attach a document might thereby harm his own interest if the court will not subsequently allow him to present the relevant document. Clearly, this sanction is effective only if it relates to a document "helpful" to the party who did not attach it, something that usually will not occur. The difficult question is determining the sanction when a party fails to disclose documents that he does not really want to disclose, since they are detrimental to him and helpful to the opposing party. An example is when the spouse who handles the family finances does not disclose all of the documents that evidence his income and the capital accumulated by the family.

In that way he attempts to lessen the portion of his spouse in the distribution of family property. In such a case the sanction that determines that he will not be allowed to present the document is not a sanction. It does not deter a party from concealing important documents that harm him, and the purpose of establishing the family court is thwarted. The important question is whether the family court is permitted to use the harsh sanction of the striking of pleadings that is provided in the general procedure.

In addition to the abovementioned constructions, the family court responded positively to this question. It determined that the sanction of striking pleadings also applies as a general rule to document disclosure and inspection in the family court.[74] This approach was expressed not only as a theoretical explanation, but also put into practice. Accordingly, the family court ordered the striking of a wife's claim for the dissolution of joint ownership in a residential apartment since she did not attach substantive documents to the claim.

---

73 Civil Procedure Rules, 1984, KT 2220 (Isr.).

74 File No. 2221/98, *supra* note 24.

C. Rejection of the Constructions by the Courts of Appeal

The constructions developed by the family courts actually circumvent the family court procedural rule preventing implementation of the general document disclosure process. Especially surprising is the use of the first construction, which views the pre-trial rule as a source of authority for adopting portions of general document disclosure.

This construction was invalidated by the judicial decision that the rule regarding pre-trial does not provide a source of authority for issuing a document disclosure order.[75] Rather, it establishes only the timing for issuing such an order on the basis of existing authority.[76] However, since the family court rules of procedure determine that disclosure orders may not be issued in a family matter proceeding, the question of timing does not arise at all.[77]

The second construction, regarding the adoption of portions of the "general provisions" including the sanction of striking pleadings, has also been rejected by the appellate court.[78] Thus it has stated, "The sanction for not disclosing documents is not the striking of pleadings, but the prohibition of presenting such documents as evidence during the legal proceeding."[79]

Undoubtedly, the family court rule preventing the disclosure procedures creates a strange situation. Due to the delicate nature of relationships between divorced spouses who continue dealing with each other in one way or another even after the legal proceeding, it is desirable to resolve the dispute as quickly and efficiently as possible. It would even be natural to expect that especially within the family court, document disclosure orders would be allowed and the sanction for not complying with them would be harsher.

Nevertheless, the interpretation of the appeals courts is unambiguous. The constructions that the family courts developed are unacceptable to them. The appeals courts therefore attempt to end the use of such constructions

---

75 File No. 12631/00 Family Court (TA), Bombach v. Bombach (Dec. 14, 2001), Nevo Legal Database (by subscription) (Isr.).

76 *Id.*

77 File No. 001384/05 Family Court (Hadera), MR v. MA (Sept. 19, 2005), Nevo Legal Database (by subscription) (Isr.).

78 *Id.*

79 File No. 12631/00 Bombach, *supra* note 75.

by the family courts and prevent the possible resulting procedural disorder. They thus place the value of "stability" above the value of "truth."[80]

The family courts have actually digressed from the rulings of the appeals courts. From the perspective of binding precedent, this has created a real difficulty that is detrimental to the required hierarchical structure of the legal system.[81] The deviation by the lower courts from the decisions of the appeals courts sends a problematic message within the judicial system. In contrast, on the substantive level it appears that the content of their rulings is appropriate and correct, and that it is desirable to implement a document disclosure procedure similar to that which is customary in the general courts.

Thus while the intention of the family courts is desirable, their actions are not. With the deviation from the binding precedent, each court acts according to its own discretion. While one adopts the disclosure procedure; a second court adopts only certain portions of it; and the third does not adopt it at all. The parties do not know how to plan their path and direct their legal steps, even with respect to procedural matters.

D. Partial Adoption of the General Procedure: A Critical Review

The second construction asserts that the family court rule excludes only the "technical provisions" within the chapter on general disclosure and enables the adoption of the "general provisions." This is a problematic argument. **First**, from the formal perspective this interpretation is inconsistent with the specific language of the regulation which did not set forth this sort of division. **Second**, the Rules of Civil Procedure and their technical aspects also reflect substantive legal principles. Included among them are the burden of proof, the burden of production of evidence, the permissible limits of infringement of privacy in a legal proceeding, and so forth.[82]

---

80 *See* Goldstein, *supra* note 21, at 471 (explaining that the Israeli system of adjudication has chosen to further the goals of certainty, the prevention of multiple litigation, and the preservation of confidential relationships, over the goal of ascertaining the truth).

81 *See* Basic Law: The Judiciary, 1984, 38 LSI 101, § 20 (Isr.) ("A rule laid down by a court shall guide any lower court").

82 For example, the rule according to which the plaintiff opens by stating his case is a derivative of the concept that the individual who brings a claim against another bears the burden of proof, and it is not only a technical determination of procedure. Thus, for example, the provisions of local jurisdiction include the idea that the plaintiff seeks the location of the defendant. They should not be viewed only as technical rules.

For example, the procedural provisions with respect to the disclosure process also reflect the tension between the inquisitorial system that advocates a broad duty of disclosure in advance, and the adversary system that leaves the disclosure and its scope in the hands of the parties. The adoption of one portion of the general rules of procedure while disregarding another fails to adequately consider the substantive concepts and the balances that the legislator incorporated within them.

Thus it is possible that voluntarily contacting the opposing party, as is customary in the adversary system, will advance a channel of communication between them that might bring about a settlement in the case. Such contacts will clearly lessen burdens on the court and not require it to delve into a disagreement that the parties could resolve by themselves. The legislator also determined that the sanction of striking pleadings is desirable only after failure to respond to a preliminary contact by the other party and noncompliance with the court's order.[83] It is possible that this sanction is too harsh if it will be imposed only for violation of the order.

The legislator weighed several considerations, balanced them, and determined one solution that from his perspective facilitates the desired justice. Adoption of one portion of the solution (the sanction) without another (the voluntary requests between the parties) is detrimental to the justice and balance that the legislator considered.

Third, it is easy to imagine the chaos and lack of uniformity that will follow this creative ruling when each judge can decide which are the "general provisions" that he may adopt, and which are the "technical provisions" that he may waive.

The importance of uniformity in rules of procedure is also reinforced by additional procedural values that experts in procedural law place at the foundation of procedure. Thus Professor Resnik writes that a lack of uniform implementation of procedural rules weakens their legitimacy and can even be harmful to the principles of democracy.[84] In contrast, uniform and coherent implementation of the procedural rules may provide a feeling that a decision is correct, even if it is not actually so:

> Consistency is also viewed as justifying and legitimating decisions. Uniform application of legal rules may prove their "correctness"; if the same

83 Civil Procedure Rules, 1984, KT 2220, r. 114(A) (Isr.).

84 Judith Resnik, *Tiers*, 57 S. Cal. L. Rev. 840, 858 (1984).

> result always appears, it may after all be "right." ... Even if the result is not correct, at least everyone is treated the "same." Consistency promotes equal treatment of individuals, thereby expressing the rhetoric of democracy, of "equality before the law."[85]

Therefore the entire document disclosure process, including orders for additional disclosure, is required and essential in light of the purpose of the family court. However, the mandatory discovery process that is practiced today provides the court with only a partial picture. Without the critical documents, both helpful and harmful, it is impossible to advance the case and resolve it with consent of the parties. In addition, it may be detrimental to justice.

However, one must examine the best way to achieve this. From the perspective of procedural law, the independent development of constructions by the family courts is problematic. New rules need to be enacted. Without an appropriate legislative solution, each of the family courts will continue to develop constructions according to its own discretion. Some of them will even decide that it is inappropriate to develop any construction, as shown above.[86] Although the flexibility of the family court is important, the guidelines for discretion should be set forth in legislation. The parties should be familiar with those guidelines so that they can plan their actions accordingly.

V. THE LEGAL SYSTEMS IN SEVERAL OTHER COUNTRIES

A. The Australian Legal System

The issue of document disclosure has been addressed by the legal systems in several countries throughout the world. For example, when preparations were made in Australia for a reform in family law, the issue of disclosure clearly

---

85 *Id.*; *see also* Lawrence B. Solum, *Procedural Justice*, 78 S. Cal. L. Rev. 181, 189–90 (2004) ("If a system of procedure is widely regarded as a source of legitimate authority, then it will succeed in guiding action. If the system is seen as illegitimate or without authority, then the system may fail. ... When we know the outcome to be unjust, the justice of the outcome cannot be the source of its legitimate authority. This conceptual point has a crucial corollary: only just procedures can confer legitimate authority on incorrect outcomes").

86 File No. 3070/02 Family Court (Hadera), M.R. v. M.A. (Sept. 19, 2005), Nevo Legal Database (by subscription) (Isr.).

required extensive revision.[87] The general disclosure procedures resulted in significant expenses as well as in delayed proceedings.[88] Parties with economic strength used the disclosure procedures in their struggles against their spouses.

Prior to the reform, the law required disclosure of every document "relevant to an issue in the case."[89] Attorneys were concerned about malpractice claims and therefore made sure to obtain every document, even if it was not especially relevant. In addition, they took advantage of these procedures to obtain significant fees from their clients.[90] This situation brought about the examination of the subject in three reports, following which a reform took place.

Changes were made in the family law, in the chapter entitled "Disclosure."[91] The outstanding changes are in legislating mandatory early disclosure.[92] This includes attaching the documents to the pleadings, connecting the procedure to the central purpose of the rules, and adopting the criteria of "direct relevance" in document disclosure.[93] Each party is required to provide the opposing party with all of the documents relevant to the matter, not only the documents upon which his pleadings rely.[94] This duty of disclosure exists for every proceeding and continues until its completion.[95]

---

87 *See* AUSTRALIAN LAW REFORM COMM'N, DISCOVERY OF DOCUMENTS IN FEDERAL COURTS 27 (2011) ("The Explanatory Statement noted an important difference between the revised Rules and the earlier Rules. The court's expectation would be that parties would not go on a—fishing expedition or apply for a general order, but would direct their mind to the higher standard and consider what is directly relevant to the disputed issues").

88 *See id.* ("The litigation tool of complete disclosure was an expensive process and was therefore timed to commence only after the Final Resolution event."); *see also* FAMILY COURT OF AUSTL, FUTURE DIRECTIONS REPORT 38 (2000) ("Under the existing system there is no significant activity between the last primary dispute resolution event (usually a conference with a registrar or a court counsellor) and the Pre-Hearing Conference. Legal practitioners put their files away during this period and there is often no work done by the court or the parties to further pursue settlement or to ready the matter for trial. That work does not resume until just before the Pre-Hearing Conference. In Registries were there are delays, that might mean that there is no activity for many months").

89 *Family Law Rules 2004* (Cth) sub-r 13.01 (Austl.).

90 *Id.*

91 *Family Law Rules 2004* (Cth) ch 13 (Austl.).

92 *See* FAMILY COURT OF AUSTL., *supra* note 88, at 42 ("The courts of Queensland have moved to change the emphasis on discovery to an emphasis on disclosure").

93 *see also Family Law Rules 2004* (Cth) sub-rr 1.06, 13.01(1) (Austl.).

94 *See Family Law Rules 2004* (Cth) sub-r 13.01(1) (Austl.).

95 *See id.* at sub-r 13.01(1)–(2) ("(1) Each party to a case has a duty to the court and to each other party to give full and frank disclosure of all information relevant to the case, in a

The parties are required to sign an affidavit in which they represent that they have knowledge of and are in full compliance with the duty of disclosure.[96] A party who does not disclose a document will not be able to present it as evidence, except with consent or by permission of the court.[97] He could be accused of contempt of court or be ordered to pay expenses. The court can also order that part of the claim be stricken.[98] The assumption is that the demand for disclosure of only relevant documents will cause lawyers to invest efforts in the initial stage of the proceeding.[99] It should be noted that in claims for distribution of family property, a broader duty of disclosure exists including spousal income, expenses, investments and economic interests in property, and more.[100]

At the basis of the proceeding is the perception that each party must know about all the property in the possession of his spouse. The mandatory early disclosure requirement does not prevent a party from applying for additional disclosure orders, a specified document disclosure order, and even an order for document inspection.[101]

Furthermore, he may request that the court order the other party to submit an affidavit as to whether a specified document exists or in which circumstances it left his possession.[102] Before making the request, the requesting party is supposed to make a reasonable effort to resolve the problem that is the subject of the request.[103] In addition, he is supposed to convince the court that the

---

timely manner. (2) The duty of disclosure starts with the pre-action procedure for a case and continues until the case is finalized").

96 *Id.* at sub-r 13.15(1).

97 *Id.* at sub-*r* 13.01(1).

98 *Family Law Rules 2004* (Cth) sub r 13.14 (Austl.). "If a party does not disclose a document as required under these Rules: (a) the party: (i) must not offer the document, or present evidence of its contents, at a hearing or trial without the other party's consent or the court's permission; (ii) may be guilty of contempt for not disclosing the document; and (iii) may be ordered to pay costs; and (b) the court may stay or dismiss all or part of the party's case."

99 *Id.* at r 1.07.

100 *Id.* at sub-r 13.04(1)(a)–(c).

101 *See id.* at sub-r 13.22(1)(a)–(c) ("Application for order for disclosure: (1) A party may seek an order that: (a) another party comply with a request for a list of documents in accordance with rule 13.20; (b) another party disclose a specified document, or class of documents, by providing to the other party a copy of the document, or each document in the class, for inspection by the other party; (c) another party produce a document for inspection").

102 *Id.* at sub-r 13.22(1)(d).

103 *Family Law Rules 2004* (Cth) sub-r 13.23 n.1 (Austl.).

request is indeed essential and will advance the resolution of the case or will decrease expenses.[104]

The reform was intended to shorten the proceeding and avoid delay.[105] Therefore, the law also sets forth which considerations the court should weigh before issuing an order requiring a party to disclose additional documents.[106] The court must examine the helpfulness of the disclosure to the resolution of the disputed issues, the cumulative expenses, the inconvenience to the parties, the delay of the case due to issuing the order, and the anticipated impact of the disclosure order on the final outcome.[107] Aside from the mandatory disclosure, one party may submit to the other an interrogatory including no more than twenty questions.[108]

B. The Legal Systems in Canada

At the very beginning of the proceeding, the legal systems in Canada require submission of Financial Statements, without any demand from the opposing party.[109] The Financial Statement is supposed to itemize all of the party's property and sources of income.[110] It is a critical element in the disclosure proceeding in family court.[111] The Financial Statement assists in narrowing the disagreements at the beginning of the proceeding and enables reaching a

---

104 *Id.* at r 13.22(2).

105 *Id.* at r 1.07.

106 *See id.* at r 13.22(3) ("(3) In making an order under subrule (1), the court may consider: (a) whether the disclosure sought is relevant to an issue in dispute; (b) the relative importance of the issue to which the document or class of documents relates; (c) the likely time, cost and inconvenience involved in disclosing a document or class of documents taking into account the amount of the property, or complexity of the corporate, trust or partnership interests (if any), involved in the case; and (d) the likely effect on the outcome of the case of disclosing, or not disclosing, the document or class of documents").

107 *See id.*

108 *Family Law Rules 2004* (Cth) sub-r 13.26(1)–(3) (Austl.) ("Service of specific questions. (1) After a case has been allocated to a first day before a Judge, a party (the *requesting party*) may serve on another party (the *answering party*) a request to answer specific questions. (2) A party may only serve one set of specific questions on another party. (3) The specific questions must: (a) be in writing; (b) be limited to 20 questions (with each question taken to be one specific question); and (c) not be vexatious or oppressive").

109 Supreme Court Rules, B.C. Reg. 221/90, r. 60A (Can.); Matrimonial Property Act, R.S.A. 1980, c. M-9, § 31 (Can.); Alta. Reg. 458/78 (Can.); Court of Queen's Bench, Manitoba Reg. 553/88, r. 70.05 (Can.); Ontario Rules of Civil Procedure, O. Reg. 131/04, r. 69.14, Form 69K (Can.).

110 *See* Courts of Justice Act, O. Reg. 114/99 (Can.).

111 Thompson, *supra* note 59, at 161.

settlement agreement at a preliminary stage. While it is the first stage of disclosure, additional disclosure mechanisms are also available to the court.[112]

However, the legislation of mandatory early disclosure transformed the right of initial questioning into a right conditioned on permission of the court that is supposed to be given only in exceptional cases.[113] The Financial Statements turned the legal system into more of an inquisitorial system and less of an adversarial system. Greater responsibility for gathering the evidence was placed on the court, especially because a large portion of the parties in family law proceedings are not represented by counsel and their ability for collecting evidence is quite limited.[114]

C. The Legal System in Several States within the United States

Under the legal system in Arizona a process was established similar to that in Australia. The duty of disclosure applies to every document relevant to each of

---

112 *See* Nova Scotia Civil Procedure Rules, Royal Gaz. 2006, r. 70.10 (Can.). For example, when a party does not comply with his disclosure obligation, the judge may order a third party to disclose documents in his possession: "Disclosure: orders to third parties. (1) Where a party has failed to make adequate disclosure ... the court officer may order a person other than a party to provide information in that person's possession, custody or control respecting the party. The information shall be limited to the party's income, expenses, assets, liabilities, employment, or address, telephone or other contact information." (2) The term "person" in sub-rule 70.10(1) includes a corporation, a public body or Her Majesty. *Id.* And for example, in a request to adjust the amount of alimony, the court ordered the husband's new wife, who is not a party in this proceeding, to fill out a financial and property statement and to appear in court. *See* Gladwin v. Gladwin, [1997] N.S.R. (2d) 159 (Can. N.S.). Aside from that, sanctions were also determined allowing the court to strike the claim of a party who does not deliver a financial declaration. *See* Ontario Rules of Civil Procedure, O. Reg. 131/04, r. 69.14 (Can.) ("Sanctions for Failure to Deliver Financial Statement or to Give Particulars (9) Where a spouse fails to comply with an order to deliver a financial statement, a new financial statement or particulars, (a) the court may dismiss the spouse's action or strike out his or her answer; and (b) a judge may make a contempt order against the spouse").

113 *See* Carole Curtis, *Philosophy and Over-view of the Rules*, SYRTASH COLLECTION OF FAMILY LAW ARTICLES, July 13, 1999, at 24 ("Both discovery and cross-examinations are now called questioning. Questioning the other party is no longer available as a right in family law cases. ... This system has been in place in the former Unified Family Court in Hamilton for many years and has been successful; in appropriate cases, the parties or their lawyers consent to the questioning. However, with more stringent disclosure requirements in the rules, and more consequences for failure to disclose, questioning a party should become a last resort and should not be required in the average family law case, as all the data needed should be available and produced through other means").

114 Thompson, *supra* note 59, at 175.

the issues in the dispute.[115] In addition, all of the parties are supposed to fill out a declaration known as a Resolution Statement within forty days of submission of the last Statement of Defense.[116] The purpose of this declaration is to narrow the disagreements at an early stage of the proceeding and to avoid prolonged disclosure procedures.[117] If one party believes that he is missing certain documents, he is entitled to petition the court and it will order compliance with a broad duty of disclosure.[118]

Under the legal system in Florida, the Supreme Court decided that the family court rules of procedure needed to be separate from the general rules of procedure.[119] In 1992, the Supreme Court established a committee to recommend new rules of procedure.[120] The committee recommended new rules intended to simplify the proceeding, expedite it, and lower the costs.[121] In 1995, special procedures were legislated for the family courts.[122] Those procedures adopted mandatory disclosure that requires automatic production of documents to the opposing party.[123]

The mandatory disclosure varies according to the party's level of income, but in principle each party is supposed to disclose all of the documents in his possession within forty-five days from the date of the last Statement of Defense.[124] If a document is not disclosed immediately, it will be impossible to bring evidence concerning that document As in the legal systems in Australia and Arizona, despite the mandatory disclosure a party is entitled to request an order for disclosure of an additional document that was not presented in the preliminary proceedings.[125]

Under the legal system in California, the relevant legislation begins with an explanation of the rationale that justifies mandatory disclosure. The rules

---

115 ARIZ. R. CIV. P. 49.

116 ARIZ. FAM. LAW. PROC. R. 49.

117 *See* Davis, *supra* note 6, at 46.

118 *Id.*

119 *In re* Fla. Rules of Family Court Procedure, 607 So. 2d 396 (Fla. 1992).

120 *Id.*

121 FLA. FAM. L.R.P. 12.000 commentary.

122 *Id.*

123 FLA. FAM. L.R.P. 12.285.

124 The question has been raised as to what extent the courts indeed enforce this requirement. *See* David L. Manz, *Financial Affidavits in Dissolution of Marriage Actions: Are They Really Mandatory?*, 79 FLA. BAR J. 70 (2005).

125 FLA. R. CIV. P. 12.380; Hastings & Reynolds, *supra* note 4, at 20 ("... a party may apply for an order compelling discovery for failure to comply with any discovery request under the family rules, including failure to comply with the mandatory disclosure").

require, as a matter of policy, the disclosure of all property at the time of separation in order to both enable equal distribution in the divorce proceeding and to correctly evaluate child and spousal support.[126] The rules seek to narrow the adversarial nature of the proceeding through the duty to fully disclose all documents. That obligation applies to all types[127] of documents in every divorce proceeding, and not only in procedures with respect to property distribution.[128]

Since this is a continuing obligation, the declarations of disclosure need to be updated whenever a new document comes into the possession of the parties. Each party must submit a declaration of disclosure to the opposing party[129] with respect to all documents in his possession.[130] In property disputes, an additional declaration of disclosure[131] must be sent to the opposing party at the end of the proceedings, prior to the judgement or the signing of a settlement agreement.[132]

---

126 See Cal. Fam. Code § 2100 (West 2004) ("The Legislature finds and declares the following: (a) It is the policy of the State of California (1) to marshal, preserve, and protect community and quasi-community assets and liabilities that exist at the date of separation so as to avoid dissipation of the community estate before distribution").

127 *See id.* ("(b) Sound public policy further favors the reduction of the adversarial nature of marital dissolution and the attendant costs by fostering full disclosure and cooperative discovery").

128 *See id.* ("(c) In order to promote this public policy, a full and accurate disclosure of all assets and liabilities in which one or both parties have or may have an interest must be made in the early stages of a proceeding for dissolution of marriage or legal separation of the parties. ... together with a disclosure of all income and expenses of the parties. Moreover, each party has a continuing duty to immediately, fully, and accurately update and augment that disclosure to the extent there have been any material changes so that at the time the parties enter into an agreement for the resolution of any of these issues, or at the time of trial on these issues, each party will have a full and complete knowledge of the relevant underlying facts").

129 *See id.* ("(c) ... each party has a continuing duty to immediately, fully, and accurately update and augment that disclosure to the extent there have been any material change").

130 *See* Cal. Fam. Code § 2103 (West 2004) ("In order to provide full and accurate disclosure of all assets and liabilities in which one or both parties may have an interest, each party to a proceeding for dissolution of the marriage or legal separation of the parties shall serve on the other party a preliminary declaration of disclosure").

131 *See* Cal. Fam. Code § 2103 (West 2004) ("In order to provide full and accurate disclosure of all assets and liabilities in which one or both parties may have an interest, each party to a proceeding for dissolution of the marriage or legal separation of the parties shall serve on the other party a preliminary declaration of disclosure").

132 *See id.* § 2105 ("(a) ... before or at the time the parties enter into an agreement for the resolution of property or support issues other than pendente lite support, or, if the case goes to trial, no later than 45 days before the first assigned trial date, each party, or the attorney for the party in this matter, shall serve on the other party a final declaration of disclosure and a current income and expense declaration, executed under penalty of perjury on a form prescribed by the Judicial Council").

When a party does not reveal all of the information in his possession, the opposing party may request that the court order him to do so.[133] If one party does not respond to the order, the law provides a number of sanctions. Included among them are preventing a party from bringing evidence concerning the same information that was not disclosed, issuing a judgment for the portion of the information that was not disclosed,[134] or setting aside a judgment that was given following the nondisclosure.[135]

As in each of the legal systems mentioned above except for the Israeli system, mandatory early disclosure does not prevent the court from issuing additional disclosure orders or from acting in any way it deems appropriate for the implementation of justice.[136]

To summarize, different systems throughout the world implement mandatory early disclosure in family law. In that respect the Israeli system is comparable to them. In some countries, this duty of disclosure is broader than it is in Israel. It may include all the documents concerning the dispute and not just those upon which the pleadings rely. In addition, in all the legal systems examined, the court is authorized to take steps following failure to comply with mandatory disclosure. Included among them are ordering specified document disclosure and inspection and striking of pleadings. Under the Israeli system, this authority is not granted to the family court. In that regard the Israeli system is an exception to legal systems throughout the world, without any convincing rationale.

---

133 *See id.* § 2107 ("(a) If one party fails to serve on the other party a preliminary declaration of disclosure ... the complying party may, within a reasonable time, request preparation of the appropriate declaration of disclosure or further particularity").

134 *See id.* ("(b) ... (2) File a motion for an order preventing the noncomplying party from presenting evidence on issues that should have been covered in the declaration of disclosure. (3) File a motion showing good cause for the court to grant the complying party's voluntary waiver of receipt of the noncomplying party's preliminary declaration of disclosure ... (d) ... if a court enters a judgment when the parties have failed to comply with all disclosure requirements of this chapter, the court shall set aside the judgment").

135 In this list, the author details a number of decisions in which a judgment was cancelled following violation of the disclosure obligation. *See* Rick C. Lal, *Family Law Corner Running Afoul of the Disclosure Statutes: Yet Another Ground for Setting Aside a Judgment*, 40 Orange County Law. 38 (1998).

136 *See* Cal. Fam. Code § 2111 (West 2004) ("A disclosure required by this chapter does not abrogate the attorney work product privilege or impede the power of the court to issue protective orders").

D. Adoption of the Process Used by the Labor Court in Israel

Although the constructions developed by the family court to circumvent procedural limitations are problematic, constraining the family court might result in benefit to a wrongdoer, nondisclosure of the truth, and an unresolved dispute. The latter part of the equation becomes more severe when considering the nature of a family dispute. Therefore, the legislator should cancel the family court rule that prevents the adoption of certain general rules of procedure regarding document disclosure. At the same time, it is recommended that the subordinate legislation in family law adopt the existing process provided by subordinate legislation in labor law. This would resolve the problem of document disclosure and also contribute to legislative harmony among the different fields of law.

The submission of pleadings in the labor court is almost completely identical to that in the family court.[137] The plaintiff must attach to his Statement of Claim a copy of every document upon which the claim relies.[138] The defendant also attaches to his Statement of Defense the documents upon which it relies.[139] Following the establishment of those rules and as appropriate, the general document disclosure process was not eliminated. On the contrary, this process was adopted into the labor court rules except for its "technical provisions."[140]

There is no need to first contact the opposing party, to wait for his response, and only then to request a court order. The court is allowed to issue an order for presentation of additional details.[141] Upon the request of a party, the court may even issue an order for disclosure or inspection of specified documents, provided that it finds it necessary for enabling an efficient proceeding.[142] The process includes a sanction and sets forth that if a party does not comply with a court order, the court may extend the time period for compliance or strike his pleading.[143]

This process is actually consistent with the spirit of the second construction formulated by the family courts as explained above. It neutralizes the "technical provisions"; does not require contacting the opposing party and waiting

137 Family Courts Law, 5755–1995, 1537 LSI 393 (1995) (Isr.).
138 *Id.*
139 *Id.*
140 Civil Law Procedure Regulations, 1984, KT 5744, 25–27 (Isr.).
141 *Id.*
142 *Id.*
143 *Id.*

for his response; and does not determine a time period for requesting a court order. This process allows for directly requesting a court order for disclosure and inspection.[144] Thanks to this neutralization, the decisions in the family dispute will not be delayed by technical matters. Second and equally important, the harsher sanction of striking pleadings was adopted in the disclosure procedures of the labor court.

The adoption of a similar process in the family court might resolve the fundamental problems described in this chapter, contribute to uniformity of the system, provide the court tools for determining the truth, and assist it in reaching more just solutions that will be more acceptable to the parties. From the *ex ante* perspective, this process might even be influential in the early disclosure stage.[145] A party and his legal counsel, who are aware of the court's authority to order broad document disclosure, will tend to attach documents to the pleadings as required by the family court rules. If they do not attach their documents, from the *ex post* perspective a later order could require them to pay legal expenses.

In addition, Israeli legislation should adopt certain other provisions from various legal systems throughout the world. First, the disclosure rules in the abovementioned legal systems determine that all the documents relevant to the dispute need to be attached, and not just the documents upon which the pleadings rely. If this provision were adopted by the Israeli regulator, it would broaden the scope of documents required for disclosure. The court should also have the authority to strike the pleading of the party who does not attach all the documents, including documents that are harmful to him. Second, of course, is adopting the authority to issue orders of disclosure, specified disclosure, and inspection despite the mandatory early disclosure procedure.

Third, as in the California legal system,[146] legislative provisions can set forth which considerations the court needs to take into account prior to issuing an order for disclosure of additional documents. Included among them are the helpfulness of the disclosure to resolving the issue in dispute, the cumulative costs, the inconvenience to the parties, the resulting delay in the case, and the impact of the disclosure order on the final outcome. With the help of guidelines,

---

144 *Id.*

145 The matter relates to the economic analysis approach to the law. *See* Alon Klement & Roy Shapira, *Justice and Efficiency in Civil Procedure—A Novel Interpretive Approach*, 7 IDC L. Rev. 75, 92 (2007) (claiming the legal proceeding can also be divided between its early voluntary stages (EX ANTE) and its later stages (EX POST)).

146 *See, e.g.*, Cal. State Bar R. P. 5.388.

orders will be issued only when needed and they will not unnecessarily delay the proceeding.

Legislative guidelines will also result in uniformity in judgments and contribute to the feeling of litigants that justice is indeed done and the court decisions are not arbitrary. In contrast, one must also consider that guidelines narrow the judge's discretion in an area in which it is desirable to grant broad discretion. Therefore, the guidelines should be formulated broadly in order to allow the appropriate extent of judicial discretion and thereby reflect an inquisitorial nature suited to the issue of document disclosure.

Fourth, it is desirable to adopt continuing disclosure, according to which each party must disclose every document that comes into his possession during the proceeding and until its conclusion. Such a duty of disclosure will narrow the gap between the factual truth and the legal truth and bring about a just distribution of family property. However, this obligation might complicate the legal proceeding and delay it due to every document that could emerge in the future.

E. The Israel Supreme Court Approved an Order to Disclose a Document

In 2013 a family court ordered a mutual disclosure of documents.[147] A request for permission to appeal that was submitted to the Supreme Court was rejected.[148] The Supreme Court determined that for disclosure of document in the family court should be done in a less formal format, which allows for deviation from the general Rules of Civil Procedure. It was further determined that the language of Regulation 258(9) of the Civil Law Procedure Regulations leads to the conclusion that with regard to family law matters access to documents should be expanded in comparison to general civil procedure. When the specific regulations of the family court procedure do not provide a solution for mutual disclosure, the court is authorized to act under section 8(a) of the Family Court Law. That section permits the court to deviate from the rules of procedure and evidence, if the court determines it necessary for the implementation of justice.

---

147 File No. 0738342-12 Family Court (Hadera), Anonymous v. Anonymous (June 21, 2013), Nevo Legal Database (by subscription) (Isr.).

148 CA 4738/13 Anonymous v. Anonymous (Sep. 13, 2013), Nevo Legal Database (by subscription) (Isr.).

This decision actually retracts the decision in the *Boteh* case.[149] The court contends that it would have been better for the subordinate legislation to regulate this matter explicitly.

VI. CONCLUSION

This chapter examines the tension between the general rules of procedure and those that are applicable in family court proceedings. It critically reviews the justification for the provision of law referred to in the chapter as the release from rules of procedure. That provision releases the family courts from the restrictions of civil procedure and rules of evidence. The chapter criticizes the use of this provision by the family courts, even when its use is less essential or not essential at all. Instead of relying upon family court rules in accordance with local procedural doctrines, the courts utilize the provision that releases them from the limitations of civil procedure. Thus the system remains unclear and the parties uncertain as to how to direct their actions.

Afterwards, the chapter examines the issue of document disclosure. The rule prohibiting the family court from issuing orders for document disclosure raises several difficulties. It constrains the family courts by eliminating the possibility of issuing an order for specified disclosure and inspection. The rule is inconsistent with the purpose of establishing the family court; the extra disclosure and transparency appropriate to the family court; the aspiration of completing cases quickly, efficiently, and as agreed upon by the parties; and the customary legal practice in systems around the world.

In addition, its interpretation by the appeals courts narrows the possibility of utilizing the release from rules of procedure as a means of circumventing the prevention of further disclosure orders.[150] The narrowing of the use of this provision is very desirable. However, leaving the courts without any authority to order document disclosure is problematic and undermines the fundamental purposes and the inquisitorial nature of the family court.

The family courts in Israel only ostensibly followed the interpretation of the Supreme Court that limited the use of this provision. They rebelled against its rulings and began developing creative constructions in order to adopt

---

149 See *Boteh supra* notes 46, 50.

150 *Id.*

particular portions of the general document disclosure process.[151] The chapter presents these constructions along with a critical review.

From the scholarly writings of procedural law experts in the United States, it appears that the law might be negatively impacted and inconsistently applied by implementing these constructions. The constructions are also detrimental to the principle of uniformity, which not only plays an important role in creating the legitimacy of court decisions, but is also integral to the concept of democracy.

The chapter suggests adopting the process currently in place in the labor court. Despite the disclosure, inspection, and mandatory attachment of documents to the pleadings, the labor court may order further document disclosure and strike pleadings in the event of noncompliance.[152] Such is the present situation in other legal systems throughout the world. Similarly, legislative guidelines can also be determined as to when it is appropriate to issue orders for further document disclosure in addition to the disclosures provided with the pleadings.

In that way the guidelines of discretion are clear and set forth in law. The parties may more easily manage their proceedings and the process is more appropriate to the environment of the procedural law. The conclusion of the chapter calls for legislative harmony in the mandatory discovery procedures and for their uniform implementation in the family courts, in accordance with legal systems around the world.

---

151 *Id.*
152 *Id.*

Glossary of Technical and Foreign-Language Terms

Functus Officio is the principle according to which decisions of officials are deemed to be final and binding once they are made. They cannot be revoked by the decision maker.

Get refers to a document in Jewish religious law which gives effect to a divorce of a Jewish couple. The requirements for a *get* include that it be given by a husband to his wife.

Different halakhic traditions are traditions that have been included in Jewish religious law. The source of their authority is Biblical and rabbinical.

Indemnification Stipulation refers to the contractual requirement that a spouse initiating a future modification proceeding will indemnify the other spouse, whether by financial payment or by return of a portion of the property received.

Ketubah refers to a Jewish marriage contract that is an integral part of a traditional Jewish marriage. It sets forth the rights and responsibilities of the groom.

Prima facie evidence is sufficient evidence to provide proof by indicating basic facts, but it might be disproved.

Privity is a relation between two parties that is recognized by law, such as that of blood, lease, or service.

Res judicata is a matter that has been adjudicated by a competent court and may not be pursued further by the same parties.

Index of Terms, Figures, and Sources

Legislation Index

Index of Cases

www.ingramcontent.com/pod-product-compliance
Ingram Content Group UK Ltd.
Pitfield, Milton Keynes, MK11 3LW, UK
UKHW021920010526
470548UK00007B/59

9 781644 695401